FINLAND

Helsingfors

Lapvik
Hango

Uto Lt.

Bogskär Lt.

GULF OF

Odensholm

Revel

Port
Baltic

ESTONIA

Dagerört

Dagö
I.

Rogekul

Moon Sound

Pernau

Osel
I.

Irben Straits

Gulf
of
Riga

Windau

RIGA

Steinort

Libau

Memel

Königsberg

RUSSIA

Lake
Ladoga

Neva

THE
BALTIC SEA

50   0   50   100   150   200
Miles   Miles

Baltic Assignment

Baltic Assignment

British Submariners in Russia
1914–1919

MICHAEL WILSON

LEO COOPER
in association with
SECKER & WARBURG

First published 1985 by Leo Cooper in association with
Martin Secker & Warburg Ltd,
54 Poland Street, London W1V 3DF

ISBN: 0-436-57801-8

Printed in England by
Butler & Tanner Ltd, Frome

To
The Memory
of
Francis Newton Allan Cromie
and
All the British Submariners
Who Gave Their Lives
1914–1919

No thought of flight, none of retreat,
no unbecoming deed that argued fear;
each on himself relied, as only in his
arm the moment lay of victory.

Milton: *Paradise Lost*

Contents

Gazetteer

The names of places in this story are those commonly in use at the time. Since then the names of some of them have changed as a result of war, revolution or political acquisition. Readers may like to identify such places with the names to be found in a modern atlas, and a guide to these changes is given below. The spelling used is that given on the British Admiralty charts of the Baltic published in 1980, numbers 2816 and 2817.

Old name	*New name*
Dago	Hiiumaa
Danzig	Gdansk
Hango	Hanko
Helsingfors	Helsinki
Libau	Liepaja
Memel	Klaipeda
Moon/Moon Sound	Muhu/Muhu Vain
Osel	Saaremaa
Pernau	Parnu
Pillau	Baltiysk
Port Baltic	Paldiski
Revel or Reval	Tallinn
Rogekul	Rohukula
St Petersburg/Petrograd	Leningrad
Windau	Ventspils

List of Illustrations

List of Illustrations

LIST OF MAPS

Preface

Whilst researching the achievements of the British submarine flotillas in the 1914–18 war I soon began to realise what an interesting story there was in the fortunes of a few submarines and their crews involved in what was regarded as only a 'side-show' in the Baltic. It was the story of the ability of the British submariners to succeed when all the odds seemed stacked against them. They managed to break into the Baltic despite the German defences, and then to operate there for three and a half years while being at the end of a supply line stretching thousands of miles back to Britain through north Russia. They managed to retain their discipline and their morale while all around them their Russian allies were turning to revolution and a readiness to end the war. They even managed to earn the respect of these self-same revolutionaries who were only too ready to murder or humiliate their own officers. They managed to survive the worst weather that a Russian winter could bring.

Leading them for the last two years was Francis Cromie, a leader in the John Buchan style, an officer who made such an impression on all who served with him; firm and correct in manner, patriotic in belief, diplomatic in his dealings with the Russians, yet leaving us with an air of mystery.

This, then, is primarily a story of submariners and their submarines. It is not a chronology of events on the Eastern Front, nor a history of the Russian Revolution and its aftermath, though of necessity both play their part in the telling of the story.

Preface

A writer incurs many debts and I am no exception. I am especially grateful to Gus Britton of the Submarine Museum at Gosport for his help in putting together this story and for his enthusiastic support. It was through Gus that I had the privilege of meeting Mr L. W. (Ben) Benson, one of the submariners of this story. He remained a submariner at heart throughout his life, and it was a great pleasure to listen to his stories of those years now long ago when he served in the Baltic with Cromie in the submarine *E19*, and through him to gain some feeling for the respect in which Cromie was held by all who served with him. I only regret that Ben's death early in 1984 prevented him seeing this story in print.

I wish also to acknowledge my gratitude to Admiral of the Fleet Sir Edward Ashmore for his interest in my story and for allowing me to quote from his father's unpublished memoirs of the period: *A Russian Scrapbook*. I am indebted to Commander Richard Compton-Hall, MBE, RN, the Curator of the Submarine Museum, for making available to me various papers and photographs held in the museum, and for his permission to reproduce them. I am also most grateful for his continual help and advice. My thanks also go to Mrs Joan Shenton and Mrs U. V. G. Betts for their help in showing me family papers relating to Admiral Laurence's time in the Baltic and for talking to me about him and the submariners of those days. Also to Mr Alan Francis of the Naval Historical Library in the Ministry of Defence.

I am grateful to the Controller HMSO for permission to quote from official reports and papers held in the Public Record Office at Kew.

To bring events up to the present day it has been interesting to hear from Torleif Nilsson and Sten Lindgren in Sweden. They have been diving on wrecks off the coast of Gotland, some of which appear to be in good condition despite the passing years since they were sunk there by Lieutenant-Commander Cromie in the submarine *E19* during October 1915.

Finally I wish to record my debt to my late colleague, Captain Michael Beeching, RN, for his help and great encouragement during the early stages of writing this book.

xii

Introduction

Halfway through the forenoon watch on 18 October 1914 lookouts onboard the German cruiser *Victoria Louise*, patrolling in the Baltic not far from the scene of Nelson's famous victory in 1801, reported torpedo tracks approaching the ship from the port side. The two torpedoes missed, but the Royal Navy, in the form of representatives from its new Submarine Branch, had returned once more to wage war in the Baltic. At the same time another link had been forged in the chain of events which had started in a Serbian town three and a half months earlier with the murder of an Austrian Archduke, and was to end more than five years later with the withdrawal of the last British troops from Russia. By geography the principal combatants in this area, the Baltic, were necessarily Imperial Germany and Russia, yet throughout most of this period of over five years the British submarines were to be active and dominant in the Baltic.

Although Nelson's victory at Copenhagen in 1801 is perhaps the best known of the Royal Navy's Baltic exploits during the Napoleonic war, it is by no means an isolated incident. Trade with the Baltic States was an important aspect of Britain's survival, and that with Sweden, which provided much of the wood for the hulls and masts of both its merchant and war ships, was of particular importance. (As the Swedish iron ore trade was to be of importance to the Germans in two later conflicts.) A second, and less well known, bombardment of Copenhagen in August 1807 had the unfortunate effect of ensuring that Denmark entered the war again on the side of France, although its immediate effect was to ensure that the Danish Fleet was captured and taken to safety in England. But, during this war it is perhaps the exploits of Vice-Admiral Sir James Saumarez which are the more notable. As a direct result of the Franco-Russian treaty of alliance signed at Tilsit on 7 July 1807, which had as one of its aims the cessation of British trade in the Baltic, Saumarez was offered, and accepted, the command of a British squadron in the area in February 1808. Flying his flag in HMS *Victory* he spent the next five summers in the Baltic, often in a completely hostile environment, sometimes with one of the littoral states as an ally, sometimes another. During this period he maintained the flow of British trade. Ships were conveyed in and out of the Baltic through the difficult passage of The Sound and the Kattegat with the nearby Swedish and Danish gun batteries often hostile. The size of some of the convoys indicates the amount of trade that took place and is an indication of the failure of Napoleon's policies; for example, on 30 May 1810, 362 ships passed into the Baltic while on 27 July that year 220 ships returned to Britain.

An even larger convoy passed through The Sound homeward bound for Britain in October that year with Saumarez himself in HMS *Victory* with six other line-of-battle ships, six frigates and other warships escorting a thousand merchantmen. Yet despite this experience, despite the proven advantages of the convoy system, in 1914 no serving officer of the Royal Navy had ever seen a convoy, or probably had ever met anyone who had been at sea with one, nor had any merchant captain ever tried sailing in close company. More surprisingly, when the German submarine campaign of 1916 and 1917 eventually forced the introduction of convoys the idea was strenuously resisted by the Admiralty. In the Baltic the Germans showed themselves to be more flexible in thought and introduced them in 1915.

Today on the small island of Hano, only some 25 miles from

the Swedish naval base of Kalskrona, a naval cemetery bears silent witness to this era of naval operations in the Baltic.

The Royal Navy was also present in the Baltic during the Crimean War against Russia in 1854–5. Operations were limited in scope and achieved little. They were notable mainly because onboard HMS *Hecla*, a six gun paddle sloop, Mate Charles Lucas won the first Victoria Cross to be awarded to a member of the Royal Navy, during the bombardment of the Russian fortress of Bomarsund in the Aaland Islands on 21 June 1854. In August the following year the Fleet bombarded the fortress of Sveaborg on the north coast of the Gulf of Finland near the city of Helsingfors, the capital of Finland and a city destined to feature later in this story. At Sveaborg a number of Russian ships were sunk, about 2,000 casualties were inflicted, but as so often during this war indecisive leadership failed to follow up the attack, making the whole affair rather pointless.

Mention to many people that British submarines operated in the Baltic during the Great War 1914–18 and if the event is recalled at all it will be with the name of Lieutenant-Commander Max Horton who was the Commanding Officer of the submarine *E9* during 1914 and 1915. Indeed, by some at that time, including our enemies, the Baltic was known as 'Horton's Sea'. A still fewer number of people may also recall the name of Noel Laurence who was present in the Baltic at the same time as Horton, and who commanded the submarine *E1*. Few, if any, will know the name of Francis Cromie, one of Britain's unsung heroes of the Great War who combined the qualities of a respected and successful submarine Commanding Officer with those of a diplomat.

This then is the story of Horton, Laurence and Cromie, together with their gallant crews and those other submariners who fought for their country, and for Russia, in the Baltic during the period from 1914 to 1918, and then on into 1919.

Certain writing conventions have been used. The names of places are those currently in use at the time of the events described; thus St Petersburg (or Petrograd from August 1914) is the modern Leningrad, Revel is now Tallinn, and

Helsingfors is Helsinki. Others are identified in the text on the first occasion of use. During the nineteenth century the Russian calendar was twelve days behind Western dates, and in the twentieth century prior to 1918 it was 13 days late. In this account all dates are given in the Western style except where it is necessary to the story, when the fact that the Old Style or Russian calendar is used is recorded.

I

1905–1914: The Years Between Two Wars

Any study of the Russian plans and preparations for war in the Baltic in 1914 must begin, paradoxically, with an event in the last days of May 1905 which took place half a world away in the Straits of Tsushima, lying between Japan and Korea. Then, a Russian Fleet, including 12 battleships, having sailed an incredible 18,000 miles from the Baltic almost to within sight of the Russian Pacific base at Vladivostok, was annihilated by the Japanese in the most crushing naval defeat of all time. Of the Russian ships that had entered the Tsushima Strait, only three escaped sinking, capture or internment. To many people it was not the magnitude of this defeat that was so surprising but rather that this hotch-potch collection of ships had managed to sail so far. The destruction of this Fleet, the second such naval disaster to befall the Russians during this war with Japan, coupled with the fall of the fortress of Port Arthur which the Fleet had been sent east to help relieve, led to a peace being signed between the two countries in Portsmouth, New Hampshire, in September. The Russians were left with the task not only of rebuilding their Fleet but also restoring shattered morale in both the Navy and the Army, and rethinking their entire strategy. That new plans could eventually include British participation in the Baltic was an idea that was not even considered in the immediate postwar years.

To make matters worse, while their Baltic Fleet had been sailing to their destiny in the Far East, European Russia had been the scene of widespread disaffection. At the time of the fall of Port Arthur to Japanese forces the Russian capital, St Petersburg, was in the grip of widespread strikes. The strikes began with a demand for a minimum wage and an eight-hour day in a munitions factory, and soon spread to a shipbuilding yard and to factories throughout the city. They began as an industrial dispute in just one factory but spread as a sign of popular disaffection against the autocracy that ruled Russia. They began with the workers of one factory wanting better conditions, but spread because of the enormous gulf that existed in Tsarist Russia between the various classes. They began peacefully but ended in blood because of the complete lack of understanding of the situation by the Tsar himself and his advisers.

The strikers decided on a peaceful march to the Winter Palace to present a petition to the Tsar stating their grievances. When this plan became known to the authorities extra troops and police were sent to the capital to be ready to deal with the situation. That the Tsar and his family had left the capital for Christmas and were at the Alexander Palace at Tsarskoe Selo, 15 miles away, and had not yet returned was unknown to the strikers and their leaders. Nor did the authorities think to inform them of the fact. Neither did the Tsar or his advisers seem to have considered that he should return to the Winter Palace so as to be able to receive any petition. So it was that on Sunday 9 January 1905 (by the Russian calendar) a great crowd of workers with their wives and children, and accompanied by numerous priests, set out through icy wind-swept streets for the Winter Palace. On arrival they found themselves confronted by the police and the Cossack cavalry. The demonstration was broken up with the loss of over a hundred lives and with many more wounded.

Over the months the story of unrest and industrial disorder was repeated elsewhere throughout European Russia. Even the Black Sea Fleet, the only major Russian naval force not affected by the naval defeats in the Far East at the hands of the Japanese, became involved with the revolutionary fervour.

Throughout the Black Sea Fleet political agitators were at work fomenting their brands of disaffection and inciting the crews to join the workers ashore in their protests against the government. In this atmosphere of potential revolution the new battleship *Kniaz Potemkin Tavrichesky* was known to be amongst the most loyal of Vice-Admiral Krieger's ships. The battleship, named after Prince Gregori Alexandrovitch Potemkin, Catherine the Great's favourite and more ruthless First Minister, had been completed at Nickolaev in 1903, displaced 12,800 tons, and was armed with four 12 inch guns in two twin turrets and had a secondary armament of sixteen 6 inch guns. Onboard on the morning of 27 June 1905 there was set in train a series of events that has been romanticised to excess and which ended with the battleship *Potemkin* (as she is more usually known) in the hands of a mutinous crew. The clash with authority began with a protest over magotty meat pronounced by the ship's doctor as being fit to eat. It was a sign of the times that even though the affair was handled badly it soon escalated to open mutiny with seven officers, including the Captain, being killed in one half hour of pitiless violence. The torpedo boat *N267*, in company with the *Potemkin* at the time, was also taken over by the mutinous battleship's crew and for a while both ships defied both the Admiral with the rest of the Black Sea Fleet, and the government. Odessa, also in a state of unrest against authority at the time, was actually bombarded in support of a revolution by extremists in the port and led to the deaths of thousands of citizens as the military regained control. Finally, the great battleship sought refuge in the Romanian port of Constanza, where the crew were allowed to remain, after scuttling their ship.

This was not the end of the troubles as far as the Black Sea Fleet was concerned. The *Potemkin*, raised from the bed of the harbour of Constanza, was returned to the Russians and taken to Sevastopol where her name was changed to *Panteleimon*. In November there were fresh outbreaks of mutiny and disorder.

Ashore, one of the regiments of infantry forming part of the garrison of the fortress mutinied. Among those released from prison by the mutinous troops was a naval Lieutenant Petr Schmidt, serving a sentence for subversive activities. He promptly led the crews of a cruiser and four destroyers in mutiny, but was eventually captured by loyal troops who quelled the uprising. Schmidt was shot with three sailor confederates on 19 March 1906, his death provoking many outbursts of sympathy throughout the country. Ten days later the four bodies had to be exhumed, taken out to sea and reburied in order to put an end to a continuous pilgrimage to the graves and the placing of many wreaths on them.

Even the rump of the Baltic Fleet that remained after Tsushima was not exempt from trouble. There unrest showed itself in the old armoured cruiser *Pamiat Azova*, a ship to be met with again later in this story. But as a result the ship lost the right to fly a special ensign, a right bestowed earlier in recognition of the services of her namesake, the flagship *Azova*, at Navarino. Her name was changed to *Dvina* on the direct orders of the Tsar.

Poor Nicholas. He had become the last (as events were to turn out) Tsar of all the Russias in 1894 and was determined to carry on the policy of his father, Alexander III, which was to prevent the spread of reform and democracy — reforms instituted by Alexander II. Yet this ultra-reactionary Nicholas II, weak willed, obstinate and suspicious of all advice, was forced to summon the Duma, or Parliament, as part of the price to be paid in restoring order within his Empire. With the war over this gesture to his peoples was to work against the rapid rebuilding of the shattered Navy. While the Tsar wanted reconstruction programmes to begin immediately the Duma would not vote the necessary money. Instead, they insisted that a far-reaching enquiry be held into the Navy's shortcomings, not only operational but also administrative.

This impasse led to two wasted years out of the all too short time that was to be available before war broke out again. Eventually the Duma, increasingly packed with the Tsar's supporters through illegal manipulation of the electoral laws, began to agree the necessary expenditure. Thus in the spring of 1908 the Minister of the Navy was voted the money for four dreadnoughts, three submarines and a depot ship for the Baltic Fleet and some other ships for the Black Sea. Even so it was nearly another 12 months for the slow moving Russian shipbuilding industry to begin work on the first of the new *Gangut* class battleships, but it was a start and the reshaping of the Russian Navy, and the Baltic Fleet in particular, had at last begun.

Although the rebuilding of the Navy had started, its ultimate shape and size continued to be hotly debated. Was it to follow the pattern of a 'big ship' navy along the lines of the one so recently discredited in actions in the Far East? Or should it comprise mainly of torpedo craft, minelayers and submarines necessary for the protection of the coasts of Mother Russia? The former concept was the one most favoured by the Tsar himself so perhaps it is not surprising that it was the view that prevailed.

By 1909 the forms of the opposing political and military national groups in Europe were beginning to take shape, and in turn this had the effect of forcing the Duma into a position where action had to be taken, however reluctantly, if the Russians were not to be left totally unprepared for any future war. A ten-year programme costing over a billion roubles was therefore put before the Duma. Even so, it was 1910 before a reduced programme of only three-quarters of a billion roubles was authorised and building could be started.

With a large building programme authorised and the finance available the completion of a new Russian Fleet was still subject to delay. The building programme envisaged by the ten-year plan was beyond the capabilities of both the Russian shipbuilding and the armament industries. Boilers, engines, armour, armament, even complete ships had to be ordered from abroad. Some of these orders had to be placed with German firms despite the fact that it was becoming increasingly obvious that in a future conflict Germany would be enemy rather than allied, and that supply of this equipment and the associated spare parts could therefore be jeopardised.

In the event two light cruisers building at Danzig became welcome additions to the German Navy in 1914.

With reconstruction of the Fleet at last under way it is timely to look briefly at other aspects of the naval reorganisation instituted after the military defeats of 1905. Until the appointment of the able Admiral Ivan Konstantinovitch Grigorovich as Minister of Marine in April 1911 little was accomplished in revising policy and plans, modernising the dockyards to cope with the new equipment to be fitted in the new ships, improving the methods of training and ensuring that an adequate supply organisation existed. Under his direction a policy was formulated that the naval centre of operations should be the Baltic with the Pacific and White Sea areas guarded only by limited coast defence forces. In the Black Sea area the only major foreseeable adversary was Turkey, and no large forces would be required to maintain a superiority over the Turkish Fleet which was in an even more antiquated state than the Russians' had been at the time of the Japanese war. Although the Baltic was considered to be the main area of operations in a future war it was thought that German superiority would mean that Russian Fleet operations would be dictated by the need to protect the capital St Petersburg — although perhaps it was a theoretical German superiority which was considered by the Russian staff and which took no cognisance of the fact that the Germans would need to maintain a large number of ships in the North Sea to counter the fleet of Russia's ally France, and that of France's ally, Britain.

Grigorovich also took energetic steps to begin stamping out the widespread corruption that bedevilled the Russian Navy's logistic support, began to reorganise the training of officers and ratings so as to take the Navy out of the era of sailing ships, and most importantly he tried to restore the morale of the badly shaken fleet in the years following the disaster at Tsushima. Yet despite all his efforts the Russian Fleet was woefully short of officers when war did break out again and was hardly comparable with their enemy in either material or efficiency. Again, despite all Grigorovich's efforts the British naval attaché in St Petersburg sent in a report just before the outbreak of war in 1914 in which he was constrained to write that

> the fundamental mistake of the Russian Admiralty is the devoting of its energy and money principally to an increase in purely material strength rather than for the more urgent problem of building up a system of honest administration and the creation of a well trained, capable, well-paid and contented personnel.

But, where would the Russian Navy have been without the untiring efforts of Admiral Grigorovich?

Once the policy had been decided that the main task of the Fleet was to defend the capital then the future of its bases could be assessed. Libau, only a few miles north of the border with Prussia, was considered to be too vulnerable in a future war with Germany and therefore no additional funds were to be made available to develop the naval dockyard. Meanwhile it was to continue to be used as an advanced base for light forces. Yet Libau was the one port that was near to the German bases, near to where the Fleet would have to be if it was to carry out any offensive policy; the distance to the German advance base at Pillau was only 122 miles, not much further to Danzig and only 400 miles from Kiel. The entrance to the port was only dredged to 26 feet which precluded its use by cruisers and larger ships but otherwise it had the potential of a fine protected naval harbour with the advantage over many other Baltic ports that it was usually possible to keep the port and its approaches clear of ice throughout the winter by the use of icebreakers.

Similar defensive reasoning was applied to the port of Riga. Despite its position on the flank of any German force operating directly against the Gulf of Finland and St Petersburg, and the fact that it lay comparatively well defended from naval attack deep within its name Gulf, it too was relegated to the role of a support base. The northern approaches to the gulf were through the Moon Sound which separated the offshore islands of Dago, Osel and the smaller Moon from the mainland of Estonia. This passage was no deeper than 15 feet, and so necessarily of use only to the smaller warships and could be easily mined. South of the island of Osel lies the southern approach to the port of Riga through the Irben Strait, which could be used by all sizes of warships in both the Russian and German Navies, and which was to figure prominently later in the war with German attempts to seize the city.

It was to be further north in the gulf between Finland and Estonia that the Russian Fleet was to have its bases. The great fortress of Kronstadt near St Petersburg at the head of the gulf was to be the heart of the defences, 770 miles from the main German base at Kiel at the other end of the Baltic. Here were the docks and support facilities for the battleships and battle-cruisers, nearby were the shipyards where the future units of the Fleet were taking shape, all protected by the great batteries and fortifications supplemented in the event of war by extensive minefields.

In 1912 the sum of 40 million roubles was authorised to make Revel a main support base for Fleet operations, with another 92 million roubles for fortifications. A complete new harbour was to be built to accommodate eight battleships together with numerous cruisers, destroyers and other light craft including submarines. By the time war broke out in 1914 its construction was far from finished and the port was inadequately equipped to form a base for any ships other than the destroyers and submarines. Even the fortifications were incomplete. Across the water on the Finnish shore lay the spacious port of Helsingfors, well protected by its fortifications and also available as a secondary fleet base.

In the event of war an outer line of fortifications to protect the Gulf, its bases and ultimately the capital of St Petersburg was planned to stretch from Hango in southwest Finland across the northernmost point of the island of Dago. By the outbreak of war little had been achieved in the construction of any fortifications at the shore ends of this line, but preparations had been made to lay the minefields that were part of the system.

Whilst Admiral Grigorovich was energetically trying to

increase the state of training of the Navy as a whole, the Baltic Fleet was lucky in being commanded by Admiral von Essen, one of the few Russian officers to have emerged from the war with Japan with any honour. When that war had broken out he had still been in his forties, and since leaving the Naval Academy he spent much of his naval career either in the Mediterranean or the Far East. Just after the turn of the century it is obvious that he must have shown his ability since he was specially selected to command the newly built cruiser *Norvik*, the pride of the Fleet, and was ordered to take the ship to the Far East. He and his ship were in Port Arthur when the Japanese attacked in February 1904, but despite the surprise of the attack he was able to fight his ship out of harbour and into close action with the enemy. In the following months the *Norvik* was frequently damaged while in action as Captain von Essen took every opportunity for meeting the enemy, impressing everyone not only with his own gallantry but also with his competence as a naval commander.

Later that year he was appointed to command the battleship *Sevastopol* and continued to show an aggression and a degree of seamanship so sadly lacking in many of his contemporaries. The *Sevastopol* was repeatedly in action, and often damaged, until with great skill Captain von Essen took her into deep water outside Port Arthur and there scuttled his ship to avoid her capture.

After the war he was sent to the Baltic to command another new cruiser, the *Rurik*. Like many other towns in European Russia at that time the naval base at Kronstadt suffered from many disturbances and mutinies, as has been recounted earlier, and it was here that von Essen once again showed the strength of his personality coupled with his own courage. Shortly after his arrival at the naval base he was met by a band of mutinous sailors as they attempted to leave their barrack block. Single handed he forced them to return to their quarters and not to join many of their fellow sailors who were running wild through the streets of the town causing an orgy of destruction, and when death could easily be the end for any officer foolish enough to get in their way. After the *Rurik* he was given command of the Baltic Fleet's minelaying squadron before becoming its Commander-in-Chief in 1908. This, then, was the man under whom the British submariners were soon to operate; a man of small stature but immense personality, an officer personally brave but more important who was professionally competent, a Commander-in-Chief who had done more than anyone to try to raise the standards of the Russian Navy after their demoralising defeats a decade earlier.

II

~~~~~~

Overtures: Plans and Preparations

17 September 1914: the 45th day of the war for the British. Forty-five days during which the nations engaged in this, the start of the first worldwide war, had seen their fortunes go first one way, then another. The Royal Navy had chased the *Goeben* and the *Breslau* across the Mediterranean only to see the German ships disappear into the Dardanelles. Turkey had yet to enter the war on the side of the Germans. In the Pacific Vice-Admiral von Spee's Asiatic Squadron had also eluded the Royal Navy. In the North Sea the Germans had been worsted in the Battle of the Heligoland Bight in late August. Submarines, a new form of warfare, has as yet made little impact on the conflict (while aircraft, the other new weapon of war, had been of even less impact), for the Germans had lost both the *U-13* and the *U-15* in their first major sortie to seek the British Fleet, the former from an unknown cause, the latter rammed and sunk by the light cruiser HMS *Birmingham*. Later the *U-21* had evened the score by sinking HMS *Pathfinder*, a small 'scout cruiser'. On the Allied side the Australian submarine *AE1* had gone missing off the coast of German New Guinea while Lieutenant-Commander Max Horton in HMS *E9* had sunk the German cruiser *Hela* in the Heligoland Bight. The BEF had been successfully transported to France

without the loss of a man or a horse through enemy action, and had then bloodied the Germans at Mons before being forced to retreat. The German advance had penetrated as far as the River Marne, faltered, and had been pushed back to the River Aisne by the French counter offensive. The Belgians still occupied the western part of their country including the great port of Antwerp and the lesser ports on the Channel coast. In the east the Russians had advanced into Prussia only to be decisively beaten in a series of battles known as Tannenberg, though they were having more success against the Austrians in Galicia. In Serbia, where the whole bloody business had started, there was fanatical fighting, and there too the Austrians had had but little to show for thousands of casualties.

On that September day an important meeting took place onboard HMS *Iron Duke*, the flagship of the Grand Fleet, in Loch Ewe on the west coast of Scotland. Those present included the Commander-in-Chief, Admiral Sir John Jellicoe, his Chief of Staff and the various admirals commanding the squadrons of the Battle Fleet. From London had come the First Lord of the Admiralty, Mr Winston Churchill, and the Chief of the War Staff, Vice-Admiral Sir Doveton Sturdee, whilst from Harwich had come the two commodores in charge of the light forces there, Roger Keyes and Reginald Tyrwhitt, commanding the submarines and the destroyers, respectively. The meeting was to review the way the war at sea was progressing, and to discuss future naval policy and movements regarding operations of the Grand Fleet in the North Sea.

The first subject under discussion was a proposed bombardment of the German island of Heligoland followed by an assault designed to capture this fortress. The island, which is about 20 miles from the entrance to the Elbe, Weser and Jade rivers where the main German North Sea naval bases were situated, is a mile long and less than half a mile wide and except at the southern limit is surrounded by high cliffs. In 1914, as in 1939, it was heavily fortified. As recently as 1913 a naval planning study had concluded that the cost of capturing the island would be prohibitive. Whose idea was this? The minutes of the meeting do not record this fact, but one can detect the restless impetuosity of the First Lord for action against the enemy in this plan; the same attitude that was to lead to similar proposals a quarter of a century later to attack the Italian-held Mediterranean islands of Pantelleria, Lampedusa and Linosa. Then, as in 1914, the plan came to nought. Naval opinion was generally against the attack on Heligoland as likely to lead to an unnecessary loss of capital ships, while the cost of retaining the island — should an assault have been successful — would outweigh any advantage gained.

The next subject for discussion was the Baltic. The idea of forcing the passage of the Skagerrak and the Kattegat with a strong portion of the Fleet and even with the added possibility of landing troops on the Pomeranian coast was not new. In the War Plans drawn up by Admiral Fisher in 1907, when he was First Sea Lord, various schemes were formulated for enforcing an economic blockade of Germany with operations in the Baltic as one of the options; an option which had been tried out as a war game in the naval college at Portsmouth the previous year. The First Lord, too, must be considered a protagonist for a scheme like this as a means of using the Fleet in an active and offensive way. As early in the war as 19 August he had written a letter to the Russian Commander-in-Chief, the Grand Duke Nicholas, in which he had mentioned a plan of this nature. However, at this meeting it was now decided not to risk a major part of the Grand Fleet on any mad-cap operations against the Germans in the Baltic in general, and in Kiel Bay in particular. It was believed that the risks from mines was too great, and that the very power of the Grand Fleet lay in its presence as a potential threat to whatever plans the Germans might consider. On the other hand Keyes suggested that there might be an opportunity for two submarines of the new 'E' class to force the passage, without undue risk, and to attack units of the German Fleet off Kiel. He was authorised to carry out a reconnaissance to determine whether or not a passage was feasible.

Keyes, ever eager for battle and never one to waste time,

took steps immediately on his return to Harwich the following day to implement the authorised reconnaissance. For this task the submarine *E1* (Lieutenant-Commander Noel F. Laurence, RN) and the *E5* (Lieutenant-Commander C. S. Benning, RN) were selected. They were ordered to leave Harwich on the 19th, spend the night at Gorleston, and then sail the following morning at daylight to meet the two destroyers *Firedrake* and *Lurcher*, which would then tow them all day as they made their way across the North Sea towards the Skaw. The submarines would then part from their helpful surface ships at dusk, proceed together overnight, and arrive next morning in the Skaw where they would part company and proceed into the Kattegat. Their task was to examine the anchorages in the Aalbok Bight and Aalborg Bay, and then cruise in the channels from the Belts. They were given a rendezvous early on the 24th to meet up with a force of cruisers and destroyers to escort them home. In fact the operation was delayed and the two boats did not leave Gorleston until the 22nd.

Both submarines carried out a thorough search of their areas and saw very little shipping, and what was seen was mostly neutral. On one day Laurence surfaced his boat and sought information from a Danish fishing vessel, which told him that German patrols in the north of the Skaw were anchored off Skagen because of the prevailing bad weather. Before setting off on an unsuccessful search to find the patrols Laurence had to transfer one of his crew to the fishing vessel so that an injured hand could receive medical treatment. The sailor was landed by the Danes in Fredrickshaven.

It is difficult to see how this reconnaissance could be said to demonstrate whether it was practical or not to force a way into the Baltic, since for obvious reasons no attempt was made to approach the passage of The Sound — the most critical part of the whole future operation. One thing that was shown was the poor mechanical state of Laurence's boat, something that was to dog his operational capability in the months to come. During this patrol one engine developed a lubricating oil leak from the crankcase to the bilges, a leak that became progressively worse the more the submarine rolled in the bad weather. It was because of this that Laurence delayed his return for two days, remaining in the comparatively sheltered waters of the Skaw waiting for the weather to moderate — his non-appearance at the rendezvous with the *E5* and the cruisers causing no little concern to those waiting for him, but otherwise little harm was done.

Keyes was undaunted and continued his planning, yet it is strange that this planning does not seem to have included the submarines themselves. With such a dangerous mission in mind it would be thought that the submarines would be allowed a period in harbour for maintenance and overhaul, allowed time for training, storing, and perhaps even some leave. But no. There was no change in the pattern of events. Indeed, to what extent did Keyes himself realise the enormous difficulties that lay ahead? Was he still thinking in terms of an immediate return to Harwich after the raid, or had he begun to think that they would have to stay in the Baltic since the return passage would be too difficult with the Germans thoroughly alerted? If the latter was the case, then the submarines would be asked to operate from a foreign base at the far end of the Baltic, over 1,000 miles from their own home base at Harwich, and with all future supplies destined to take the even longer route to north Russia and then suffer the delays and frustrations of an archaic and limited transportation system between Murmansk and Petrograd. Despite Churchill's earlier letter to the Russian Commander-in-Chief there is little evidence to suggest that the Russians were privy to any change in plan or were invited to acquiesce in the proposal.

From the papers still available it is also not clear when Keyes selected the actual submarines that were to make the trip, so taking the Commanding Officers into his confidence, or even who authorised the increase from two to three submarines. Despite the doubts about the mechanical reliability of Laurence's boat, the *E1* was one of those eventually selected to try and force their way into the Baltic. The *E5*, the other boat to have made the reconnaissance of the Kattegat with Laurence, was not chosen, instead the *E9* (Lieutenant-Commander Max

Horton) and the *E11* (Lieutenant-Commander Martin Nasmith) were selected.

Who were these three Commanding Officers that Keyes had selected to carry out his daring scheme? All three had entered the Navy just before the turn of the century, all three joined submarines in October 1904, all three served their country with distinction during the war and served again in high rank during the next conflict. Yet, as individuals they could not have been more different.

Laurence entered the Navy at the age of 17 from the Nautical Training College on the Thames — better known as HMS *Worcester* — going quickly to a ship of the fleet, HMS *Diadem*. During his training he did well in all his examinations and gained additional seniority. A well built man, standing over six foot in his socks, he must have had trouble finding any comfort in the cramped small submarines of his time, and for which he had soon volunteered. His ability as a submariner was soon evident with his appointment in command of first the *A1*, then the *D1* and *D2*, followed by a short period back in general service after which he commissioned the *E1* on completion of building. Keyes regarded him as a most skilful and determined submariner. Keyes' high opinion of him was such that he was one of seven officers, either serving in submarines or with submarine experience and knowledge, appointed to assist Keyes who was himself a non-submarine specialist. Laurence was a reserved and rather formal man. He seldom joked or laughed aloud, a smile was about as far as he would go, yet he had what has been described as an 'imposing presence'. He was a man of tremendous competence and immense integrity. He nevertheless took great interest in the men under him and though a strict disciplinarian was a popular and trusted captain.

Even in the early stages of the war Horton's reputation as a submariner was second to none, for his exploit in sinking the *Hela* became well known. Before the war his actions had put him in the front rank of submarine Commanding Officers. For example, during the autumn manoeuvres of 1912 Horton had skilfully taken his boat, the *D6*, up the Firth of Forth and 'torpedoed' two 'enemy' warships lying at anchor above the bridge. With his own total devotion to the Royal Navy he expected the same standards from not only his own crew but also from everyone else. Yet he was a loner with few real friends, somewhat unorthodox and an inveterate, but lucky, gambler.

The third member of the trio, Martin Nasmith, had not only served with Laurence on Keyes' Submarine Advisory Committee but had also been an instructor at the submarine training base at Gosport. Under his guidance the art of attacking with a torpedo had been changed from hopeful guesswork to an applied science of relative velocities, angles and ranges. With his background he should have had better luck in the opening weeks of the war in the Heligoland Bight, yet his submarine, the *E11*, had nothing to show for several hazardous patrols against the enemy. Lady Luck had not smiled on this cheerful and determined officer who as a result of his frustrations and disappointments had vowed that he would abstain from smoking and drinking until he had sunk an enemy warship. It was, in fact, to be in another theatre of operations far from the Baltic that he was to be released from his vow and to gain high distinction.

Routine operations continued. Any preparations that could have been taking place onboard the three submarines were interrupted by events elsewhere. In Belgium the German advance was causing great concern in those early days of October 1914 and the important port of Antwerp was threatened. If that city fell it would open the way for the Germans to advance on the Channel ports of Ostend and Zeebrugge, and that would place the German Army, and ultimately Navy, far too close to England for the liking of either the Admiralty or the government. Reinforcements for the British Army in France were despatched from England in the form of the 3rd Cavalry Division and the 7th Infantry Division. Their task was to try and hold the two Belgian ports on the Channel coast and stabilise the left of the Allied line. As was the case when the main body of the BEF was sent to France in August, these troops all arrived safely with no interference from the

German High Seas Fleet or submarines. Nevertheless, as part of the forces deployed to protect their crossing two submarines were sent to Zeebrugge in case the Germans did try to attack these tempting targets. Originally the *E4* was ordered to Belgium with the *E11*, but in the event the former patrolled off the Terschelling Lightship while the *E1* went to Zeebrugge. The submarines were to remain in harbour until informed of the enemy's approach when they were to proceed to sea. The idea was to cut off the enemy's retreat to the north and force him westwards over a newly laid minefield. Such precautions proved unnecessary, the Germans stayed away. With a lack of understanding of the pressures involved Keyes reported at this time to the Commander-in-Chief that 'the two submarines at Zeebrugge are really resting, and will be available for service elsewhere when relieved'.

Keyes himself travelled to Zeebrugge to view the landings and to be on hand in case the submarines were required to counter a German sortie. So, by a twist of fate, he was able to view the port with the full might of the British Army making a peaceful landing. For it was here nearly four years later that the action for ever associated with his name was to take place when the landing parties of sailors and marines from HMS *Vindictive* stormed the mole while the blockships were positioned in an attempt to block the canal to Bruges and so prevent the German submarines based there from regaining the open sea.

Meanwhile, what of the *E9* destined with the *E1* and *E11* to try and break into the Baltic? Since the beginning of the war the British submarines had been keeping watch in the Heligoland Bight for any movements of the High Seas Fleet from its bases. But, since the sinking of the *Hela* by the *E9* in September their only reward had been fleeting glances of their elusive quarry, which had apparently abandoned the use of the Bight as an exercise area. More and more the Germans were using the safety of Kiel Bay for their training. More and more the British submarines were being worried by the growing area of minefields, and suffering from the exceptionally heavy gales which raged at the end of September. Conditions onboard these early submarines, where the designers had made only limited concessions to the needs of accommodation and none to comfort, were basic in the best of weather. During these autumn gales life for those onboard was indescribably grim. The air soon became foul because of the lack of ventilation caused by the need to keep the conning tower hatch shut for long periods in the short steep seas, which added to the usual smells of oil and cooking. There was the eternal problem of condensation, the water from those seas that pooped the submarine, and the violent motion. For weary men coming off watch there could be little respite, as sleeping space was at a premium, the sailors finding somewhere to rest where they could. Even when dived the boats were uncomfortable, still rolling when at a depth of 60 feet, and with accurate depth-keeping impossible.

However, as the Germans seemed reluctant to send their larger ships into the Bight Keyes and Tyrwhitt planned to lure them out into a submarine ambush. The plan was to attack any destroyer patrols that could be found with a force of light cruisers and destroyers from Harwich, in the expectation that the Germans would then support their patrols with some larger ships sent out from their bases in the Weser or Ems. The submarines *E3* and *E6* together with Horton's *E9* were to set the trap, lying in wait off the mouth of the River Ems. The operation was planned for 5 or 6 October, depending on the weather, and the submarines were sailed to take up their positions. However, 24 hours later when the weather was considered unsuitable the raid was cancelled, but there was then no way of informing the submarines.

So it was that at 10.30 a.m. on the 6th Horton in the *E9* was in a position off the west Ems waiting for signs that the raid was taking place and hoping, no doubt, that a worthwhile target would present itself for *E9*'s torpedoes — perhaps even a battleship! It had been an anxious time for Horton and the Commanding Officers of the other two submarines, with bad weather adding to the normal hazards of the area. In the years before the war the author Erskine Childers had dramatically used this area as the setting for his novel of espionage and daring deeds, *The Riddle of the Sands*, a book which Horton with his usual thoroughness had read with interest, his seaman's eye noting the navigational problems confronting the story's hero. Now, not for the first time since war had been declared, he was coping with these same problems himself. With two German destroyers in sight he had waited with increasing impatience to see what happened as the presence of the British force made itself felt. As they were still there at noon he guessed that the raid had been cancelled and anticipating that there would be no bigger targets in the area, he began his own attack. His targets were the two small destroyers, *S116* and *S117* of the 7th Half Flotilla. Of only some 420 tons displacement they had been built between 1902 and 1906, and had an armament of three 4 pounder guns and three 18 inch torpedo tubes. Twice his target altered course just as Horton was about to fire. Then he found himself in a position about 500 yards just forward of the beam of the *S116* and fired both his bow tubes. One torpedo struck the destroyer amidships and she broke in two and sank in three minutes. When Horton next put his periscope up all that was to be seen was about 15 feet of the destroyer's bow sticking vertically out of the water. The commanding officer, Korvetten-Kapitän Freiherr von Ziegesar, and nine ratings perished, the remaining 55 officers and ratings were picked up by the *S117* and the *S118*, another sister destroyer which arrived on the scene shortly afterwards. In those days there was nothing the remaining destroyers could do for a deliberate counter-attack as long as the submarine remained submerged and invisible. The destroyers had no hydrophone to find the submarine nor depth charges with which to make an attack. All they could hope to do was to keep the submarine submerged until its battery was exhausted, when it would be forced to surface and could be attacked by the destroyers' guns. So it was that *E9*, with batteries almost exhausted, crept away to the west, surfacing later in the afternoon to return to Harwich. With this success, the second in two months, Horton had established himself firmly as the leading British submariner with one cruiser and one destroyer to his credit.

Perhaps it was at this stage, with the *E9* back from her successful patrol in the Bight and the *E1* and *E11* back from their 'rest period' in Zeebrugge, that Keyes broke the news to his three Commanding Officers that they were about to take part in an extraordinary operation. In any case, if the expedition were to be mounted and the submarines were to have the opportunity of making their presence felt once they had entered the Baltic before the seas froze over for the winter, then time was at a premium. But still the Admiralty had not finally approved that they were to go! Keyes' plans were submitted to the Chief of the War Staff on 10 October and amplified in a second letter two days later: the operation to take place as soon as a spell of fine weather appeared imminent.

Keyes' submission on the 12th is remarkable on two counts. First, he stated that his plan was for the submarines to leave at daylight in tow of *two* destroyers, with a destroyer to look out ahead and another on the starboard flank, the implication being that only two submarines were to take part. Was this really still his intention at this late stage before departure? Was it put in this way perhaps since the Admiralty had never changed its instructions after the 17 September meeting, where Keyes himself had stated that there might be opportunities for two 'E' class submarines to attack the Germans in Kiel Bay? There is no record of the Admiralty sanction for the third submarine to take part. Secondly, Keyes refers to a plan to send cruisers and destroyers into the Kattegat so that the submarines may meet with friendly forces there on their return. This rendezvous was to be on the seventh day after the departure of the submarines from Yarmouth. Was it really a possibility that the submarines were still intended to attempt the return passage so soon after entering the Baltic? Were the Russians still in the dark concerning the idea that the submarines would remain in the Baltic to operate from Russian bases? If so, this lack of liaison with Britain's Allies was to have near-disastrous consequences in the weeks to come. In these circumstances it is hardly surprising that the Naval attaché in Petrograd, Commander H. Grenfell, RN, after a visit to the Russian Commander-in-Chief,

Admiral von Essen, following the arrival of the submarines, wrote:

> he [von Essen] would have been even more pleased had he received timely notice of their coming, or been informed as to whose orders they were intended to be subordinate.

With hindsight, and with the knowledge of the detailed planning that takes place today before even the smallest scale operation, the total indecision only days before the submarines left seems almost beyond belief.

A mere 24 hours later Keyes issued his written orders to the three submarine Commanding Officers, having at last received approval from the Admiralty to his plans. They were to sail that day for Gorleston, take on fuel from the oiler *Ialine* and then leave at daybreak next day under the tow of the destroyers who would tow them until dusk towards the Skaw. Their object then was to arrive off the entrance of The Sound, unseen, to pass through The Sound if possible by night, to avoid the German patrols at the southern end of The Sound, and to attack the German Fleet believed to be exercising in the area. The orders concluded that when the submarines became low on fuel they were to proceed to Libau, where they would be expected, and to operate from their until they received fresh instructions. In addition they were given a recognition signal for use in the North Sea when they returned after 1 November. Here, only hours before departure, was yet another variation on the plan, with the submarines expected to stay in the Baltic operating from Libau until some time in November or later.

But, the die was cast. The great enterprise was about to start.

III

~~~~~~

1914: Into the Baltic

So it was that on the afternoon of Tuesday 13 October 1914 three submarines led by Laurence in the *E1* slipped from their berths in Harwich harbour, where the depot ship HMS *Maidstone* had mothered them and the other submarines of the VIIIth (Overseas) Flotilla, and headed quietly out to sea. To many of those watching it must have seemed another case of three submarines leaving harbour for another patrol, probably in the Heligoland Bight. Just how many of those onboard the submarines themselves realised the significance of the occasion, let alone realised where it would all end, will never be known.

As they left harbour over on the port hand at Shotley were the huts and buildings of the Boy Seamen's training establishment, HMS *Ganges*, where in the first hours of the war the youngsters and their instructors had crowded the pier to cheer the destroyers of Commodore Tyrwhitt's force leaving for the first sweep of the war into the North Sea, and the submarines *E6* and *E8* leaving for their first war patrols in the Heligoland Bight. Now, just over two months later, such events had become commonplace and evoked no such enthusiastic demonstration. Then again on the port hand further across the Stour estuary were the seaplane hangars of the new Royal Naval Air Service base at Felixstowe which had become operational in the year before the war, and from where the naval fliers now maintained a precarious patrol off the coast watching for any move by the enemy. Finally, a friendly wave to the crew of the *Cork* lightship signified farewell to Harwich, and they were on their way. Ahead was the unknown, but first there was an easy stage of only 40 miles up the coast to Gorleston at the mouth of the River Yare and just outside Yarmouth. There they berthed in turn on the small oiler *Ialine*, herself smaller than each of the submarines she was to top up with fuel. Built in Holland the year before, she had been taken over by the Admiralty at the outbreak of war and stationed at Gorleston to supply oil to the ships and submarines in the area.

Already things had started to go wrong. The starboard engine of Nasmith's *E11* had a defect, to repair which involved replacing a cylinder and its liner. Repair work began immediately and it was hoped to have it completed with the minimum of delay. Indeed, when Laurence reported the situation to Keyes that evening he was confident that all would be well, and proposed that the three submarines should leave at 5.0 a.m. on the 15th, the weather being suitable.

But when the time came for the three submarines to leave, the *E11*'s repairs were not complete, despite heroic efforts by the boat's engine room staff over the previous 36 hours. Nasmith believed that he would be ready to sail at 9.0 a.m., only four hours after the other two boats. As the plan was for the three submarines to pass through The Sound at two-hour intervals Laurence thought that this further delay was acceptable since the *E11* would still be able to pass into the Baltic as the last boat of the three. As will be seen this was leaving too much to chance and later Laurence was to be criticised for this action by Keyes, who thought that waiting another day would have been more prudent as all the boats would have been able to set out together.

In the event plans were to be disrupted even further and such armchair driving was only an academic exercise. Keyes himself had, at the last minute, dispensed with the requirement for destroyers to tow the submarines on their first day's passage across the North Sea. The submarines were on their own. Then, at 9.0 a.m. when the *E1* and *E9* were in the area

of Smith's Knoll, the *E1* suffered an engine defect, and since Laurence was unsure just how long it would take to rectify he sent the *E9* on ahead expecting to catch up later that day. Despite the fact that repairs were completed and he was able to get under way again just one hour later, it was to be the last these two submarines were to see of each other for many days. As for the *E11*, repairs took even longer than expected and it was 3.0 p.m. before she was ready to sail from Gorleston — six hours later than expected and ten hours after the other two. As the three submarines were now sailing independently it is perhaps appropriate to follow their fortunes in a similar manner.

Laurence, with his engine again repaired, set off from his position near Smith's Knoll and by 1.30 p.m. on the 17th had rounded the Skaw into the Kattegat and was to the north of the entrance to The Sound. Despite the delay in the North Sea he was the first to reach a position from whence he could attempt to break through ino the Baltic. Thus far according to plan. Since entering the Skagerrak he had had to dive frequently to avoid being seen by the many merchant ships sighted, all of which he believed to be neutral, but who were all potentially able to betray his presence to the Germans. As soon as it was dark he proceeded southwards through The Sound, through the Flint Channel and into the Baltic, a passage that was completed surprisingly easily by 11.30 p.m., and is best summed up in Laurence's own words:

At dark the passage of The Sound was commenced and safely accomplished by 11.30 p.m. The German patrol was seen burning searchlights ahead, and as I did not wish to find myself at daybreak with exhausted batteries, I deemed it inadvisable to dive past them and so went to the bottom off Moens Klint. At daylight (18th) rose to the surface and found a German destroyer close to us. Proceeded submerged to the southward.

Later, just after nine o'clock, Laurence sighted what he thought was the German cruiser *Fürst Bismarck* and began to manoeuvre the *E1* into an attacking position. Nearly an hour later he found himself well placed only 500 yards on the port beam of this old cruiser, which he had wrongly identified and was in fact the *Victoria Louise*. The *E1* was fitted with only one bow torpedo tube (as were her next seven sister boats; a second bow tube was not fitted until the *E9* was built), but she did have two beam tubes which Laurence fired at the German cruiser at one minute intervals. He believed that the first torpedo ran too deep and under the German ship, the second missing only yards ahead. Certainly the *Victoria Louise* was not hit, though the torpedo tracks were seen by the German lookouts both on the ship's quarterdeck and in the crow's nest. The Germans claim that the first torpedo passed not under the ship as Laurence thought but close astern, while the second only missed as the cruiser swung to starboard under full helm, and then ran parallel with the ship for some minutes before sinking at the end of its run. (The torpedo itself is several yards ahead of where its wake and track appear on the surface of the water.) A brilliant attack thwarted only by the alertness and good fortune of the German lookouts in sighting the torpedoes and being able to warn the bridge to take avoiding action in time. To the German luck may be added the fact that the torpedoes were running deeper than Laurence thought, a situation that foiled several British submarine attacks in the early days of the war. It was caused by the unappreciated fact that the warheads were heavier than the peacetime practice heads and so caused the torpedo to run up to four feet deeper. But was it a wise move by Laurence?

As a result of this attack the Germans were now certain that the British had infiltrated one or more submarines into the Baltic — for it was thought, correctly, that the attacker could hardly have been Russian. Before this there had been several false reports of British naval units, both surface ships and submarines, readying themselves for an attempt on the Baltic. Now these reports were confirmed. Even the September reconnaissance by the *E1* and the *E5* had been observed and reported to the German High Command. The day before

Laurence's attack (the 17th) German destroyers of the 19th Half Flotilla* had intercepted a steamer at the entrance of The Sound and her Master reported having seen a British submarine in the Skagerrak. Another destroyer of this Half Flotilla stationed at the southern entrance of The Sound reported that a submarine had been sighted about five miles west of the Falsterbo Reef lightship — surely the same destroyer sighted by Laurence when he came to periscope depth at daylight. Thus the Germans were truly alerted and had positive evidence that their North Sea foe had entered into the Baltic war, as opposed to the many scares and false reports that had occurred almost since the start of the war. If as intended Horton and Nasmith had each followed on two hours behind Laurence as planned then little would have been lost except perhaps the main chance of a surprise attack by three submarines on the 'safe' Kiel Bay exercise areas of the German High Seas Fleet. But in view of all that had gone wrong so far with the planned timetable it was too much to assume that both the *E9* and the *E11* were also safely into the Baltic when the *Victoria Louise* was attacked. Indeed they were not, and their chances were correspondingly reduced.

As might be expected, the Germans reacted strongly to the presence of enemy submarines so near to their main base. The report from the *Victoria Louise* of the unsuccessful attack on her reached Prince Henry of Prussia, the German naval Commander-in-Chief in the Baltic, at 10.30 a.m. and immediately he issued orders for increased patrols to try to catch the submarines and to make it even harder for any more boats to attempt the passage through The Sound into the Baltic. The forces available to him included the airship PL19. The inclusion of this vast zeppelin in the search dispositions is an indication that the potential of these craft for anti-submarine warfare was appreciated by the Germans even at this early

*The Half Flotilla consisted of the *G.134*, *S.120*, *S.123*, *S.125*, *T.97*, *T.102* and *T.127* under the command of Kapitan-Leutnant Graf von der Reike-Volmerstein. The *V.25* had also been with this Half Flotilla when it was formed, but was now with the 17th.

stage of the war, and its use here may well be the first time that a joint sea and air search force was deployed. Prince Henry also wanted to mine the southern approaches to The Sound, as had been done in the Belts in the early days of the war. However, the German High Command vetoed this proposal as 'it would be useless against submarines, and commerce must be maintained'.

What had happened to Horton in the *E9* which should have followed two hours behind Laurence? On the day following his separation from his Senior Officer in the middle of the North Sea he had sighted the coast of Jutland by mid-morning and had then proceeded northwards so as to round the Skaw at midnight. During that day he had had to dive three times to avoid being sighted by neutral merchant ships. Then, shortly after sunset, but before the light had completely faded, Horton had sighted what he thought could have been the wake of another submarine, though nothing was in sight. To be on the safe side he dived immediately, staying quiet and hidden for half an hour until it was completely dark, though postwar German records do not indicate that one of their boats was in the area at the time.

The following day he proceeded cautiously through the Kattegat first towards the Swedish coast and then southwards towards The Sound. However, he was unable to make much progress as there were a large number of merchant ships in the area, and also a Swedish cruiser which by chance remained in his vicinity for most of the day, all of which caused him to remain dived for the day. Just before sunset he surfaced again and once more was able to head towards The Sound on his main engines, although meeting with a 'continuous stream of traffic proceeding in both directions'. Under these conditions he must have been sighted and only Horton's keenness to press on into the Baltic with Laurence according to Keyes' plans could have prompted this indiscretion. Even so at 11.30 p.m. that night he was still three miles north of the Kullen Light and some ten miles from the start of the narrows north of Helsingborg on the Swedish coast. But enough was enough. Horton decided that as he would not be able to clear The

Sound before daylight he would postpone his passage until the following night. It is interesting to note that he records in his report that he considered that the other two boats would have been similarly impeded by the necessity of remaining hidden from the constant stream of merchant ships. Yet at this time Laurence in *E1* had just cleared the southern entrance to The Sound.

Horton remained on the bottom all the next day, the 18th, while his colleague was making his unsuccessful attack on the *Victoria Louise* and causing the Germans to react so strongly to this incursion into their private backyard. At sunset he was able to return to periscope depth again, carefully survey the area through the periscope and noting that there was no shipping in the area he was able to surface before once more trying to pass through The Sound. One can only guess at the conditions onboard the *E9* at this time, and the relief of the crew to have fresh air circulating through the boat again after 17 hours dived. With the boat lying quietly on the bottom most of the crew would have been able to sleep wherever they could find a suitable space or just sit around so as to conserve the oxygen as much as possible. Yet even under these restful conditions the air would have gradually become more and more foul, mingling with the all-pervading smell of diesel oil and the sick-making smells from the unemptied sanitary buckets, for the heads (the usual naval term covering the landsman's toilets) could not be used with the submarine below 30 feet. Condensation and water trickling from any of the inevitable small leaks would have contributed to the misery of all onboard.

It was a calm night, with no moon, so good progress could be made. All went well at first and by 11.0 p.m. they passed Malmo, where the lights still burnt in neutral Sweden, and they began the really dangerous part of the whole passage as they entered the narrow and shallow Flint Channel. For this Horton trimmed the submarine down until the upper deck was awash and only the conning tower of the *E9* showed above water to mark its passage, while to cut down the wash and the noise he reduced speed and proceeded on one engine only.

Just before midnight, when the *E9* was southwest of the Drogden lightvessel, Horton sighted a destroyer only 150 yards away on his starboard bow. Luckily the destroyer was lying stopped and also her lookouts failed to see the small silhouette of the submarine. Quietly Horton took the submarine down to periscope depth, hoping to creep past this German sentinel. But before even the periscope standards were underwater the *E9* hit the bottom — they were resting on a shallow patch marked 4½ fathoms on the chart. Now they could only hope and there they remained for 20 minutes wondering what the German would do next. By that time the German had drifted to within 70 yards of the stranded submarine. Keeping the submarine only inches off the bottom Horton slowly edged the *E9* towards deeper water. Hardly daring to hope that his luck would hold he watched the depth gauge move slowly from 10 feet (this was not the depth of the keel, but the depth at which the gauge was fitted on the hull, just below the normal surfaced waterline), to 15 feet and on to 20 feet as the submarine bounced along the bottom towards safety. Incredibly they were not seen. At 3.40 a.m., by now the 19th, Horton was able to give his weary crew a short rest while the submarine lay on the bottom with a safe 48 feet showing on the depth gauge. But it could only be a short break before they once more headed south into the Baltic. At dawn Horton came to periscope depth to find German destroyers both ahead and astern of him — part of the enemy's reactions to Laurence's attack the previous morning. But Horton was through The Sound and was able to surface by mid-morning to ventilate the boat and to start charging his batteries. There was a destroyer only six miles away which caused him to dive again for a couple of hours as it passed close to his position, but again he remained unseen. At dusk he once more dived to spend a restful night on the bottom — only the first of many nights he was to spend at sea in the Baltic before he saw England again. Two boats had made their way into the Baltic, what of the third?

Martin Nasmith, the Commanding Officer of the *E11*, must have watched the other two submarines slip quietly from their berths in Gorleston early on the morning of the 15th with feelings of frustration mingled with the confidence he had in his own crew to repair his engine in time for him to sail so as to keep his part of the plan. But it was not to be. Nine o'clock came and they were not ready. As the engine was being put together again additional defects became apparent. So the hours ticked by adding to Nasmith's mounting impatience, until at 3.0 p.m. when at long last all was ready for the *E11* to set sail. Twice more going across the North Sea Nasmith was delayed by defects to one or other of his engines and it was the afternoon of the 17th before he rounded the Skaw into the Kattegat, too late to try to pass through The Sound that night as planned. In fact it was the afternoon of the following day before he was ready to make an attempt on the passage, just as Horton, too, was doing at this time. By then there was intense activity by the Germans and this coupled with the large amount of merchant shipping in the area made the operation extremely hazardous. At one time four steamers were sighted in an apparent line abreast formation. Was this the fortuitous formation of four innocent merchant ships, or were they naval auxiliaries wire sweeping for a submarine? Nasmith was luckily able to work the *E11* around the flank of this group and so never had to find out the answer to this problem. After dark he tried to press on with his navigation lights burning hoping that he would look like a merchant ship on passage! But the Germans were trying the same trick, and he had to turn at full speed from a destroyer which was only recognised as such at the last minute. Although both the *E11* and the destroyer were in neutral waters at the time Nasmith claimed that the enemy had deliberately tried to ram him rather than try to sink him by gunfire, hoping no doubt that if successful the event could be described in the niceties of diplomatic language as an accident. Early in the morning of the 19th another destroyer was sighted at close quarters and reluctantly an exhausted Nasmith took the *E11* to the bottom for the remainder of the night and decided to leave an attempt on the passage of The Sound for the following night.

Having failed in the first attempt to transit into the Baltic it was essential for the *E11* to charge her batteries before any further attempt could be made. So Nasmith took the submarine back to periscope depth after only a short rest and began to creep out of neutral waters towards the open sea. While he was doing this he sighted a submarine on the surface, and believing it to be the German *U-3* he attacked with two torpedoes, both of which missed. Later the *E11* herself was attacked, but the torpedo missed ahead, leaping out of the water at the end of its run, as Nasmith himself reported. Both that day, and on the following two, the *E11* was constantly hunted by the enemy in the Kattegat and was unable to try to approach the northern entrance of The Sound for another attempt to pass through into the Baltic. On one occasion Nasmith sighted a German seaplane flying towards him in a shallow dive as if to make an attack and the *E11* had to dive quickly to avoid any possible consequences. Luckily for them, perhaps, the rather primitive seaplanes of those days were not only unable to keep in contact with a submarine once it had dived but also were unarmed. Nevertheless it had been a nasty shock.

Then on the 22nd when Nasmith came to periscope depth at dawn he was surprised to find the horizon clear of enemy ships, but reluctantly he felt that he had better return to Harwich and hoped to be allowed to try later to enter the Baltic. He arrived back on the 24th. It was perhaps one of the hardest decisions he had had to make so far during the war; the temptation to try just once more must have been very strong, but with his crew exhausted after days of hunting and the enemy well alerted it was considered that he had acted correctly.

There is one postscript to this attempt. It was not the German *U-3* that Nasmith had tried to torpedo but the Danish *Havmanden*, which also had the number '3' painted on its conning tower. Nasmith, supported by the Admiralty, firmly denied for many weeks that he had attacked a Danish vessel, and he was not convinced otherwise until parts of one of the torpedoes which had exploded on the beach were examined and proved to be one of those issued to the *E11*. The Admiralty made a reluctant apology to the Danes early in 1915, and there the matter ended.

Later in the morning of the 18th after his attack on the *Victoria Louise* Laurence sighted another of the patrolling cruisers, and for six hours he tried to work the *E1* into an attacking position. But the Germans were thoroughly alert and the cruiser was making frequent and large alterations of course and speed, and Laurence was unable to get sufficiently near. The next day he spent south of the island of Bornholm where he failed to make contact with the enemy, though this was one likely area of operations that had been suggested to Keyes by Naval Intelligence. Hoping for better luck he headed towards Danzig. There on the morning of the 20th, while the *E1* cruised in the bay, Laurence was able to see through his periscope three cruisers lying in an inner basin. There were the *Amazone, Lubeck* and *Augsburg*, recently returned from a raid towards the Gulf of Finland in which the Russian cruiser *Pallada* had been sunk by a U-boat which had accompanied the German cruisers. Once more Laurence was unable to attack and he turned finally for the Russian base at Libau.

After the *E9*'s safe passage of The Sound in the early hours of the 19th, Horton took the boat eastward on the 20th, also with the intention of seeking out the enemy in Danzig bay. While still south of the Swedish coast he did sight one cruiser about ten miles away but was unable to make positive recognition, and it may have been either Swedish or German. The cruiser was going in the opposite direction to the *E9* and between them lay the Roume Banks, and Horton was forced to let it go. The following day, Trafalgar Day, he was once more forced to give up his quest for the enemy, this time because of trouble with the insulation on the starboard main motor. He too decided it was time to head for Libau.

While the *E1* and the *E9* were on their way eastward the Germans continued their activity south of the entrance to The Sound and around Kiel Bay. Just as there had been several unsubstantiated reports of U-boats around Scapa Flow, so now the Germans were left chasing shadows around their own main base. The destroyer *V27* gave a graphic account of one such hunt in which fire was opened on a submerging conning tower. Then the destroyer *S31*, which also arrived on the scene, joined in the hunt for this submarine which was 'clearly seen'.

Laurence arrived at Libau on the afternoon of the 21st, and though he does not say so in his report, the Russian officers he met must have been somewhat surprised to see him. Horton arrived the following morning and was met by a tug which escorted the *E9* into harbour. It was after their arrival that both officers were told that the dockyard had been largely destroyed and stocks of coal, stores and ammunition burnt, as the port was expected to fall into German hands at any time. In August, soon after the outbreak of war between Germany and Russia, the British Ambassador in St Petersburg reported to the Foreign Office that the Libau forts were rumoured to be destroyed, but this information does not seem to have been passed on to the Admiralty, nor do the Admiralty appear to have made any enquiries of the embassy about conditions at the port before the submarines left England.

No submarines had been lost, two submarines had arrived at a Russian base while the third had returned safely to its British base having been unable to enter the Baltic. To that extent the operation had been a success. Now it was to be seen just how the two submarines in the Baltic could exploit this success and make their presence felt. So far luck had been on their side, and it is appropriate for the First Lord of the Admiralty, Mr Winston Churchill himself, to sum up the events so far in this story. Commenting — as was the prerogative of the First Lord — in red ink on an Admiralty docket containing the reports that were eventually received from both Laurence and Horton, he writes in masterly understatement:

These are probably the most skillful (sic) submarine pilots in the world. To send these submarines in to the Baltic without telling them of the Libau minefield or what they were to do if they did not return [to England] was bad staff work. The Russians also were imperfectly acquainted with their project and possible arrival.

IV

~~~~~~

1914: The First Campaign

When the *E1* and the *E9* arrived at Libau the two Commanding Officers expected that the port was to be their base in the months to come. But it was not to be. The story has already been related that the two submarines had passed through a German minefield in the port approaches, and that much of the port had already been destroyed by the Russians in case of a sudden German advance, though in fact it was not to fall until early in May 1915. Even so the Germans had already twice bombarded the port and the Russians themselves had obstructed the entrances with blockships, inadequately, for small ships and submarines could still make their way in and out. Rear Admiral Zagoryanski-Kisel's command was virtually defunct and Laurence received instructions from the Russian Commander-in-Chief to take the two submarines and join him in the Gulf of Finland as soon as possible. Meanwhile Keyes far away in Harwich was writing to the Admiralty after the return of the *E11*

> . . . I consider that it would be advisable to keep *E1* and *E9* in the Baltic throughout the winter. Libau is practically an ice free port, and their presence should be a source of continual annoyance and anxiety to the enemy. *If this is approved* [author's italics] I would like to go into the matter fully with the Russian Naval Attache and make

arrangements to send torpedoes and a liberal supply of spare parts to Libau, via Archangel.

At least he was correct in assuming that their presence would cause the Germans some concern, but he also shows that once again the plans for the submarines were to be changed. What had originally been thought of as a few days' raid into the Baltic, then operations for a few weeks, had now become a proposal to stay all winter. Only now were thoughts being given to the provision of replacement torpedoes and the vital spare parts necessary to keep these submarines operational. Still the Naval Staff in England were unaware of what the Russians planned for their advance base at Libau — a prewar plan that expected the port to be either untenable or captured early in any conflict.

After waiting in vain for the *E11* to arrive, and having received orders from the British Ambassador in Petrograd to proceed to Lapvik, the two submarines left Libau on the morning of the 25th. They must have left with heavy hearts as still no word had been received as to the fate of the *E11*, and they could only hope for the best whilst fearing the worst. Besides resting, re-storing and making good the myriad of minor defects while in Libau the British submariners had had their first opportunity of meeting their Russian counterparts for the *Krokodil*, an oldish boat of 1905 vintage, was also present. Now she too left the stricken port to go direct to Lapvik while the two British boats first went south to try once more to attack the Germans in the Bay of Danzig.

The Germans had appreciated that the arrival of the British submarines might encourage the Russians to assume the offensive but were determined not to let this factor deter their own plans. Thus fate decreed that as the British left Libau to seek the Germans off Danzig so the Germans left that port to carry out their plans. This involved a sweep by the old training cruisers towards the port of Windau and the approaches to the Gulf of Riga in the hope that this would draw the Russian Fleet to sea. To cover this eventuality the remaining cruisers and destroyers with the submarines *U-23*, *U-25* and *U-26*

41

were placed in ambush positions just to seaward of the Russian protective minefields across the entrance to the Gulf of Finland. It is of interest that two seaplanes were specially embarked onboard the flagship, the cruiser *Friedrich Carl*, for this operation. They would be hoisted out by the ship's crane and then flown off to scout up the Gulf towards Revel and Helsingfors for signs of the Russian Fleet.

The Russians failed to rise to the German bait, while Laurence and Horton met with no success off Danzig. Both Commanding Officers were considerably hampered by fog which persisted most of the time they were in the area. Horton sighted one destroyer while lying off Hela Point on the 28th, while on the same day Laurence managed to approach within 500 yards of, perhaps, the same destroyer. He fired one torpedo which missed, and also was not seen by the Germans for the event has gone unrecorded by them. However, the *E1* had been sighted two days earlier and it was this rather than Laurence's unsuccessful torpedo attack which had the dramatic effect of causing the German High Command first to order the recall of the training cruisers, including the lucky *Victoria Louise*, from the current operations, then ordering them to Swinemunde rather than Danzig, where they were soon paid off, their crews being distributed amongst the rest of the Fleet. Both the submarines left their patrol that night and heading up between the coast of Sweden and the island of Gotland proceeded towards Lapvik. Once more luck was against them, somewhere in the darkness they must have passed close by the German squadron returning from their fruitless sortie. Neither side saw anything of the other.

The two submarines met up again on the morning of 30 October and then with an escort of a Russian destroyer proceeded in company towards Lapvik. Even now Horton's troubles were not yet over for when only 20 miles short of his destination he had to slow down with yet another engine defect, this time a cracked cylinder liner in his starboard engine which caused it to run hot. It was now obvious that both boats would need some time in harbour for repairs before they could be considered for further operations. At

Lapvik the British submarines were given a generous welcome by the Russians and the crews found that the old unarmoured cruiser *Ruinda*, of 3,540 tons and built in 1885, had been made available for use as a temporary base ship. Before the war she had been used for trials with diesel engines and now the expertise of her staff and some of the spare parts carried might be available to help keep the engines of the two 'E' class submarines running.

The day after his arrival Laurence found that a destroyer was put at his disposal and he was taken to Helsingfors to meet the Russian Commander-in-Chief, Admiral von Essen, personally. Von Essen's early career has already been mentioned and the Russians were most fortunate to have this able officer in command in the Baltic. Yet the Baltic Fleet was operationally subordinated to General von der Fleet, the Commander of the Russian Sixth Army and responsible for the defence of the capital. Von Essen was required to act as directed by the General, saving that the Tsar himself would take the final decision on any use of the Fleet's battleships. It was an impossible position for this proud sailor, and hardly one designed to allow the best use of the Fleet. The Fleet at his command consisted of four pre-Dreadnought battleships, five armoured cruisers, four light cruisers, 62 destroyers, 12 submarines and numerous other craft such as minelayers. Only the destroyer *Norvik*, named after an earlier command of von Essen's which had been sunk in the war with Japan, now built in Russia to a German design, was the result of the vast rebuilding programme finally authorised after the débâcle of 1905. The remaining ships of this programme were still incomplete in the builders' yards.

Since this is primarily the story of submarines and submariners it is perhaps appropriate to look more closely at the submarines of the Russian Baltic Fleet with which the *E1* and the *E9* were now to join for operations against the enemy.

The Russian Navy had been experimenting with submarines, or submersible warships, since the time of the Crimean War. Yet, at the outbreak of war in 1914 the Russian submarine Fleet, unlike that of the British or the Germans, was woefully inadequate for the tasks of war. In the time between the fall of Port Arthur to the Japanese in early 1905 and the Armistice later that year the Russians transported 14 boats along the Trans-Siberian railway to Vladivostok, and by March seven of these primitive submarines were said to be operational. More were made ready before the end of the war. It is questionable the effect these boats had on Japanese plans for operations against the remaining Russian naval base in the Far East, or indeed what effective use could have been made of these boats in the event of a Japanese attack. But what is important to note is that at a time when the Royal Navy had its *Hollands* and the 'A' class submarines and the German *U-1* had not even been laid down, the Russians were actually proposing to use their submarines in active operations against the enemy. Unfortunately postwar development did not maintain this advantage.

Just before the war ended in 1905 the Russians ordered four large boats to be built to the design of the American Simon Lake — the *Alligator, Drakon, Kaiman* and *Krokodil*. Designed for long range with good sea keeping qualities that hopefully would take them to the coast of Japan they incorporated an armament of four torpedo tubes and two guns into their displacement of 410 tons (surface), 482 tons (dived). The displacement of the contemporary British 'B' class submarines was 287/316 tons. In the event the boats were too late for the Pacific war, required considerable modification by their crews after delivery and never came up to expectations in performance, but were to form half the operational strength of the Russian submarine flotilla in the Baltic in August 1914.

Two other boats that were to be listed in the Russian order of battle on the outbreak of war were the *Makral* and *Okun*. Designed by a naval engineer named Bubnov who had begun work on submarines in 1901 they were laid down in the Baltic Yard at St Petersburg in 1904. Yet despite their small size of only 140/177 tons they were not finally delivered to the Navy until 1909. Each boat had only one unreliable petrol engine driving a dynamo, failure of which left them almost helpless. To add to their shortcomings, not only were their hydroplanes

unreliable but also because of their small size they were poor
seaboats.

The operational force of submarines was completed by the
Akula and *Minoga*. The *Minoga* was another small boat laid
down in 1907 and completed in a relatively short time by 1909.
Unlike the other Russian submarines in the Baltic at this time
she was fitted with a diesel engine and mechanically was
capable of longish patrols, but her small size limited her
operations as the crew conditions onboard rapidly became
untenable. She was fitted with two bow torpedo tubes but
trimming problems in the small craft made it impossible to fire
them both without a longish interval between shots while trim
was regained. The *Akula*, on the other hand, was the latest
and best of the Russian submarines. Laid down at the same
time as the *Minoga* she was over twice as big and had not been
accepted into service until the spring of 1911. Fitted with two
diesel engines she carried enough fuel to give an endurance of
about a thousand miles, her range being limited more by a lack
of lubricating oil — no reserves were carried, the extra space
being taken up by additional torpedo stowage. Although only
fitted with two bow torpedo tubes she was capable of carrying
eight torpedoes.

In addition to these eight operational submarines of the
Baltic Fleet, three older Holland type boats of 1904 vintage,
the *Sterlyad*, *Peskar* and *Byeluga*, were organised into a Training Division.* Until a year previously these three submarines
had formed part of the two Operational Divisions with training being carried out in the small *Sig* and the experimental
Pochtovy. While the *Sig* was a small if conventionally designed
boat built in 1905 the *Pochtovy* was a remarkable vessel built
by public subscription to a revolutionary design to try for a
high underwater performance, a design more like those of the

*Apart from the eight boats of the two operational divisions there is some
confusion not only as to the exact number of Russian submarines in the
Baltic but also as to which ones were in commission. The names given here
(at variance with some other sources) are taken from Part I of 'War Vessels
and Aircraft', British and Foreign, issued by the British Admiralty.

German Dr Walter in 1944 than Russia in the early years of the century. To achieve this hoped-for performance she was built with large capacity high pressure air bottles fitted in place of the batteries to enable the submarine to continue to use the petrol engines whilst dived. Leaving a great wake of air bubbles coming to the surface the submarine's performance was not up to expectations and she was soon paid off and scrapped.

A large number of more modern submarines ordered as a result of the post-Japanese war rebuilding programme were still completing at the time of the arrival of the two British submarines in the Baltic, their building delayed by the incompetence and shortages experienced in the Russian shipyards and now by the non-delivery of parts from Germany. Consequently the Russian submariners, although professionally competent, were handicapped with the need to operate only eight old and not very efficient boats. By the end of the 1914 campaign they had failed to gain any success despite carrying out 14 patrols. On the debit side the *Akula* grounded during her first patrol causing damage to one propeller shaft which was never fully rectified.

By comparison the heroines of this story, the *E1* and the *E9*, were much more efficiently designed despite their apparent faults with recurring engine defects. The Royal Navy, after initial protestations that submarines were the weapons of weaker nations and that all submariners ought to be treated as pirates, had entered into a steady and logical programme of construction and development. After the *Hollands*, which were built by a British shipyard to an American design to evaluate the idea of submarine warships, came the British designed 'A' class, followed logically over the years by the 'B' and 'C' classes, each in turn an improvement on the preceding class and each class becoming a little larger. With the 'D' class there was a radical change of design in that the ballast tanks were taken from inside the main pressure hull and placed in saddle form around it, thus giving greater strength and diving depth, in addition to more space inside the hull. Two other changes at this time came with the introduction of

the diesel engine to replace the smelly and potentially dangerous petrol engine, while an increased endurance gave the
submarines a new offensive role as opposed to the more traditional one of coast defence.

The 'E' class was designed in 1910, the *E1* being laid down
in Chatham dockyard in February 1911 and completed at the
end of April 1913. Nine of this class had been built by the
outbreak of war. The first eight boats were of 178 feet overall
length with a surface displacement of 655 tons, and were
armed with four torpedo tubes including two beam tubes.
Their two diesel engines gave a surface speed on trials in
excess of 15 knots. With a reserve of buoyancy of 80 tons
they were considerably more seaworthy than any of their
predecessors, and with a range of 3,000 miles at 10 knots they
had an endurance which tended to be limited more by that of
the crew than the boat. Thus these boats can be compared
with the largest of their Russian counterparts, the *Alligator*
class, whose displacement was only just over 400 tons.

As the size of the submarines increased there arose doubts
among many submariners concerning the viability of the end-
on attack at short range since it was felt that it would become
more and more difficult to manoeuvre clear of the target after
firing. Such was the strength of this feeling at the time the 'E'
class were designed that it was seriously considered whether
bow tubes should be retained. In the event two beam tubes
were fitted and only one bow tube. Later modifications to the
class, beginning with the *E9*, included lengthening the hull by
three feet and fitting two bow tubes one above the other.

The increase in size of the boats over the years, coupled
with the adoption of the saddle position for ballast tanks, did
give more room inside the submarine for crew and equipment.
But as always seems to be the case with warship design, the
additional equipment left little additional space available for a
crew which had almost doubled from that carried in the 'C'
class. Even so conditions onboard were still spartan at best, at
worst they compared unfavourably with the grimmest messdecks of Nelson's navy. Ventilation had been improved but
did not prevent the eternal condensation while at sea nor

eliminate the pervading smell of stale food and bodies mixed with that of fuel oil. A small wardroom space was allocated for the use of the officers and while the crew had their own small kit lockers sleeping space was still a problem. Reload torpedoes and stores stowed in every possible nook and cranny added to the general cramped conditions. Yet the men, all volunteers, were true professionals of their trade: dedicated to their boats and keen to show their ability against the enemy.

While the two British submarines were recovering from their long journey from England the Germans were not inactive. They apparently were unaware of the fact that the *E1* and the *E9* were temporarily non-operational and considered that they would be using Libau as a base for their patrols. Consequently a submarine blockade of the port was instituted, the U-boats operating from Danzig. Then the Germans attempted to complete the sealing of the port by adding more blockships of their own to those the Russians had already sunk in the entrances. This too was only partially successful and while supporting the operation the cruiser *Friedrich Carl* was lost in a Russian minefield.

By 13 November both the British boats were ready for sea again and returned to Helsingfors where they were ordered to proceed 'for offensive actions against the German Fleet in the Baltic, near Bornholm and to the West of it'. They were delayed one day by a gale but on the 15th Laurence considered that the weather had moderated sufficiently for them to sail in company for their first patrol in the Baltic. As darkness fell that evening the two submarines parted company as *E1* altered course to pass down the east coast of the island of Gotland whilst the *E9* carried on eventually to pass between the island and the Swedish coast. In the rapidly gathering darkness they soon lost sight of each other, now on their own until meeting up again a week later on return to base; lone hunters in the sea as all submariners prefer to be.

Laurence's bad luck continued; once again he had a fruitless search accompanied by the usual story of mechanical mishaps to the boat's machinery. Damage to the starboard engine took 36 hours of hard work by the crew to repair, lying on the bottom one night to keep the boat steady with the weather rather than the Germans as an enemy while heavy machinery could be lifted, inspected and repaired in comparative safety and peace. Of the Germans he did catch sight of four destroyers late one afternoon, but no worthwile target accompanied them. Although the sea was empty of signs of the German Fleet there was plenty to indicate that commerce was continuing and he reported a large number of merchant ships at sea passing between neutral Sweden and Germany.

Horton's patrol was also unsuccessful, although he did make one attack on a German cruiser. Shortly after midday on the 17th he sighted through the periscope a two-funnel cruiser to the south of him which he took to be the *Gazelle*. With the enemy zigzagging extensively it was not easy to manoeuvre the *E9* into an attacking position, but Horton managed to do this and some 12 minutes after first sighting the target he fired two torpedoes at her when only 500 yards away just forward of the enemy's beam. Unfortunately both torpedoes ran wild, breaking surface just after firing in the heavy seas still running after the recent gale. Horton thought he had been seen for the cruiser altered course towards him at this time, so preventing a second shot using one of the beam torpedo tubes. In retrospect this alteration of course must have been a coincidence for the attack appears to have gone unnoticed and is not mentioned in the German records.

Both submarines arrived back at Lapvik on the 22nd with the bitter cold of a Russian winter already becoming very apparent to the British sailors unused to such conditions. After the war, when it was possible to study the German records, it was seen just how unfortunate the British had been on this unsuccessful sortie, for only days before they left Helsingfors units of the German High Seas Fleet, normally used for operations in the North Sea, had taken the opportunity of exercising in both the eastern and western Baltic, only returning to Kiel the night before the two British submarines were finally able to sail on their patrols to look for them.

Once again a period in Revel followed these two patrols, taking advantage of the limited facilities in the dockyard to make essential repairs to the submarines' engines. To Laurence and Horton it was obvious that the whole reason for their presence in the Baltic could be jeopardised if they ran out of torpedoes, and so far there had been no word that Keyes had been able to arrange for spares to be sent from England to replace those already fired. There was only one solution: use Russian torpedoes. In the two weeks available extensive tests were made to try out these torpedoes in the British boats, and with some minor modifications, it was found that they were entirely satisfactory.

By 10 December they were ready again and left Revel for Helsingfors to receive their orders from the Commander-in-Chief for their second patrol. They were to sail at daylight on 11 December, arriving to the eastward of Bornholm two days later, and attack any German warships in the area. If by the 14th they had made no attacks they were to show themselves and ensure that the enemy were aware of their presence. The plan was for the submarines to act in conjunction with a minelaying operation in the Bay of Danzig by the Russians. While the two submarines were to act as bait off Bornholm, and maybe even score some success themselves, Rear-Admiral Kerber, with his flag in the cruiser *Rurik*, was to operate with two other cruisers adapted for minelaying, the *Admiral Makarov* and *Bajan*, in company as one group while the minelayer *Enisei* and the two cruisers *Oleg* and *Bogatyr* formed another. Although the *Bajan* was in the event unable to sail because of a shortage of coal, the remaining minelayers laid a total of 424 mines during this operation on the 14th and 15th, unhindered by the Germans.

Before the submarines sailed Russian intelligence informed them that two German armoured cruisers were at anchor off the island of Rügen whilst a light cruiser patrolled towards Falsterbo and a gunboat off Moen. A spin of the coin decided that Horton in the *E9* should seek out the two armoured cruisers whilst Laurence took the *E1* to attack the patrols.

Shortly after midday on the 13th the *E1* was lying stopped on the surface about 20 miles off the coast of the Danish island of Moen, where the high white chalk cliffs — Moens Klint —

were plainly visible for some 30 miles to seaward, when a German destroyer was sighted coming towards zigzagging wildly. Laurence immediately dived and began the task of manoeuvring his submarine to gain an attacking position. It says much for his skill that just ten minutes later he was in an ideal position only 600 yards off the destroyer's beam. He fired one torpedo — 'more', he wrote in his report, 'with the hope of letting him know of our presence than with any hope of hitting'. As he had anticipated the torpedo missed and he was given no opportunity of a second shot, even though the destroyer remained in his vicinity for another half an hour hoping no doubt for some chance to ram the submarine or shoot at it with its guns.

Laurence waited until after dark before surfacing and immediately began the routine of recharging the submarine's battery. Within minutes trouble once more struck this unlucky submarine when the port intermediate shaft connecting the diesel engine to the electric motors fractured, leaving the submarine with only one usable engine. Laurence considered that he had accomplished his purpose as the enemy must have been fully alive to the presence of at least one submarine off Bornholm, and so began the long journey back to Lapvik. Two days later he was getting worried about the clutch between the engine and the motors on the starboard side, and if this too became defective he would be left without engines and be limited only to the endurance of his batteries. To be safe he asked by wireless for a Russian destroyer to meet him and escort him back, but although one was sent it failed to make the rendezvous with the submarine and Laurence carried on alone.

Meanwhile the *U-25* (Korvetten-Kapitän Wünsche) had been sent by the Germans to patrol off the Bogskär lighthouse at the entrance to the Gulf of Finland to watch for any sign of the Russian Fleet putting to sea. After some days of fruitless patrol, the lot of so many submariners, Wünsche was fortunate to sight another submarine also on the surface on the morning of 16 December. In a heavy sea and with the wind blowing at nearly gale force the U-boat manoeuvred for a bow attack and remained unseen by the lookouts on the exposed bridge of the *E1* for it was the *E1* that was being stalked, until firing one torpedo at a range of only 300 yards. Laurence thought that two torpedoes had been fired at him, for the German was sighted at the moment of firing, and combed the tracks to reduce the chance of a hit and then dived. Now it was the German's turn to become a target so he too dived. With both the submarines dived and with the chances of even catching a fleeting glimpse of the other's periscope in the weather prevailing being negligible, let alone being able to make an attack in such conditions, there was little that either Commanding Officer could do. Both submarines crept away and two hours later Laurence dared to surface again so as to continue to Lapvik where he arrived that evening.

Horton too had mainly bleak skies and a horizon empty of enemy warships to compensate for the cold days on passage and on patrol. He also returned to harbour on one engine. As night closed in on 13 December he surfaced to recharge his batteries having completed a search in Tromper and Prorer bays in the island of Rügen for the two armoured cruisers reported to be there. Soon afterwards the port engine had to be stopped because of the intense vibration that had suddenly started in the propeller shaft. The fault was diagnosed as the loss of one or more blades from the propeller — a fact that was borne out when divers checked this on his return to harbour and it was found that there was only one blade and a small part of the boss remaining. Nevertheless Horton managed to stay on patrol for another two days hoping that a target would appear for him before he too turned towards Lapvik where he arrived on the morning of the 17th.

Horton was not to stay in harbour for long, despite the loss of the *E9*'s port propellor. No sooner was he alongside than interception of German wireless traffic indicated that their forces were active in the area, and Horton begged to be allowed to go to sea to try to cut them off on their return to base. Finally permission was given and he sailed that evening for a maximum of 48 hours. By then it was too late, for though the Germans had been at sea they were by this time on their way back to Danzig; indeed it was simply by bad luck that neither Laurence nor Horton had met with them earlier when the two submarines were returning to Lapvik.

The Germans had decided to investigate reports that the Russians, contrary to the conditions of the Treaty of Paris of 1856, were fortifying the Aaland islands. These islands, at the southern end of the Gulf of Bothnia, were considered vital to the Russians in two respects. Firstly, Russian merchant shipping leaving the coast of Finland near Hango and Lapvik could proceed with little risk between the numerous islands almost to Swedish territorial waters, and this trade with Sweden was becoming more and more important to the Russian war effort as the war progressed. Secondly, the islands were less affected by winter ice than other Russian bases and the Germans considered that they could easily afford a winter haven for submarines with a depot ship for support. In fact during this reconnaissance the German cruiser *Lübeck* reported seeing some submarines proceeding to sea from near the small island of Utö; that they were not the *E1* or the *E9* leads to the supposition that they were Russian, though unfortunately no records are available to confirm or deny this. It is known that the German forces were not attacked.

Both British submarines were now suffering badly with engine defects and it was decided that both should go from Lapvik to Revel for repairs. The *E1* arrived there on 18 December, the *E9* following on the 22nd. Now it was the turn of Engineer Lieutenant Cecil Simpson to show his true worth as he toiled to co-ordinate the facilities of the dockyard to ensure that the boats were ready for sea again as soon as possible. In those days individual submarines did not carry their own engineer officers and it was due to the forethought of Laurence before leaving England that Simpson had been brought to Russia in the *E1* for just such an occasion as this. For the next three weeks this dedicated officer worked tirelessly, and had it not been for his efforts the time spent in Revel for repairs would have been much longer. One can only speculate on the improvisation employed, the cajolery and pleading necessary to get the dockyard officials to authorise the work as a matter of urgency, together with the efforts needed to keep the dockyard workers hard at work to complete the tasks before winter really set in and frozen seas prevented further operations. Simpson's own charm, zeal and example did just that.

When these refits began no spare parts were available from England; they did not arrive until 10 January 1915. The Russian dockyard was persuaded to cast a new propeller and nut for the *E9*, a task that was only completed on the day that the spare at last arrived from Chatham. The *E1* was delayed until a rough machined forging for the intermediate shaft also arrived from England, was turned up and fitted to replace the one broken on Laurence's last patrol. The *E9*'s engine clutches were carefully refitted and replaced under Simpson's patient supervision, the task being completed before any spares arrived. That these spares were not available earlier can only be attributed to the lack of long-term planning by Keyes and the Admiralty before the submarines left Harwich, and to the frequent changes in plan. It will be remembered that it was originally envisaged that they would only be in the Baltic for about a week, and so no spares would have been necessary, but then it was considered that they could operate from Libau for about a month, and then again changed to the stay of months over the winter and into the following spring of 1915.

One other event marked this period in Revel. On the last day of 1914 both Laurence and Horton were named in the half yearly list of promotions to Commander. In both cases it was not only a mark of their professional competence but also a recognition of the effect their energetic approach to operations in the Baltic had had on the Germans, though both officers had been singularly unlucky so far in terms of warships sunk.

Horton's boat was completed first on 15 January 1915 and he sailed from Helsingfors on patrol on the 24th. By this time the winter weather had really begun to set in and was considered by the Russians to be hardly suitable for submarine operations. There was a light southerly wind but the temperature had dropped to an energy-sapping ten degrees below freezing, and the *E9* required the help of an ice-breaker to get from Helsingfors along the coast and out of the Gulf. In places the ice was already four to six inches thick and with the wind from the south the northern shore of the Gulf tended to be thick with broken pieces which had drifted ashore and then piled up one on another. Once clear of the Gulf Horton headed towards the island of Gotland intending to go on down towards Bornholm. During the short winter's day the leaden grey sky gave every indication of the snow to come while even the moderate sea appeared heavy like a thick broth with half-formed ice. Any spray blowing towards the bridge froze as soon as it struck either man or submarine. The canvas screens around the bridge which were to protect the personnel on watch and which were usually removed before diving became an immovable block of ice six inches thick. The bridge telegraphs to the engine room became frozen solid and could not be used. No one had ever dived a submarine in conditions quite like this, but Horton believed, correctly as it turned out, that once dived the slightly warmer sea under the surface would melt the ice and leave the boat to operate normally. The main danger was the conning tower hatch where one man was continually employed ensuring that the hatch and its seat were kept clear of ice.

The sub-zero temperatures were only part of the misery that had to be endured during the winter months at sea. However well wrapped up they thought they were the unfortunate personnel standing their watch on the bridge would find the icy water trickling its way down the neck, up the wrists or even into their boots. They would stand on that small platform called the bridge only feet above the stormy seas chilled to the marrow, trying to dodge behind the waist-high protection as the waves sent the spray flying towards them, then once more staring out with salt-rimmed eyes over the angry seas ever watchful for the enemy. The wind itself adds to the numbing coldness on such occasions, for it is often forgotten that for every knot of wind speed the freezing temperature is effectively lowered by another degree and a half. Imagine then the effect of even a 30 knot gale! Then there was the rolling. It always has the ability to tire a man more than anything else at sea; the sailor can never relax while the submarine rolls with a maddening rhythm, ever ready to catch the unguarded moment so that moving about, eating and even sleeping become a time of watchfulness. At the best of times the 'E' class submarines had little to recommend their comfort; a winter gale in the Baltic could only have produced conditions that could have had little equal elsewhere.

The Germans too were at sea, once more carrying out a reconnaissance towards the Aaland islands. On the way the cruiser *Prinz Adalbert* went ashore off Steinort in the early hours of the 24th. Horton was diverted to attack this promising target, but as the German got off after only two hours and began to return to Danzig there was nothing in sight by the time the *E9* arrived the next day.

The 29th found the *E9* once more off the island of Moen in a worsening gale which added to the misery of all onboard. In mid-afternoon Horton dived to attack a destroyer which was sighted coming towards him, the only enemy warship that appeared to be at sea in the prevailing weather. Lieutentant C. M. S. Chapman, who as Horton's First Lieutenant was responsible for keeping the submarine at the correct depth, struggled with the heavy swell to prevent the submarine breaking surface and betraying her presence to alert the enemy or else going too deep so that Horton couldn't see through the periscope. Eleven minutes after sighting the destroyer, the *S120*, a torpedo was on its way, fired with the submarine only 600 yards away and just forward of the destroyer's beam. All seemed to be well, and then with the submarine's trim upset by the firing the periscope dipped in the swell and Horton was unable to watch his target. To the cheers of the ship's company an explosion was heard at the right time after firing and they assumed that the torpedo had hit the enemy destroyer. When the periscope could next be used the target was not in sight and shortly afterwards Horton saw another destroyer approaching the area. Horton claimed to have sunk the destroyer he had attacked and this was confirmed by both the Russian and British Admiralty who congratulated him on his feat in successfully attacking a fast zigzagging target in such bad weather. Later it was found that the attack had not been successful, for the torpedo must have dived to the bottom and exploded there, quite close to a startled destroyer.

Horton returned to Revel on 1 February to the acclaim of both the British and Russians. In his report he commended his officers for their resource and cheerfulness under very novel and trying conditions. One of those he mentioned was a Russian Lieutenant, Otto von Essen, the only son of the Russian Commander-in-Chief who was onboard the *E9* as a liaison officer to assist with the language and with local conditions.

It was Laurence's turn next, and he sailed on 8 February. In appalling weather conditions he waited for 24 hours in Port Baltic (now Paldiski, on the coast west of Revel) while the gale eased and then sailed for a patrol area east of Gotland. Once again troubled with defects he returned to Revel on one engine, with bow caps damaged by the passage through the ice, and with his progress forever being hindered by the growing fields of pack-ice. Assisted by an ice-breaker he returned on the 15th. The campaign of 1914/15 was over.

What had been achieved? In material terms there was on the credit side only the destroyer claimed as sunk by Horton on his last patrol. But the effect on the Germans and the Russians cannot be measured in precise terms. The Russians were obviously impressed by the individual professional skills of the British submariners and by their determination to take the war to the enemy at every opportunity. Yet, while keen to emulate their new colleagues they were still limited by the inadequate performance of their own boats, and hoped for better things from the submarines now nearing completion. Apart from a series of successful minelaying operations the Russian Fleet had been inactive, leaving the Baltic in general to the Germans with their fleet of mainly old and second class ships, but one capable of being reinforced rapidly through the Kiel Canal from the High Seas Fleet. With these ships the Germans had maintained an offensive policy right up to the entrance of the Gulf of Finland. The arrival of the British submarines had not changed this policy but had been a considerable worry to them for they recognised that the British would not be content to remain on the defensive. It was now to be left to the time when the spring thaw cleared the ice fields for these Allied expectations and German fears to be realised. In the meantime the British submariners settled down to an isolated existence far from home in a harsh climate quite unlike anything experienced before.

V

1915: The Opening Moves

With the Russian bases immobilised by the winter ice the British submariners settled down to await the coming of spring. It was to be a new and testing experience for them with the Russian weather proving a far more terrible adversary than the Germans. Although there was plenty of work to be done to keep the submarines in good operational shape and to repair the many defects, mostly to the engines, boredom was to vie with the cold as the chief enemy. There was little for either officers or ratings in the way of entertainment; the chances of sport were minimal due to the frozen state of the grounds and heavy snow, contacts with the local population were limited by language problems and even English language books and newspapers were hard to come by with news of the war heavily censored in what papers there were. Inevitably the sailors formed their own concert party and this taken with the chance to see the occasional silent film show would prove to be the highlights of the winter. Letters from home were erratic and slow, parcels even slower. They all felt forgotten and neglected and the fact that morale remained as high as it did was due not only to the leadership given by Laurence, Horton and the other officers, but also to those special qualities shown by the British sailor throughout the ages — an inbred good humour allied to his ability to adapt to the prevailing conditions.

Back in England during the winter months there were changes in the air that were to affect the isolated British submariners. Most immediate was the departure in February 1915 of Roger Keyes from his post as head of the Submarine Service, an appointment held since 1910. It is no part of this story to assess the overall achievements of Roger Keyes as Commodore (Submarines); that debate will surely continue for many years to come. Suffice it to say here that he brought to the job his charm and powers of leadership which marked his many commands throughout his long career, and he added a touch of showmanship that in the closing years of peace convinced most of the rest of the Royal Navy that the submarine was something more than a new toy for the unorthodox. It is, however, in the technical and wartime operational fields that his leadership of the submarine service is most often questioned. Now in Sydney Stewart Hall the submarine service had back the man who in 1910 was relieved by Keyes, and who would once more bring the considered calculated approach of the technical expert to the problems facing the several submarine flotillas.

As the English spring gave way to summer both Winston Churchill and Admiral Fisher found themselves in increasing disfavour over the Dardanelles campaign until they too were forced to resign from the Admiralty. Churchill himself never doubted the wisdom of sending the submarines into the Baltic, but perhaps regarded it as only a prelude to a much larger operation. Even while planning the Dardanelles landings he once described the ultimate object of the Navy as access to the Baltic (in Cabinet, 25 January 1915). Yet with the departure of the men who had conceived the idea of using submarines in the Baltic, there was, fortunately, no wavering in the intention to use them to the full in the ice-free months of 1915.

For the Germans the winter had been a period of refit and training, carried out largely in the knowledge that the Russians could not interfere as they were ice bound in their harbours, but with a nagging doubt about what the British planned to do. For this reason the patrols at the entrance to the Baltic from The Sound and in the Kattegat had to be maintained, even in the gales and snow storms that frequently covered the area.

By the early months of 1915 both the Germans and the Allies had realised that the war was not going to last just a few months, and this fact was to influence the German plans for the summer campaigns of 1915. In France the Western Front had settled down to the almost static siege-like conditions that were to continue for the next three and a half years. Perhaps, so the German Staff thought, the Eastern Front offered greater chances of striking victories. So it came about that the Army, in conjunction with the Austrians, would mount an offensive eastwards in Galicia and it would be supported by another thrust towards Riga and then the Russian capital of Petrograd. The Navy's main objective was to assist in capturing Riga.

Whatever the Russian plans for the summer of 1915 their Navy could do nothing until the spring thaw allowed the ships to leave their winter bases. Nevertheless, it must not be forgotten that it had been Russian policy for some years that the main duty of the Baltic Fleet was to guard the capital, and that support to the right wing of the Army, even though it might be said to be indirectly defending the capital, was of only secondary importance. In 1914 all proposals by the Commander-in-Chief to take offensive action against the Germans at sea or against their coastal areas had been vetoed by the Army Headquarters to whom he was subordinate. Indeed, the Tsar reserved for himself the final say as to whether any battleship should leave the area of the approaches to Petrograd. Any Russian offensive action had been confined to several successful minelaying operations and to patrols carried out by both British and Russian submarines. The Germans considered it unlikely that this pattern of operations would change in 1915, as was to be the case.

With the German naval bases being comparatively ice-free it was natural that the Germans should make the initial moves in the 1915 campaign. In mid-April the submarine *U-26* (Korvetten-Kapitän von Berkheim) was sent to test the ice conditions towards the Gulf of Finland and then to attack any enemy shipping off the Swedish coast, and because the Germans had not then adopted a policy of unrestricted submarine warfare he was instructed to ensure that any attacks on merchant ships were made in accordance with the Geneva Convention. At the same time a force of cruisers and destroyers was to escort the minelayer *Deutschland* to lay a minefield on the route that the Russian battleships would be likely to take when leaving the Gulf of Finland. The *U-26*, however, reported that the ice conditions were not suitable for minelaying in the planned areas for there were still dense ice floes, some blocks reaching as much as eight feet above the water. Consequently an alternative area to the west of Dagerort was mined while the supporting ships and submarines dispersed to attack shipping. Unfortunately for them most of the shipping on the ice-free routes around Sweden and towards Finland had been stopped by the Russians when radio intercepts had provided them with the intelligence that German units were in the area. The only success came on the 23rd when the *U-26* stopped and sank the small Russian steamer *Frack*.

Only two days later with rapidly improving ice conditions the *U-26* was able to penetrate towards the Gulf of Finland almost as far as the longitude of Port Baltic before beginning the return passage to Kiel.

It was the beginning of the end of winter, the limits of the ice were receding quickly and though the ice was still heavy in the harbours where the fleet had been laid up for the winter it began to be possible for the Russian ships to break out of their berths and for some movement to take place outside the harbours with the assistance of ice-breakers. For those who have never experienced it the intense cold of a Russian winter is difficult to imagine. Even the Baltic coast in late April when the spring thaw is underway is no place for the unwary traveller and the British submariners must surely have wondered when they were to feel the warmth of the sun again.

Laurence, as Senior Officer, was the first to take advantage of the improving weather conditions and early on the morning of 27 April the ice-breaker *Peter The Great* towed the *E1* from Revel through the still heavy ice floes off the Estonian coast towards the more open waters of the Baltic. His orders from the Commander-in-Chief instructed him to try to intercept the battlecruiser *Lützow*, which was expected to sail from Danzig to Kiel, passing to the north of the island of Bornholm, between 29 April and 5 May. (These dates, which are given here in the Western fashion, replace those of the Russian calendar used in Laurence's orders.) Unfortunately the intelligence was in this case at fault, for no battlecruiser was at sea and Laurence spent a fruitless few days north of Bornholm. On the 5th he decided to go and seek out the enemy and moved further west towards the Danish coast. There were plenty of merchant ships to be seen, but Laurence was not interested in attacking them and hoped only for the sight of some major unit of the Kaiser's navy.

On the morning of 8 May his chance came, seemingly his last chance for that patrol, for he had already decided that he would have to start back for Revel that night as he was running out of provisions. Over the horizon came the light cruiser *Amazone* and the *E1* was carefully worked into a position 1,200 yards on her beam, a long way off track for the rather erratic torpedoes of the day. Nevertheless he fired his single bow torpedo at this tempting target. In his report he stated that it was more in the hope of frightening the enemy than with a chance of hitting him. He failed on both counts as not only did the torpedo miss, but it also went unreported by the cruiser.

Two days later, weary but nearly back at his base, Laurence was roused by the cry from the bridge of 'Smoke on the port quarter'. Eventually in the pale early morning light he was able to identify four battleships, a perfect target if only he could get near enough. But the Germans were too alert having been warned of the presence of possible Russian submarines in the area, and they remained too far off for Laurence to attack.* He waited in the area until darkness fell once more,

---

*In a similar situation in November 1916, when commanding the submarine HMS *J1* on patrol in the North Sea, Laurence sighted the German 3rd Battle Squadron, and scored a hit on two of the ships.

hoping that the enemy ships might return, before he continued to Revel.

Horton had followed his partner to sea a day later. He too was troubled by ice while off the Estonian coast, he too spent an unproductive patrol waiting for a German squadron that had been reported by Intelligence but which was not sighted. In the cold of a northerly gale it was a miserable beginning to the new year's work. Then as he turned towards Dagerort, where there was a small Russian lookout and radio relay station, to see if there were any new orders for him, the gale died away to be replaced by thick fog. Not wishing to navigate past the many Russian and German minefields that lay in his way without first accurately fixing his position he had to wait for the fog to lift. With the fog gone there was more discomfort as the northerly winds returned bringing heavy seas for the submarine to contend with.

New orders were indeed waiting for him at Dagerort and he returned as rapidly as possible to Revel to refuel and re-store in readiness for a prolonged period at sea. On land the German army had begun an offensive against the Russian forward base at Libau, and they had already retaken the port of Memel which the Russians had captured only weeks previously. Horton was ordered to act in conjunction with the Russian minelayers and supporting cruisers operating in the area off Libau. The Russian cruisers had an inconclusive action with a German cruiser early on the morning of the 7th, but the *E9* was not involved. Later that day, in foggy conditions, Horton dived to attack the destroyer *S20*, on patrol with a sister ship the *S23*, but despite firing both his bow torpedoes at a range of only 500 yards he was not to get a hit. The enemy saw the bubbles of the discharge and was able to turn away and avoid the torpedoes.

That night the now desolate base of Libau was evacuated by the Russians. Most of the port facilities had been destroyed earlier in the war, stores evacuated or burnt, harbour entrances closed with block-ships and all remaining small vessels scuttled. In one of the locks they sank the old submarine *Sig*, no longer of fighting value, but hopefully of value if it would help to deny the Germans use of part of the port for some while. German units entered the harbour early on the morning of 8 May and in the course of this the new destroyer *V107* hit a mine and was badly damaged. Subsequent salvage was hindered by gale-force winds and the vessel became a total loss.

Once the news of the fall of Libau was known Horton was ordered to take the *E9* and operate against the enemy ships which were expected to be proceeding on the route from Danzig or Memel to the newly captured port. On the 10th he sighted smoke on the horizon and after manoeuvring the submarine all day in an effort to close the enemy ships he had to abandon the hunt. The same four battleships that had earlier eluded Laurence on his way back to Revel now went unscathed once again. However, Horton's luck was to be better the next day.

That morning he sighted two large and one small transports escorted by three cruisers and several destroyers returning from Libau. Horton had to use the full dived speed of the *E9* to close these tempting targets, slowing down from time to time so that he could use his periscope without leaving a feather in the calm water which could be sighted by an alert lookout. Passing under the leading destroyers he fired both his bow torpedoes at the cruiser *Roon*. Both missed, but Horton was now in a good position to attack the transports which followed some three miles astern of the cruisers. So as to have the advantage of the sun behind him he crossed the bows of the advancing transports while remaining inside the protective screen of destroyers, hoping that in this way it would be more difficult for the Germans to see the periscope each time it was put up to take an observation. At the right time he fired his port beam torpedo at the leading ship. It would seem that he could hardly miss at such a close range, but he did. Once more the torpedo had travelled deeper than its set depth and had passed underneath the target without exploding. Turning to starboard he fired his stern tube at the second ship and claimed to have hit her just forward of the funnel. By this time the Germans had discovered the area where their attacker was hiding and whenever Horton's periscope appeared it came under intense fire from the escorting destroyers who also turned inwards hoping to ram the submarine. Continuing his swing to starboard Horton was then able to fire one of his bow torpedo tubes which by prodigious work by the crew in the forward part of the submarine had been reloaded after his first attack. Once more he had the satisfaction of seeing a large explosion which he believed sank the ship, but then had to go deep to avoid the persistent attacks of the destroyers. For some time he was forced to stay deep until he had crept away from the enemy's attempts to sink him, but on returning to periscope depth he could only see two of the three transports, confirming his opinion that one had been sunk. He returned to Revel to replenish with torpedoes, stores and fuel, arriving on the 12th.

For all Horton's confidence in his success it is interesting to note the German account of this action. The cruiser *Roon* claimed to have seen the first salvo of two torpedoes fired at her, and watched them pass close astern while taking avoiding action, while the destroyer *S141* tried to counter-attack by following up the torpedo tracks. The transport *Inkula*, also attacked, saw one torpedo explode near the ship, presumably on hitting the bottom, while another torpedo track passed close astern. No ships were sunk.

Horton was allowed a week in harbour to replenish and recuperate before setting out again. In the meantime the German activity continued off the newly captured port of Libau, together with minelaying operations towards the entrance of the Gulf of Finland. It was while supporting one of these operations on the 14th that the light cruiser *Thetis* was twice attacked by the Russian submarine *Drakon*. The *Thetis*, with some destroyers, was escorting the *U-4* towards the Gulf of Finland while the minelayers were carrying out their work further south. Neither of these two attacks was successful, despite the fact that initially the cruiser was towing the *U-4* and had to stop in order to slip the tow. The Russian commander fired at too great a range and the tracks were easily seen and avoided in the calm sea.

At this time the Russian Navy and their British submariner allies suffered a great loss when the Commander-in-Chief, Admiral von Essen, died on 20 May after a short illness. Without his undoubted ability in the years before the war the Russian Navy would have made a much less viable recovery from the disasters of 1905 than was the case; without this energy and drive his Fleet would have surely achieved very little in the opening months of the war. He led the Fleet by personal example and the fact that too many of his officers were still content to rely on the privileges of their rank and birth was the fault of the system rather than the efforts of this great admiral. His body was taken by the destroyer *Pogranichnik* to Petrograd where he was buried. In a letter written as war broke out and marked 'to my wife in the event of my death' he included the words 'I go with a quiet conscience that I have done all that depended on me to get the utmost out of what was placed in my hands. We' — that is the Fleet he commanded — 'will do our duty to the end'. A fine epitaph for this great man, but regrettably it was not to be so for his Fleet.

Vice-Admiral L. F. Kerber, von Essen's Chief of Staff, became the temporary Commander-in-Chief until the appointment by the Tsar of Admiral B. A. Kanin. Kanin, born in 1862, had entered the navy in 1879. Since 1913 he had commanded the Minelaying Squadron of the Baltic Fleet, and in consequence had been extensively engaged on operations since the outbreak of war. Although for the most part these operations had been successfully completed, and while Kanin was considered to be a competent officer and the best available candidate for the post, he was an uninspiring personality. In the troubled times ahead the loss of the firm decisive hand of von Essen was to be felt keenly.

During Horton's next patrol from Revel (20–29 May) he was fortunate to meet up with the enemy again to attain an attacking position. Once again his targets were the two transports *Indianola* and *Ikula* which he had attacked on his previous patrol. Because of shortages of British torpedoes the two RN submarines were having to take a number of Russian ones with them, and it was one of these that Horton fired at the rear ship. To the astonishment of all the torpedo broke surface soon after firing and ran on the surface with a slight bow-up angle making a large — and easily sighted — bow wave.

It was Laurence's turn next, sailing as Horton returned for a position off Libau. Hardly had he reached his position than it was discovered that the starboard main motor shaft, linking his motors to his diesel engine on that side, was fractured. By that time of year there was as much as 20 hours of daylight every day, and a submarine off the enemy coast was liable to have to be dived for long periods. It was essential therefore to have both engines working properly to ensure that a full battery charge could be completed every night. Reluctantly Laurence decided to return to Revel for the repairs that in the event took till late July to complete. It was this defect that was to dog the fortunes of the *E1* for the remainder of her time in the Baltic.

Before Horton could get to sea again the small Russian submarine *Okun* brushed with the enemy off Windau. Once again the *Thetis* was the target and once again the ship seemed to bear a charmed life. As the submarine was lining up to attack the cruiser she must have showed too much periscope which was instantly seen on the destroyer *G135* only a hundred yards away. Immediately turning the destroyer rammed the submarine. It was to be an amazing escape for the Russian as the submarine heeled over to twenty-five degrees under the impact and had her periscope bent over at right angles, yet apart from a few small leaks where some rivets had sprung she remained intact and was able to return to harbour. The torpedoes she fired all missed.

As the *E9* sailed for her next patrol news came through that the Russian minelayer *Enisei* had been torpedoed not far from the Odensholm lighthouse while on passage from Revel to Moon Sound. She had gone down very quickly and there had been heavy loss of life. Horton immediately proceeded towards the area and early the following morning was delighted to see the offending U-boat on the surface still in the area not far from where the Russian went down. The two submarines must have sighted each other at much the same time for as

Horton dived to attack so did the *U-26*, and the chance of action was lost in a stalemate.

However, it was a different story the same afternoon when the masts of two warships were seen on the horizon. Once more Horton dived to attack and manoeuvred to close the range and to gain a position on the enemy's beam. Gradually it became clear that it was not just two warships but a small group consisting of a light cruiser, the ubiquitous *Thetis*, four destroyers and a collier. Incredibly though it seemed to Horton, the group had stopped to allow two of the destroyers to coal while the cruiser and one destroyer patrolled to seaward and the remaining destroyer inshore. Horton noted that there was one point on each sweep when he would be able to fire simultaneously at the cruiser with his beam tube and at three coaling ships with his two bow tubes. It says much for Horton's ability as a submariner that he considered such a plan to be feasible, even more that he was able to carry it out after an afternoon of patient manoeuvring. He deserved better of fate for once again the *Thetis* was to escape as the first torpedo ran erratically. (Despite later damage the *Thetis* did survive the war.) Of the other two one crashed home against the stern of the collier *Dora Hugo Stinnes*, blowing a large hole in the ship and sending a great cloud of coal dust skywards, while the second struck the bow of the destroyer *S148*. Surprisingly the collier did not sink immediately but went down an hour and a half later, all but two of her crew being saved. The destroyer was left down by the bows, with the damaged hull badly twisted and only the upper part of the forecastle remaining above water. Gradually the crew were able to transfer weights so as to bring the stern down and the propellers back into the water. Once that was done the ship was able to steam slowly stern first away from the area.

The rest of the patrol was uneventful and Horton returned to Revel on 7 June, where he was allowed a week's rest before being sent out again. The *E1* was under repair and so virtually the whole burden of offensive support for the Russians remained with Horton and his *E9*.

The remainder of the month was occupied with sporadic

mining sorties by both sides and with the Germans additionally probing towards the Russian defences in the Irben Straits
leading from the Baltic into the Gulf of Riga. On land the
Germans advanced northwards from Libau towards Windau
whose capture would help to open up the Straits and would be
a prelude to an all-out assault on Riga itself. So it was that the
E9 was next sent to look for a battleship which was reported
damaged off the coast south of Libau, but was in all probability
the damaged destroyer *S148* being towed back to Germany for
repairs, which had long since left the area by the time that the
E9 got there. Later Horton tried to attack the cruiser *Augsburg*
but was unable to get close enough. The Russian submarines
were active too but still failed to open their score with a
successful attack when the *Alligator* attacked the lucky *Thetis*
and the *Okun*, repaired after the damage incurred earlier,
brushed with the *Augsburg*.

The series of moves by both sides reached a climax on the
morning of 2 July when in thick mist off the coast of Gothland
the Russian cruisers, led by the flagship *Admiral Makarov*,
came upon an inferior German squadron. The fog undoubtedly
hindered the Russians and prevented them from achieving a
notable victory as first one side then another gained advantage,
with the Russians generally considered to have been in a
superior position by afternoon. The German minelayer *Albatross*
lay damaged and aground on the coast of Sweden where she
and her crew were soon to be interned, while the *Augsburg*
and the *Roon* had been damaged. In response to signals for
assistance two of the older German armoured cruisers, the
Prinz Adalbert and the *Prinz Heinrich*, sailed in support. It
was at this stage that Horton and the *E9* entered into the
battle.

On the previous day Horton had deliberately not attacked
three tempting targets, in the shape of heavily laden merchant
ships proceeding from Danzig to the west, as he did not want
to betray his presence in the area. Then at 2.45 p.m. on the
afternoon of the 2nd his forebearance was rewarded when he
sighted through the periscope an enemy squadron of two large
ships escorted by destroyers. They were only about four miles

away and Horton immediately began his attack routine. The sea was glassy calm and any carelessness could easily have enabled the enemy to detect his periscope. It could only be used for very quick observations with just a few inches showing above the water while the submarine was going dead slow to prevent the telltale feather giving him away. Under these conditions it must have been tempting to try for a long-range shot but that was a foreign idea to a man of Horton's character. He remembered his earlier attacks when the Germans had seen the bubble caused by the torpedo discharge and had had plenty of time to turn away and avoid his torpedoes, or when the torpedoes themselves had run erratically off course. He pressed on in until the range was only 400 yards on the starboard bow of the leading ship.

'Fire!' Both bow torpedoes sped towards their target. With full wheel Horton then tried to swing the submarine to port so that his beam torpedo tube would bear and another torpedo could be sent towards the enemy. But it was too much for the delicate trim of the submarine already lightened by the firing of the two bow torpedoes. The *E9* broke surface exposing her conning tower to the surprised gaze of the German destroyers. Horton just had time to see his first torpedo explode by the forward funnel sending smoke and debris mast high before he had to cope with a destroyer racing in towards him hoping to ram. He heard rather than saw the second torpedo explode as his First Lieutenant desperately flooded trimming tanks and took the submarine down into the comparative safety of the depths to strike the sea bed as the destroyer rushed by, only just missing them.

For the next hour Horton was kept down by the destroyers, but in the absence of hydrophones to detect the submarine and depth charges to attack their activities were more annoying than dangerous. One brief look through the periscope revealed only one large ship in sight so that Horton had every reason to hope that his two torpedoes had sunk the target. Slowly the hunt drew away until all the German ships were lost to sight in the mist.

Onboard the *Prinz Adalbert* the disturbance of the torpedo

discharge had been noticed in the calm sea as had the tracks of the torpedoes themselves. It was just as well that Horton had pressed his attack to close range for the German captain had no chance to take avoiding action. The first torpedo tore a large hole in the ship, flooding the forward boiler room and some nearby compartments and thereby putting out of action all the gunnery control order instruments. The rudder jammed and had to be controlled manually from aft. At first it was thought that the second torpedo also hit but it must have dived to the bottom, exploding close to the ship nearly under the port quarter, the concussion being felt throughout the ship. The *Prinz Adalbert* was able to limp back to Danzig where a portion of the air vessel of one of the torpedoes was found on the quarterdeck. The inscription in English clearly identified the nationality of the attacker!

While the damaged *Prinz Adalbert* was returning home through the fog Horton's day was not quite over. During the evening he sighted the three German cruisers returning from their earlier engagement with the Russians which had prompted the sortie by the *Prinz Adalbert* and her consort. Fortune did not smile on him for a second time in one day the Germans were going too fast and he was unable to bring the *E9* closer than two miles.

By the 4th he had returned to Revel to be greeted as a hero. On the Tsar's orders he was sent for and decorated with the Order of St George, Russia's premier award for bravery against the enemy. But for the *E9* there now had to be a period in harbour to repair the many small defects which had started to appear. With the *E1* still being repaired there was no British submarine available for operations until nearly the end of the month.

So far the naval war in the Baltic during 1915 had consisted of skirmishing by both sides, dominated by the German attempts to support the advance of their enemies up the coast from Memel to Libau and on towards Riga. That the British submarines in particular had had little in the way of success to show for the many tedious hours on patrol was due more to the unpredictability of their torpedoes than to any bad management on the part of either Laurence or Horton. One thing was certain: the Germans were aware of their presence. From that morning in October 1914 when the *Victoria Louise* escaped from Laurence's torpedoes just south of The Sound the Germans were in constant fear that these two submarines would alter the maritime balance of power in the Baltic with just one true-running torpedo. Despite the tell-tale bubbles on discharge giving warning of attack, or the faulty running of the torpedoes, there had been some successes to give substance to the German fears.

Now the summer's battles were to reach a critical stage. The German Army reached and captured the port of Windau on 18 July and shortly afterwards were in control of the southern shores of the Irben Straits. It was to be up to the German Navy now to force the Straits giving their ships access to the Gulf of Riga and the chance to attack the Russian flank during the forthcoming battle for the vital centre of Riga itself.

On the Russian side their naval forces in the Gulf were reinforced by the move of the elderly battleship *Slava* (launched in 1903, 13,566 tons displacement, 4×12 inch guns) to the area at the end of July, a move covered from seaward by both British submarines. It was under these circumstances that at 9.0 p.m. on the 30th off Libau, Laurence in the *E1* sighted a group of what he took to be three transports in line ahead. In a text-book attack he fired on the leading ship and scored a hit with his torpedo. He turned to fire at the second ship in the line but was forced deep at the crucial moment by the third ship apparently heading straight towards him to ram. These ships had been specially fitted out by the Germans as minesweepers and the *Aachen* took the full force of the torpedo and one of her holds, the engine and stokehold rapidly filled with water. Fifteen minutes later the ship had sunk. Although there was a heavy sea running the other two ships rescued all but five of the *Aachen*'s crew. Contrary to Laurence's belief that one of the ships had tried to ram him the Germans believed that the *Aachen* had been mined and remained in ignorance of the *E1*'s presence.

By 8 August the first German attempt to force the Straits had had to be abandoned after the minesweepers had failed to clear a way through the many minefields which were defended by the *Slava* with supporting destroyers and gunboats. Two German minesweepers, the *T52* and *T58*, were mined while the *Thetis*, ever in the thick of events, and after so many escapes from torpedoes, was damaged by another mine, as was a third minesweeper. On the Russian side the *Slava* was damaged by shellfire from German heavy ships whose newer guns outranged the Russian ones.

German submarines too were active off the entrance to the Gulf of Finland and to the west of the Gulf of Riga. The small *UC-4* laid mines, the *U-9* had a success against a Russian coaster while the *U-26* was missing — probably mined — after sinking another steamer. The *U-10* had a lucky escape when she was sighted on the surface by the *E1* and moved off only moments before Laurence was in a position to fire.

On the 12th fortune favoured the *UC-4* which, lying stopped with a defective gyro compass, was sighted by Horton some 40 miles to the west of Dagerort. He closed to 300 yards before firing his two bow tubes, but then had the mortification of seeing the tracks of both torpedoes pass under the conning tower and the stern of the German, which immediately dived. A third torpedo fired from the beam tube passed over the target!

On the 16th the Germans began another attempt to force their way into the Gulf of Riga through the Irben Straits. For this purpose their Baltic Fleet had been reinforced by some of the newer heavy ships from the High Seas fleet, including the new battleships of the *Thuringen* class and the battlecruisers *Seydlitz* and *Moltke*. Helped by fine weather the minesweepers cleared their way through the several mine barrages and net defences. Attempts by the Russians, led by the *Slava*, to disperse the minesweepers were thwarted by the *Posen* and *Nassau* who not only outgunned the Russian ship but also outranged her. With the way clear through the minefields the German capital ships and destroyers were able to enter the Gulf, where despite all the efforts of the German destroyers the damaged *Slava* was able to escape behind further defences to the north of the Gulf in Moon Sound. Other German forces penetrated as far as the port of Pernau, in the northeast corner of the Gulf, and obstructed the entrance by sinking two block-ships. Other units bombarded the Russian forces covering the approaches to Riga. Then, as it was obvious that these forces had no prospect of a decisive action with the main Russian Fleet which lay passive in their bases in the Gulf of Finland, the Germans decided to withdraw. It was an inevitable action as they had no safe haven for refuelling in the area, but among the Russian staffs in Petrograd it was hailed as a victory. A number of German ships had been hit and two destroyers sunk, while the Russians had lost two gunboats, one with all her crew. The threat of submarines was ever present in the German Admiral's mind, but although the *Makrel*, *Minoga* and *Drakon* were deployed in the Gulf they played no active part in the battle. To seaward both the *E1* and the *E9* were on patrol together with two recently completed Russian boats, the *Bars* and *Gepard*.* There, as the battle was drawing to a close, the *E1* was to have a success, giving rise to far-reaching results at both ends of the Baltic.

At 08.10 a.m. on 19 August the *E1* was conducting a periscope watch in her patrol position to seaward of the approaches to the Irben Straits. The sea was calm but the visibility was poor, when suddenly a squadron of battle-cruisers was sighted coming out of the mist and heading towards the submarine. There was little time for any man-oeuvres for already the Germans were only 4,000 yards away. Laurence just had time to get into a firing position and remained undetected, for it was only the disturbance of the torpedo discharge that alerted the Germans in the flagship *Seydlitz* that they were under attack. The German captain

---

*During 1912 the newly constructed Noble Lessner Yard in Revel laid down 12 submarines of a type designed by Professor Bubnov: 650/784 tons, designed speed of 18/9.5 knots, six 21 inch torpedo tubes, two 75 mm and one 45 mm guns. Building time had been extended because of a shortage of parts, some of which including engines had originally been ordered from Germany.

could do nothing but hope for at 200 yards range there was no time to swing the big ship out of the way. But the mighty ship steamed on unscathed as the torpedo passed close by the bow and straight into the path of the *Moltke*, disposed on the *Seydlitz*'s quarter. The torpedo hit, but the tiny warhead on Laurence's sole 18 inch bow torpedo did not make much impression on the 25,000 ton battlecruiser — the forward torpedo room was flooded with eight men killed but her speed was scarcely reduced. Nevertheless the immediate reaction of the German commander was to return to Danzig and safety so that the damage could be inspected and repaired. Indeed in only a month she was ready for sea again and back at her base at Kiel.

Laurence himself once again narrowly missed being rammed by one of the escorting destroyers and was prevented from firing a second shot from one of his beam tubes because of the large number of destroyers that combed the area before the big ships once again disappeared into the mist. It was a classic attack by Laurence which by its lack of greater success highlighted two inherent weaknesses of the *E1* design: the continual alerting of the enemy by the bubbles on discharge and the poor results to be expected against a heavily armoured ship when limited to a bow salvo of only one 18 inch torpedo. The first of these faults was to continue to plague our submariners for some time while the second had in part been rectified in the *E9* and subsequent boats of the class which were fitted for a bow salvo of two torpedoes. It was not to be before the building of the *H20* class later in the war that 21 inch tubes with their heavier warheads were to be fitted to British submarines.

News of this attack on the *Moltke* was flashed to Naval Headquarters at Kiel where at the same time reports were being received of another British submarine which was aground on the island of Saltholm, apparently while trying to enter the Baltic. The unfortunate sequel to this incident will be related in the next chapter, and can be taken as an indication of German apprehension regarding the activities of the British submarines in the Baltic.

A third result of this attack on the *Moltke* was the subsequent withdrawal of the units of the High Seas Fleet from operations in the Baltic. Thereafter they played little part in the Baltic war, being retained as a Fleet 'in being', a threat poised at the supremacy of the Royal Navy in the North Sea. So while Laurence's attack only caused minimal damage to the *Moltke*, the long-term consequences far outweighed these material results.

Returning to Revel Laurence was regarded as the saviour of Riga and was summoned to the Tsar to be invested with the Order of St George. There was further honour for Laurence when in December the annual parade of the Order took place before the Tsar in Petrograd. Representatives from every Corps in the Russian Army, the Baltic and Black Sea Fleets were present. After a religious service they all marched past their Emperor, among them the tall, immaculate figure of Noel Frank Laurence.

VI

~~~~~~

Reinforcements

While Horton in the Baltic had been establishing himself as an ace submariner, back in London the Admiralty had been considering the problems involved in reinforcing the two British submarines already in the Baltic. The advantages would be twofold: it seemed to be one way of taking the war to the enemy with a fair chance of success, while at the same time it was one of the few methods of giving practical aid to our Russian allies. The main risk lay in the need to force the passage of The Sound between the coasts of Denmark and Sweden with an enemy waiting to foil any such attempt, more alert and ready even than he had been the previous year when Laurence and Horton had taken the *E1* and the *E9* into the Baltic, leaving a frustrated Nasmith with *E11* still in the North Sea and having to return to Harwich. What is not clear, even today, is the extent which the Russians sought such reinforcements or indeed were aware in advance of the intent to send them.

It is interesting to note that the Naval attaché in Petrograd, Commander H. Grenfell, RN, had written to his ambassador in early June 1915 proposing just such a reinforcement. He considered that with the port of Libau already in German hands it would not take much effort on the part of the German Army to advance further up the coast to capture Windau, providing they were backed by a German naval squadron. The loss of Windau by the Russians would in turn threaten their base at Riga and the whole area surrounding that bay. With the Russian reverses further south in Galicia this seemed to be a logical step and was backed up by reports of more modern heavy naval units being sent to the Baltic by the Germans as the stalemate in the North Sea led to an inability of the Germans to use them there. It was considered that the presence of additional British submarines would deter the Germans in such a plan, not only because Horton and Laurence had shown their greater aggressiveness *vis-à-vis* their Russian colleagues but also because the new Russian submarines were still not complete, though at that time it was hoped that two would be ready for operations shortly. Meanwhile, the Naval attaché wrote in his report, they had only one of their old submarines operational.

This letter was forwarded to the Admiralty by the ambassador, Sir George Buchanan, where it met with a less than enthusiastic response. The new First Lord, The Right Honourable Arthur James Balfour, while stating that he would like to send another submarine into the Baltic, dismissed the proposal as all available submarines were being sent out to the Mediterranean for operations in the Sea of Marmora. Yet even so this letter was no official approach to the Admiralty by the Russians, merely an appreciation by Commander Grenfell. Had he consulted the Russians before writing? There is no indication that he had done so, yet surely he must have discussed the situation with many of the Russian staff whom he would have known in the course of his duties.

Only a month after the First Lord had summarily stated that no submarines were available the Admiralty changed their minds. In a letter to Captain Wolkoff, the Russian Naval attaché in London, the Admiralty stated their intention to send two more 'E' class submarines into the Baltic and sought information about Russian and German minefields, routes and recognition signals. Captain Wolkoff was instructed that the news should be communicated to as few people as possible, both in London and Petrograd. In London the Foreign Office were not told of the plans nor was the information given to the ambassador and his attaché in Petrograd.

Yet chance too was now to play its part in the scheme of events. Despite their victories in Galicia the Germans had failed to destroy the main Russian armies, although they had been severely mauled and had suffered appalling loss. Now they were preparing to launch an offensive against the northern portion of the line with Riga as the objective, and, as predicted by the Naval attaché in his letter in June, the assault was to be backed by heavy units of the High Seas Fleet loaned from the North Sea area of operations. Whatever else may be said for the Russian forces during this war their Intelligence service was generally good and predictably it became aware of the German intentions. It was at this stage that the Russians asked for help to relieve the pressure either by sending more submarines to the Baltic or by action elsewhere. This request was received by the Admiralty on 15 August,* the day that the two submarines were eventually due to sail.

The two submarines selected for this operation were the *E8* (Lieutenant-Commander F. H. J. Goodhart, RN) and the *E13* (Lieutenant-Commander G. Layton, RN). How much preparation were they allowed before departing on such an operation which would leave them isolated thousands of miles from their home base? Like the *E1* and the *E9* before them it would seem that they were expected to go to the Baltic with minimal forewarning or preparation.

Goodhart in the *E8* was no novice submariner. Together with the *E6* he had taken his submarine to the Heligoland Bight in the early hours of 5 August 1914 for the first RN submarine patrols against an enemy, the two submarines being towed across the North Sea by two destroyers so as to conserve their engines. Since then the *E8* had been a frequent visitor to the area conducting many tiring patrols under conditions of foul weather, increasing danger from mines and with decreasing chances of a target. Layton had less wartime submarine experience than his colleague for the *E13* had not

---

*According to Corbett's Official History. The Germans give the credit for this news to a Dutch newspaper story published on the 12th. Either date is immaterial, the letter to Captain Wolkoff was written on the 8th.

completed building until the first Christmas of the war but nevertheless he was destined to reach high rank in the Royal Navy. A quarter of a century later he was to be involved in the débâcle of Singapore, the defence of Ceylon from the Japanese attacks of Easter 1942, and was to retire after being the Commander-in-Chief of Britain's premier naval base at Portsmouth. Now these two Commanding Officers and their crews were to be sent to the Baltic with all too little time to prepare and little beyond their experience and common sense to guide them through the dangers, while still no one appreciated the difficulties of supporting them when they had arrived at Revel.

The two submarines left Harwich in the early evening of 15 August and in company headed out across the North Sea towards the Skagerrak. They had been instructed to avoid all shipping in order to reduce the chance of alerting the German patrols both in the Kattegat and to the south of The Sound. By the 17th they were having to dive frequently to avoid neutral shipping and it was during one of these dives that they lost contact one with the other. By chance the two submarines still happened to make the passage through The Sound at roughly the same time, but being separated it is appropriate to follow their stories individually, and because that of the *E13* is the more eventful to look at her adventures before those of her consort.

Despite losing contact with the *E8* and being forced to dive frequently the 17th was a relatively peaceful day for Layton and his crew as they made their way stealthily southwards through the Kattegat until by early morning the following day they were in a position to make the final dash through The Sound into the Baltic. Accordingly they spent the day quietly on the bottom, resting for the dangerous passage they had to make in the coming night. At 4.15 p.m. they began to move southwards, remaining dived until dark when Layton surfaced and proceeded at greater speed on his diesel engines. Naturally he could show no lights. To the need for following the winding channel was added the hazard of avoiding the numerous merchant ships, fishing vessels and patrol boats, any of which could so easily put an end to the whole operation. To port the Swedish coast was dark and uninviting: few house lights, no navigational beacons. To starboard the more friendly Danish coast was ablaze with light. Once he was forced to dive for a destroyer going north; it was burning its navigation lights so Layton assumed it to be Danish, but could not be certain. By 11.0 p.m. he was off the Swedish port of Malmo and paused to fix his position accurately before starting on the next phase. Then increasing speed again he headed into the Flint Channel that would take him clear into the Baltic. Within minutes Layton sensed something was wrong with his compass and reduced speed once more while the main gyro-compass was checked against the magnetic. There was something drastically wrong: the gyro had a defect and they were steering 20° to starboard of their correct course and heading straight into shallow water off the Danish island of Saltholm. Ordering the helm hard over Layton desperately tried to avert disaster. It was too late. Before the coxswain could even obey the order the submarine struck and came to a shuddering halt.

For the next six hours Layton tried everything he knew to get his submarine out of the shallows into deeper water but she was stuck fast. Not long after 5 o'clock the next morning the Danish torpedo boat *Narhvalen* arrived on the scene and her Captain informed Layton that under International Law he would be given 24 hours to leave Danish territorial waters. After that the *E13* and her crew would be interned. The Danish ship then left taking onboard the *E13*'s First Lieutenant, Lieutenant Paul Eddis, to report the situation at Copenhagen. A German torpedo boat, the *G132* (Leutnant zur See Graf von Montgelas), then arrived on the scene and remained nearby until two more Danish ships arrived. The German then withdrew and signalled a report of the situation to the admiral commanding the Coast Defence Division at Kiel. Soon a third Danish torpedo boat arrived, and all three — the *Støren*, *Søulven* and *Tumleren* — anchored close to the stricken British submarine.

One can only imagine the consternation at Kiel when von

Montgelas's signal was received. Here was proof that the Royal Navy was sending at least one submarine to reinforce its Baltic flotilla, and it was possible that there would be at least one more. At the other end of the Baltic the Germans had begun operations against the Russians in the Gulf of Riga, and by coincidence the news that the new battlecruiser *Moltke* had been torpedoed and damaged by a British submarine (the *E1*) was received in Kiel at about the same time. No risks could be taken and Rear-Admiral Mischke ordered the destruction of the British submarine which was aground so near to Germany's premier naval base, even if not actually in German waters.

On Saltholm Layton and his crew continued their efforts to lighten the *E13* sufficiently to get her off the island and to avoid internment. At about 9.30 a.m. two German ships were seen approaching the scene from the south, the *G132* returning with a consort. When the leading torpedo boat was about half a mile away Layton saw a commercial flag signal hoisted. Before it could be read and understood from the signal book those on the bridge of the *E13* were horrified to see the enemy had fired a torpedo at the stranded submarine. After what seemed ages but was in reality only a few seconds the torpedo hit the bottom short of its target and exploded harmlessly. Worse was to come. Immediately afterwards the German opened fire at a range of only 300 yards. Because of the list on the submarine it was useless for her to try and fire one of her beam torpedoes at the enemy. There was no escape. Layton had no alternative but to order his crew to abandon the submarine which was already severely hit. Those who could swim were ordered to make for the shore or for the Danish ships nearby, the rest took shelter in the water on the side away from the Germans. Even then the shelling and machine gunning continued and only ceased because of the prompt action of the *Søulven* which slipped her anchor and steamed into the space between the two belligerents. Their work done the Germans then withdrew, leaving the Danes to rescue as many of the British sailors as they could. The submarine was badly damaged with 14 shell hits and was burning inside. Fourteen

British sailors were dead or were to die of their wounds, others were wounded and one was missing. It would have been worse but for the bravery of one Danish sailor who jumped into the sea and saved the life of an exhausted petty officer, an act for which he was recommended to receive the Albert Medal.

In Copenhagen feeling ran high against the Germans for this wanton and criminal act inside Danish waters. The dead were sent home to England in the SS *Vidar* accompanied by a captain in the Royal Danish Navy, and as an additional mark of respect the ship was escorted by three ships of the Danish Navy as it left Copenhagen. For Layton, Eddis, who had rejoined his surviving comrades, and the remainder of the crew there stretched the dismal prospect of internment for the rest of the war, for by the strict interpretation of International Law the *E13* had not left Danish territorial waters within the stipulated 24 hours.

Layton refused to give his parole and schemed to return to England and resume the fight against the Germans who had destroyed his ship and killed so many of his men. It was not long before the opportunity he was seeking arose. Using the age old trick of leaving a bolster in his bed to confuse the guards he escaped from the naval barracks in Copenhagen, made his way to Bergen in Norway and arrived back in Newcastle on 1 November. Eddis too withdrew his parole and escaped back to England, survived the war only to be killed when the submarine he was commanding was sunk in an accident in 1924.

The British government made several attempts during the war to secure the release of both the crew and the submarine which had been salvaged and taken to Copenhagen. They used the argument that the damage to the *E13* was aggravated by the gross and unprecedented breach of International Law by the German torpedo boat. That the submarine had not left Danish waters within the time limit was therefore the fault of the Germans not the British, and they should be released. Whatever the Danes may have felt privately about the case they could not agree with the British government's argument

Captain Cromie (*Photo: L.W. Benson*)

HMS *E19* shortly before leaving for the Baltic, summer, 1915. (*Photo: L.W. Benson*)

HMS *E19* in dry dock. Note the two bow torpedo tubes mounted one above the other. Compare the side by side tubes in the 'C' class submarine.

A submarine in winter. Icing was a severe problem even in harbour. (*Photo: Submarine Museum*)

HMS *E18* arriving at Revel after passage from Harwich, 1915. (*Photo: Submarine Museum*)

Members of the Submariners' Concert Party, Christmas 1915.
(*Photo: Submarine Museum*)

and there the matter had to rest until the end of the war brought freedom once more for the survivors of the *E13*. The submarine herself was eventually sold for scrap to a Danish firm.

Unbeknown to Layton and Goodhart the two submarines were not far distant from each other when the unlucky boat with the unlucky number came to rest on the Danish sandbank. At that time the *E8* had been proceeding trimmed down so that only her conning tower showed above water when she was sighted by a patrolling warship at a range which Goodhart estimated as only 200 yards. Goodhart gave the order to dive. Almost immediately there was a bump as the submarine touched bottom. A glance at the depth gauge showed that they were in water which was barely deep enough to cover the conning tower and which would be too shallow to prevent them being rammed if a ship should come right over the top of them. Luckily the destroyer passed over the bows of the submarine and gave Goodhart time to start to work his way clear and into deeper water which would befriend the submarine. All night the battle of wits went on with an enemy patrol nearby every time that Goodhart tried to come to the surface, and with the water often too shallow for safety though just deep enough to hide them. One scrape on the rocky bottom left the *E8* with the starboard propeller racing madly as the blades were stripped off. It seemed unbelievable but when Goodhart put the periscope up at 7.15 the following morning the horizon was at last clear — there were no enemy patrols in sight and they were clear into the Baltic. Yet their troubles were far from over. The submarine's batteries were almost flat and if not recharged soon the boat would be helpless. The predicament of the *E13* aground near Copenhagen increased the activity of the German patrols and also meant that they were thoroughly alert. The presence of neutral shipping was another worry for Goodhart; he could not afford to be seen by any of the numerous merchant ships in the area for it was almost certain that they would report his presence to the next German warship they saw.

Cautiously Goodhart made his way towards Bornholm,

intending to pass to the north of the island before altering course for Dagerort where he would rendezvous with the Russians. All he could do was charge his batteries on the surface when he could, then to dive and make cautious progress till the danger was over and he could once again surface.

Once past Bornholm the going was easier though there was to be one more scare. On the morning of the 21st a German light cruiser was sighted coming towards them, a chance meeting that left the *E8* happily undiscovered. On the following morning, just after breakfast, Goodhart was only too pleased to meet Horton in the *E9* and a Russian destroyer, his escort on to Revel. The pleasure of the meeting and the feeling of pride in having successfully fought their way into the Baltic must have been tempered for the *E8*'s weary crew by the news of the fate of the *E13* and some of their comrades.

Emphasising the lack of co-operation between the British Admiralty and any one else, the ambassador in Petrograd first read of the *E13*'s misfortunes in the local newspaper, and assumed that this was perhaps just one of several British submarines trying to enter the Baltic. He was constrained to telegraph to London:

> If it is the case that British submarines are being sent into the Baltic it would be advisable to give the Russian authorities timely notice of date and port of intended arrival so that arrangements can be made to conduct them through the Russian minefield.

Two more submarines were ordered to the Baltic in September, the *E18* commanded by Lieutenant-Commander R. C. Halahan, RN, and the *E19* whose commanding officer was Lieutenant-Commander F. N. A. Cromie, RN. Halahan had been commanding the submarine *D6* at the outbreak of war, and had carried out several patrols to the Heligoland Bight in the first autumn and winter of war. With the need for experienced commanding officers to take over the new submarines completing in early 1915 he had been sent to Barrow to commission the new *E18*. He had so inspired his crew of the *D6* with his own brand of leadership that when he left to take over his new boat all his senior ratings volunteered to go with him, and such was the faith in him that most were allowed to do so.

While Halahan had been gaining his war experience in the Heligoland Bight Cromie had been fretting in Hong Kong where he commanded the local flotilla comprising the depot ship HMS *Rosario* and three 'C' class submarines. Like so many of his fellow officers in both the army and the navy Cromie was worried that the war would be 'over by Christmas' and that he would have been left out. But since experienced submariners were needed at home and there was no need for submarines in the Far East, the three boats in Hong Kong were reduced to care and maintenance status and their crew sent back to England. Once there Cromie soon found himself up in Barrow standing by a new submarine which was building in the yard.

Francis Newton Allan Cromie was born in Ireland in 1882, the son of an officer in the Hampshire Regiment who was later to become the Consul-General at Dakar, and whose wife was the daughter of the Chief of Police in Pembrokeshire. With this background he had a Welsh education at Haverfordwest Grammar School before joining HMS *Britannia* as a Naval Cadet in May 1898. In those days there was no fine college buildings as may be seen today, but rather two old wooden three-deckers moored in the Dart.

There can be no doubt about Cromie's experience as a submariner, for he had been one of the first to volunteer for service in boats, having done so in 1903. By the following year he was commanding his own submarine. In 1906 he had been awarded the Royal Humane Society's Bronze Medal for his courage in trying to save the life of a sailor who had been washed overboard from the submarine *A3*. Later he was to command the training flotilla of 'A' class submarines at Devonport with the ageing HMS *Onyx* as a depot ship. At the time he was still only 28 years old but he took endless

87

trouble training his younger charges in their cumbersome obsolete submarines. Even at that stage of his career he stood out as a leader; tall, good-looking and with curly black hair and dark eyes his manner though always polite appeared slightly aloof, concealing his intense dedication to the task. Whilst many submariners contented themselves with a grubby white sweater Cromie, with a certain flamboyance and vanity, always sported a spotless white silk scarf while on more formal, and cooler, occasions the astrakhan collar to his great-coat picked him out from the crowd. In the same way he wore carefully groomed side-whiskers, and had a penchant for wearing his medals — the Bronze Medal and his China Medal with Peking Clasp and Mention in Despatches for his work as a young midshipman with the Naval Landing Brigade during the Boxer Rebellion. Surprisingly, for a man of his day, he neither drank nor smoked, underlining his professionalism and flourish with a strong self-discipline.

Unlike their predecessors, Cromie and Halahan had some warning of the plans to send them to the Baltic and were thus enabled to grant their crews four days leave before they sailed. Although their final destination was kept secret crews were warned that they were to set off on a dangerous mission. Halahan used the deception of telling his crew that they were being detached to work with the Grand Fleet from Scapa Flow. Even so, news of the exploits of the submarines in the Baltic and the Dardanelles had reached the flotilla in Harwich, as had the news of the fate of the *E13*, and some at least of the crews of the two submarines were making shrewd guesses as to their destination. From Harwich the two submarines went to Newcastle where they arrived on 30 August ready to make the final dash across the North Sea.

It was here that an earth was found on the starboard main motor of the *E19* which nearly prevented Cromie from proceeding any further. Luckily a new armature was available from Vickers' yard at Barrow and was rushed across the country by lorry. Now all that was required was for work of fitting it to be completed in time before the order to go was received. Unable to get the civilian shipyard workers at Elswick to work long enough hours to complete this, Cromie set his own crew to do the job, 12 hours on and 12 off, with Cromie himself ever on hand to revive flagging spirits. The work was done in time and a thankful Cromie arranged for two pints of beer to be made available at the dockyard canteen for each man of his weary crew.

But there was to be little rest for the *E19*'s crew for hardly had they taken advantage of Cromie's refreshment when orders came for them to sail 'within the hour'. Both submarines left Newcastle in the early evening of 4 September 1915 and headed out into the North Sea towards the Skagerrak.

Onboard the *E18* with Halahan was a young Sub-Lieutenant, L. H. Ashmore (later Vice-Admiral Ashmore, CB, DSO), as the Navigating Officer, and it is fortunate that he has left his personal account of the eventful passage of the *E18* through The Sound into the Baltic. The story which follows is based on this account.

Before leaving England Cromie and Halahan had agreed that once the Skagerrak was reached each boat would proceed independently of the other, diving by day to preserve secrecy. All went well except that both submarines found many more merchant ships in the Kattegat than they had expected. However, the *E18* reached the entrance to The Sound at daylight on 8 September and once they had fixed their position from the light buoy marking the entrance, Halahan bottomed the boat while the crew rested for the ordeal ahead during the coming night.

Young Ashmore recalled that the day was the longest 12 hours he had ever experienced. The interminable hours of waiting for the start in the ominous silence of the boat with all machinery stopped were hard to get through with patience. The First Lieutenant disappeared from the tiny wardroom to busy himself as only First Lieutenants can; Ashmore returned to his charts and pored over them till he could see the details still with his eyes shut and knew by heart the corrections that had to be applied to the little magnetic compass which would be all he would have available on the bridge during the passage. The gramophone would be turned on to liven the deadly stillness but it quickly palled. Sleep was impossible and books could not hold the attention.

Halahan had two alternatives: to surface as soon as it was dark and then press on through The Sound and the Flint Channel in one continuous run, or to get only as far as the entrance to the Flint Channel, the really intricate portion of the passage, during the first night, and after a further day lying quietly on the bottom, tackle the Flint Channel on the second night. He decided on the former.

As darkness fell that night the *E18* was brought cautiously to the surface. All seemed clear and the order was given to start the diesel engines. A cough and a splutter as they came to life and then with a steady rumble the submarine slid forward on her dangerous journey. Although on the surface Halahan had left the boat trimmed down with her hull only just awash and little more than the conning tower showing.

The night was fine and clear with no moon — ideal for this purpose — and the *E18* steered for the Lapegrund light vessel, where at the neck of The Sound the Danish town of Helsingor faces the Swedish Helsingborg across the narrow strip of water. Passing between the light vessel and Helsingborg the submarine ran so close to the shore that Halahan and Ashmore on the bridge felt that they could clearly see the Swedish families strolling on the front in the warm summer air.

So far all had gone well, and there was time to wonder how the *E19* was faring, little knowing that she had by chance entered The Sound at much the same time as the *E18* and for a short time had the other submarine in sight. Then ahead of the *E18* loomed a line of lights stretching right across the fairway, apparently some form of obstruction. No such thing was shown on the charts so Halahan went gingerly forward, peering into the darkness to discover the meaning of the lights. At almost the last moment it was seen that they were marking a line of open boats stretched from shore to shore. There was nothing for it but to dash through at speed as it was fairly certain that this must be the patrol of fishing craft the

Germans were reputed to maintain in the area. As the submarine sped through the line the wash nearly swamped one of
the boats and capsized another, while two men in a third
shouted and waved their hats. Whether they were indeed
Germans passing the alarm or Danish fishermen protesting
at their night's fishing being ruined was never established.
Events of the next half hour made the former explanation
seem the most likely.

They were now approaching the northern end of the Flint
Channel. To starboard could be seen the lights of Copenhagen
whence the searchlights were continuously sweeping back and
forth over the channel entrance. As the beams fell across the
submarine they seemed to show up the grey, glistening hull
with stark clarity. Each time it seemed certain that the Danes
would spot them and that the beam would settle back on the
submarine. Each time it passed on and Halahan sighed with
relief.

Then to the southward, starshell blossomed in the sky,
lighting up the whole area and, as Ashmore recalls, making
them feel so very naked under their white glare. It was clear
that the German patrols were ready and waiting. There was
still time to turn back and wait in the hope of a quieter passage
the following night. But Halahan gritted his teeth and kept
grimly on.

Ashmore was too absorbed with the problems of navigation
to worry much about anything else. In the flat expanse of
shallow water of The Sound there is nothing to mark the
course of the narrow Flint Channel except, in normal times,
a succession of light buoys at frequent intervals. These had
all been removed so there was nothing to steer on. Using the
primitive little magnetic compass to take bearings of lights on
the Danish shore and the Malmo lighthouse opposite, whose
shape showed up clearly against the starlit sky, although the
Swedes had extinguished its light, he fixed their position
repeatedly with anxious care, knowing that a small error could
put them aground.

Thankfully they at last ran out into more open waters, but
were by no means out of danger when the Flint Channel had

been safely traversed. Indeed they were only then at the most hazardous point. There was still insufficient water to dive yet from here the first enemy destroyers could be expected and it seemed that they were thoroughly alert.

Ashmore knew that until the Drogden light vessel was on a particular bearing on their quarter the submarine could not safely dive. The bearing of its two dim lights, which had replaced its proper signal, drew aft with agonising slowness. At intervals Halahan's voice, tense with impatience, would stab across the small bridge.

'Can we dive yet, Sub?'

'No, sir. Not yet. Not till the bearing of the light is right.'

It was an anxious time for Halahan. Unable to dive as he was, discovery at that stage would be the end. And suddenly, there indeed was a destroyer, overtaking a bare 200 yards to starboard. It seemed unbelievable that they had not been sighted from her. Any moment she could turn to ram the submarine. Halahan called down to Petty Officer Bagg at the wheel: 'I've got the wheel, Coxswain. Steering from the bridge.' To Ashmore he added quietly: 'I'll ram the bastard if he turns towards us!'

Then in silence the two officers watched the black shadow draw slowly ahead and melt into the darkness. A sigh of relief broke from them as they realised that the danger was past. Every minute now was taking the submarine into deeper water, but there was still too little for safety when another destroyer loomed up ahead.

'How's that bloody bearing, Sub?' Halahan gritted.

'Another few degrees yet, sir, before deep water.'

To hell with it. We've got to get down decided Halahan and sounded the diving klaxon. Ashmore dropped quickly down the conning tower ladder into the control room followed by Halahan, slamming and clipping the hatch shut behind him. Hardly had they reached the control room when the submarine hit the bottom with a tremendous crash with only ten feet of water showing on the gauge. There was barely water to hide them, let alone for safety, but whatever his feelings

Halahan remained outwardly calm. As looks of dismay and alarm spread over the faces of the control room crew, he turned to one of the sailors nearby and said in a voice utterly confident and calm,

'Get me a cup of cocoa, will you, Welsh.'

At once all trace of anxiety left the faces of the men around him and they turned quietly to carry on with their various duties.

For the next two and a half hours progress was of a sort to make any submariner's hair stand on end. With both motors at half speed they bounded along the rocky bottom at some four knots, rising nearly to the surface one moment and scraping along the bottom the next. At last at half past three on the morning of 9 September they ran thankfully into deep water. The strain of the long night can hardly be imagined by those who have never had to undergo such conditions, for Halahan who carried all the responsibility it must have been worse and he must surely have been near to nervous exhaustion.

An hour later it was daylight and Halahan decided to risk proceeding on the surface, not only so that he could put as much distance between himself and the German patrols as quickly as possible, but also so that he could recharge his almost exhausted batteries. But it was not to be long before he was forced to dive by the appearance of a German cruiser and a destroyer. By nine o'clock he decided to try again. The different water density, now that they were in the Baltic, made the submarine's diving trim a matter of guesswork, and as the submarine came up to periscope depth the First Lieutenant was unable to check her rise. Just as Halahan at the periscope had sighted an enemy cruiser, the *Amazone*, close at hand, the conning tower broke surface. The submarine was spotted instantly and the cruiser opened fire with altogether too much accuracy for comfort, the second round bursting alongside the partially surfaced submarine putting out all the lights in the forward part of the boat and bringing down a quantity of cork and paint flakings from the deckhead.

With batteries almost exhausted Halahan could neither attack the cruiser nor try to sneak away; he could only hope to lie on the bottom and remain undetected so that he could creep away after dark. But dark was a long time away, and though the *E18* lay immobile, giving no opportunity for the German hydrophones to track them, the submarine's crew could hear the propellers of the *Amazone* and a destroyer, the notorious *G132*, thrashing about overhead as they passed and repassed the spot where the *E18* was lying, till their nerves were as taut as bowstrings. Finally the First Lieutenant asked to put the periscope up so that in the clear water he might be able to see what was giving them away and enabling the Germans to stay in contact. As the periscope slid up he put his eye to the eyepiece and peered carefully through it, first aft then forward. Then he saw the cause of their trouble, a thin stream of bubbles rising to the surface just forward of the conning tower. A quick inspection of the ballast tank blowing valves disclosed one of them not quite shut. A slight turn of the valve and the escape of air was cut off. The result was soon apparent. The propeller noises above became fainter and fainter and finally died away. It was extremely lucky that the German ships had no depth charges, which were then in the early stages of development by both sides, or the *E18* would have been a sitting target.

By dusk the batteries were almost done for and the air in the boat was dangerously foul. Halahan could delay surfacing no longer. As the conning tower hatch was thrown open and the blessed sweet air came streaming into the boat Halahan leapt on to the bridge and quickly scanned the horizon for tell-tale signs of the enemy. Then the diesels coughed into life, putting a much needed charge into the batteries and driving the submarine on into the Baltic away from the active enemy patrols. They were about to congratulate themselves that they were safely through when the dim shape of another destroyer was sighted on the starboard bow. Desperate to get a charge into the battery Halahan decided to stay on the surface, hoping to pass undetected. Once again his luck held and peering over the front of the bridge he was able to watch the black silhouette of the enemy warship drawing aft as they passed unseen.

Some hours later, in the small hours of the following morning, from the after end of the bridge there was an urgent cry from the lookout, 'Destroyer right astern!' Swinging around Halahan could see the white turmoil of the bow wave of a ship heading towards the *E18* at high speed. The raucous cry of the klaxon sent the bridge watchkeepers tumbling down through the hatchway and the boat was on her way down long before Halahan slammed the conning tower hatch behind him. As the depth gauge pointer whirled quickly round there was the roar of propellers as the ship passed directly overhead. For the next few minutes there was a hushed expectancy in the boat as the crew waited for the next move by the Germans and gave thanks for the escape from ramming. There had only been split seconds between them and ramming, yet they had been unseen, for the German hurried on and did not return to the scene.

Once more they surfaced and proceeded to make an undisturbed rendezvous with both the *E9*, which had been sent to meet them with a Russian destroyer, and also the *E19*, which had arrived some two hours earlier.

By comparison Cromie's passage in the *E19* into the Baltic had been much easier. He had started his attempt, as has been related earlier, at roughly the same time as Halahan and had even had the *E18* in sight for a short while. Then the searchlights and the star shell display started up ahead and Cromie wisely decided that the night was too lively for two submarines to get through together. So he decided to retire, let things quieten down and to try again the following night. The next night, the 14th, he tried again. In the Flint Channel he too had to dive hurriedly to avoid a destroyer, and as the depth was only 16½ feet at the time he too had bounced along the bottom with not enough water covering him for safety should the destroyer try to pass over the top of the conning tower.

Later that morning he sighted the same light cruiser, the *Amazone*, which had so shaken Halahan and his crew the previous day, together with the destroyer *S122* patrolling astern. Feeling that it was time to show some aggression against these persistent patrols Cromie fired two torpedoes at the destroyer as she came in to try and ram him. Unfortunately both missed. Then the Germans called in the assistance of a zeppelin to help with the hunt, and in the clear water this enabled the destroyer to remain in contact longer than Cromie would have wished. The airmen even joined in and dropped two small bombs, neither of which caused the submarine any worry. By dusk all was clear and Cromie was able to surface and take the *E19* towards the prearranged rendezvous off Dagerort.

Although passing through The Sound 24 hours after Halahan, Cromie had the clearer run and arrived at the rendezvous first to meet with Horton in the *E9* and the Russian destroyer. It was with no little anxiety that they waited for the *E18* to arrive since Cromie was all too well aware of the activity in The Sound ahead of him. Horton had been waiting for them since the 9th and had even had time to stalk a cruiser, the *Augsburg*, which had passed not far from the rendezvous. As luck would have it the cruiser had altered sharply away from the submarine's position just as Horton was creeping into a firing position, and passed 4,000 yards away from him, too far for a torpedo shot.

In triumph the two new arrivals proceeded to join their comrades in Revel. Onboard the *E19* Telegraphist Benson could begin a letter to his young bride back in Scotland telling her of his safe arrival and of his plans to organise the boat's football team. An innocuous sounding message to the censor, but eventually it told an anxious Mrs Benson that her husband was in the Baltic; a description of the boat's cricket team would have heralded his arrival at Mudros off the Dardanelles.

So the British submarines had been reinforced by three additional boats, and one had been lost. Great skill on the part of the Commanding Officers had combined with a lot of luck to bring about this success. But it had become very obvious that future reinforcements would have to find another way into the Baltic or face unacceptable losses in the attempt. German patrols were becoming more and more effective and in 1915 the absence of an underwater weapon was perhaps the only reason for Goodhart, Halahan and Cromie — and their crews — being able to join up with Laurence and Horton.

VII

~~~~~~

Interlude

There were now five British submarines based at Revel —
the ancient capital of the province of Estonia — which was
believed to have been founded in the early thirteenth century
when King Waldemar II of Denmark built a strong castle
there. By 1915 it was a city of nearly 75,000 people with a large
commercial port and was a busy naval base for the Russian
Fleet. The naval, or outer, harbour lay between vast curved
breakwaters on two sides, a mole on a third while the fourth
was another stone breakwater dividing it from the commercial
port. The commercial harbour, once busy with ships trading
all over the Baltic, with England and elsewhere in northwest
Europe, now relied on a limited trade with Sweden to help
keep the Russian economy from collapse. On the other hand
the naval side had become one of the main operating bases for
the Baltic Fleet. Yet the fortifications and defences were far
from complete. The planned coastal batteries of 35.6 or 30.5
cm guns were not even started, though a few 15.2 or 12.0 cm
guns were in position. There was no dock available to take
cruisers or larger ships, repairs for these vessels necessitating
their going to Kronstadt.

Laurence was the Senior British Naval Officer of this small
flotilla, but he was under the operational command of the
Russian Commodore Podgursky who was responsible in his
turn for all submarine operations to the Russian Commander-

in-Chief, Vice-Admiral Kanin. Administration of the British submarines was a wholly national matter and this once more reflects the way the submarines had been sent to the Baltic in 1914 with little thought for their future support. For the boats and their crews were still considered part of the 8th Submarine Flotilla based on HMS *Maidstone* at Harwich. All communications had to be sent by telegraph or by a postal system that was anything but fast or regular. One can only guess at the complications caused by this requirement, and it was to be the subject of many letters in the months to come before any change was made. The long route via Archangel for stores and spare parts with the added burden this placed on the long-suffering Engineer Officer, Lieutenant Simpson, has already been mentioned. Even replacement uniforms were in short supply and garments of Russian naval origin were by now being used by the British sailors, either with or without some modification to British style.

There was one other aspect which affected the operations of the British submarines. To all intents and purposes they were merely additional units of the Russian Fleet. In harbour all dealings with Russian officials in the dockyard and with Russian staffs had to be conducted in a language of which the British officers were totally ignorant, at least in the early days. All operation orders and signals were also in Russian. Each submarine therefore carried an English-speaking Russian officer and a telegraphist to help them surmount these difficulties. Among these likeable and helpful men was Lieutenant von Essen, son of the late Commander-in-Chief, serving in the *E9* with Horton, and who had already been commended by Horton as has been related previously. For the telegraphists it was a much-sought-after job. It carried the privilege that they were allowed to live with their British crew in harbour, eating the better British rations, enjoying the more enlightened standards of discipline in force in the Royal Navy, and being eligible for British decorations, prize money and bounties. With a Russia technically 'dry' for the duration of the war there was one extra perk: they became entitled to the British rum ration, or rather, since the rum brought from

England in the *E1* and the *E9* had long since been drunk and not replaced, there was a ration of vodka.

There is a story, possibly apocryphal, which illustrates the problems faced by the British submariners so many miles from home. It is ascribed to Horton, as are so many stories of those times, but if it is true it probably was the work of Laurence as Senior Officer. Apparently, during the first winter stocks of rum used for the official daily ration for the sailors of the *E1* and the *E9* ran out. Resupply from England was either held up somewhere in Russia or else had not even left the dockyard at home. Besides its effect in giving a temporary respite from the intense cold the daily ritual of the rum ration had an effect on morale out of proportion to all else and it was important to try and replace it. But officially Russia had gone 'dry' at the beginning of the war and so not even vodka could be obtained for the British sailors. The officers pursued their request to the highest levels until eventually it reached the ears of the Tsar himself. As in so many matters the Tsar was ill advised and unconcerned over such minor detail in the life of the humble sailor — Russian or English. Why should the British sailors be treated differently from the Russians who had no vodka? 'If they are so cold,' he is reputed to have said, 'why can't they wear two shirts?' Nevertheless it is to the credit of the Russians that the matter was resolved and despite the ban on its sale to Russians a supply was made available to the British submariners. Later, this privilege was destined to become another source of friction with British and Russian sailors in adjacent messes, the one with a ration of vodka each day, the other without.

The arrival of three extra submarines also meant changes in the accommodation arrangements for the crews when they were in Revel. There was just no room in the old *Ruinda* for everyone so a sloop, the *Voyne*, was provided as overflow accommodation. Even so time in harbour was hardly a period of pleasant relaxation. During the day there was work to be done in the submarine, but later there was only a spartan existence in these two old ships bereft of all the comforts usual in a similar ship in the Royal Navy. Even later when the two ships were replaced by the cruiser *Dvina*, one of the ships involved in the mutinies of 1905, life was little better, though it did have the advantage that all the British crews were then living in one ship when in harbour.

As had been the case in the *Ruinda*, so in the *Dvina*. There was a Russian crew to man and work the ship, leaving the British sailors just to look after their own part of the 'hotel'. The officers shared a common wardroom with their Russian opposite numbers, while among the sailors the British had their messes on one side of the ship with the Russians on the other side, the two being separated only by a thin bulkhead. Even in harbour the Russians provided their allies with food rations which were in keeping with what they had been accustomed to, and which by their superiority amply demonstrated the gulf that existed in conditions in the two navies. It will be recalled that it was the question of dubious victuals that ignited the proverbial powder keg on board the *Potemkin* in 1905, and conditions had changed but little in the intervening years.

Besides the three additional British submarines there were other submarine reinforcements during that summer of 1915. Mention has already been made of the *Bars* and the *Gepard*, the first two of the Russian submarines laid down before the war to be completed. It was hoped that these and their sister submarines would take some of the load off the British submarines and the inefficient and elderly Russian boats that had yet to score any success in the Baltic war. The table on p. 102 shows the comparison between these new boats and the 'E' class used by the British, the two being similar in size but with the Russians carrying a more formidable armament.

The plans for the *Bars* called for the installation of four 550 hp diesel engines to be used for the main propulsion system while on the surface and for recharging the batteries yet the backwardness of Russian industry was such that it was unable to supply this equipment which had had to be ordered from Germany. With the outbreak of war deliveries had been suspended and the Russians were forced to transfer 250 hp engines from the Amur River monitors to the submarines.

	E9 Class★	*Bars*
Length	181 ft	223 ft
Beam	22½ ft	14½ ft
Draught	12½ ft	13½ ft
Surface displacement	667 tons	664 tons
Dived displacement	807 tons	753 tons
Surface speed	15¼ knots	11½ knots
Dived speed	9½ knots	6¾ knots
Torpedo tubes	4×18 inch	6×21 inch
Guns	None as built (fitted later)	2×75 mm 1×45 mm AA
Diving depth	200 ft	165 ft

★The *E1* and *E8* were slightly smaller and had one less bow torpedo tube.

But what of Russia herself after nearly 12 months of war? The outbreak of war in 1914 had united the Russian people in a patriotic fervour that had not been seen before and crowds had even sank to their knees to shout 'God Save The Tsar' when he appeared on the balcony in Palace Square. But by the summer of 1915 the Army was in serious trouble, having yielded ground on all fronts and suffered untold casualties. The economy was unable to cope with the demands of a major war of twentieth-century proportions; inflation was rife, the food shortage was critical and discontent with an ineffective and corrupt government was becoming more manifest. Food shortages in both Petrograd and Moscow had provoked riots in April and with news of military disaster to fan the fire of discontent scapegoats were sought, many being hounded from their jobs, or worse, imprisoned. Inevitably the Jews were blamed, but so were any Russians with German sounding names. Indeed one can speculate on the fate of the able Admiral von Essen, the former Commander-in-Chief of the Baltic Fleet, if he had continued to live.

Worse, there was friction between the military and government fanned by the suspicion that neither were doing all that they might to win the war. Morale was low and strong action was needed. A lead was required from the Tsar.

On 5 September the Tsar was at last stirred to action, but instead of trying to heal the differences between the military and civilian factions he stepped in and took over as Commander-in-Chief from the respected Grand Duke Nicholas, his uncle.

Today I have taken supreme command of all the forces of the sea and land armies operating in the theatre of war. With firm faith in the clemency of God, with unshakable assurance in final victory we shall fulfil our sacred duty to defend our country to the last. We shall not dishonour the Russian land.

Fine words. But he had now firmly established himself with the Army and thus his reputation with any future military reverse or victory. It was also unfortunate that he had little military background, no experience of war, and understood even less. As Chief of Staff he appointed General Alexeyev, a man who had worked his way up from the ranks by sheer merit, no mean feat in the Tsarist army. But despite this he was indecisive and lacked moral courage and did not have the strength of character to bolster the will of the weak and vacillating Tsar. After the strength of the Grand Duke it was to be a disastrous combination.

In the background around the throne there was the strange figure of Rasputin. The rough peasant 'man of God', who had gained an entrée to the Palace through his uncanny ability to control the bleeding of the haemophilic Tsarevich, had an unnatural influence on the actions of the arrogant and autocratic Empress. She in turn exerted a strong influence with the Tsar so that ministerial appointments were, in the long run, decided by Rasputin's whim. It is said that one of the Tsar's reasons for displacing the Grand Duke Nicholas was his displeasure with the way his uncle maintained an outspoken

criticism of Rasputin, for not only was the Grand Duke replaced as Commander-in-Chief but he was sent far away from
Petrograd to command the Army in the Caucasus. Whatever
the reason for the Grand Duke's downfall the association of
the Empress with Rasputin was to harm her reputation more
than any other act, and with her the Tsar was to suffer too.

This, then, was the Russia that Cromie and the other 'new
boys' had come to; a nation of discontent, an army short of the
many necessities of war, a government incapable of construc-
tive action and a Tsar lacking in the essential powers of
leadership to take his country back to the high road of success.
Surprisingly in this saga of deficiency the Baltic Fleet was an
example of comparative success, for after the battles of Riga
they felt that it was their actions that had saved the city and
had sent the Germans running back to Danzig.

VIII

~~~~~~

The Months of Success

Goodhart's first task after arriving in Revel was to have repaired the propeller which had been damaged during the *E8*'s transit through The Sound in August. He then carried out one patrol to seaward of the Irben Straits during the first days of September which served to let him and his crew become acquainted with the conditions in the Baltic and at the same time added to the Russian defences in the area in case of a renewed German assault. Horton was also at sea during this time but like Goodhart saw nothing and suffered the vagaries of the local weather: a strong northwesterly gale with heavy seas and overcast skies one day, calm and hazy the next, with increasing wind and heavy seas again to end the patrol.

Goodhart was unlucky not to be in Revel to share the general pleasure when Cromie and Halahan arrived in the *E19* and *E18*, since he had left for a patrol earlier the same day. The morning of 15 September was bright and sunny with only a light breeze and the crew of the *E8* waited with impatience for their first sight of the enemy. Then, shortly after their midday meal, there he was right ahead, a small German submarine. Without wasting a moment the bridge watchkeepers dropped into the control room, the klaxon blared twice and the *E8* slid out of sight. Goodhart cautiously began the intricate business of getting his boat into the right position to fire his torpedoes against the unsuspecting German. But things went wrong; he got too close and then the enemy spotted his periscope and he too was gone beneath the waves, leaving neither antagonist the chance for further action. The German was the *UC4* returning from carrying out a difficult mine-laying operation in the northern approaches to Moon Sound. Luck was with the *UC4* on this patrol for her Commanding Officer reported that on the outward passage he had evaded an enemy submarine off Dagerort and two more on her return before sighting the *E8*'s periscope only a hundred yards away!

The following day Goodhart tried to close and attack a cruiser which he identified as one of the *Graudenz* class but he could get no closer than five miles. Such were the frustrations to be suffered; one day too close, the next too far away. In fact he had incorrectly identified his target for it was not one of the *Graudenz* class — one of which, the *Hela*, had been sunk by Horton in the North Sea in the early months of the war — but the similar but older *Augsburg*.

Halahan too had troubles with identification as well as the frustrations of being unable to attack during his first patrol. 22 September was a day which he would remember for a long time. Just after breakfast his lookouts reported a submarine also on the surface right ahead of the *E18*. This submarine dived and began what appeared to be an attack on the British boat, but for some reason Halahan was confident enough not to dive and afterwards he wrote laconically in his report 'I avoided this easily as she was showing a large amount of both periscopes'. No German submarine claimed such man-oeuvres or was anywhere near the area at this time. Could they have been Russian? No sooner had Halahan evaded this attack when smoke was observed on the horizon to the west. This time Halahan dived and began his attack on what he thought was a *Deutschland* class battleship and two cruisers, one on each quarter of the big ship. When the enemy were only about four miles off and Halahan was in a perfect position for an attack when they got closer they suddenly reversed course and steamed away. It seemed inexplicable until Halahan looked round to the eastward and to his fury saw a Russian submarine on the surface only two miles off. To him this seemed the explanation of the Germans' abrupt manoeuvre and one can imagine the temptation to let his ally have the torpedoes which should have been on their way towards the enemy. Instead he closed the Russian's position and tried to identify himself by firing a red Verey light, but she dived and was seen no more. Could this have been the submarine encountered earlier? Unfortunately history neither gives us the answer nor records the name of the submarine. But Halahan too had wrongly identified his target, which had not been as grand as he had thought. Instead of a battleship and two cruisers it was the light cruiser *Bremen* and two destroyers.

Following the failure of the last German attack on the Gulf of Riga in August the Russians had been expecting a renewal of the German offensive on land against the city. Most civilians had either fled or been evacuated from Riga in the first weeks of August, leaving only the indigenous Baltic Germans in the city waiting for the German Army to arrive. Yet the land fighting had died down with German troops held outside the city. At sea the unsettled and unseasonal autumn weather with its quickly rising seas limited the operations to which the Germans were prepared to commit their ships. For despite the inaction of the Russian battlefleet and many of their heavy ships it was still a force 'in being', and also, on paper, superior to the German Fleet in the Baltic. The Germans had to be able to make full use of the speed of their ships and of the destroyers escorting them; but this became impossible in the sudden violent autumnal storms interspersed with periods of poor visibility. With Riga apparently safe, at least for the time being, Admiral Kanin may have felt free to change the target priorities of his enlarged British submarine flotilla and the new Russian boats. Certainly policy was changed, but unhappily the documents still available do not indicate on whose orders this was done. What is known is that on the 28 September the Russian *Bars* with HMS *E8* and *E19* sailed from Revel to prey on German merchant shipping which had until then traded unhindered between Germany and Sweden.

This was not merely a case of the individual Commanding Officers looking for easier targets but a fundamental change involving the whole concept of submarine warfare as foreseen by the Naval Staffs up to that time. It must be remembered that in reviewing the likely course of a future war, submarine attacks only on warships had been considered by the British Admiralty prior to 1914; a submarine war on commerce had not even been considered. Indeed in 1913 when Lord Fisher, then in retirement, had written a memorandum in which he prophesied that the Germans would use their submarines to attack our merchant fleet, both the then First Lord of the Admiralty, Mr Winston Churchill, and the First Sea Lord, HSH Admiral Prince Louis of Battenburg, had rejected the whole idea as abhorrent. At that time the Germans too had no intention of using their submarines other than against warships, not necessarily from chivalrous feelings but because the small number of U-boats possessed by the Germans was earmarked for other duties.

Despite the high-sounding words uttered in the days of peace it was not long after the outbreak of war when the first merchant ship fell a victim to attack by a submarine. On 13 October 1914 the *U17* under Kapitänleutnant Feldkirchner had achieved this distinction for Germany when he stopped the small British steamer *Glitra* (866 tons) off the coast of Norway near Stavanger. After searching the ship in accordance with International Law the steamer was sunk by opening the seacocks. The crew had been given ten minutes to abandon ship, the boats subsequently being towed by the submarine for a short distance towards the coast, where they were later picked up by a pilot vessel and the crew taken to Stavanger. Later Feldkirchner had second thoughts about his actions and feared that he would be disciplined on his return to harbour for his excessive zeal, although the German Naval Prize Regulations of 1914 did permit the destruction of an enemy merchantman if it was deemed inexpedient or unsafe to take her to a German-held port as a prize. Instead his conduct was approved and the whole question of attacks on merchant shipping was re-opened. A memorandum was sent by the staff of the High Seas Fleet to the Chief of the Naval Staff in Berlin, Admiral von Pohl.

As England completely disregards International Law there is not the least reason why we should exercise any restraint in our conduct of the war. We must make use of this weapon, and do so in the way most suitable to its peculiarities.

Consequently a U-boat cannot spare the crews of steamers but must send them to the bottom with their ships. The shipping world can be warned and all shipping trade with England should then cease within a short time.

In itself this was an extreme and ruthless view for that stage of the war. Nevertheless it puts the onus for breaches of International Law on the British government in the first place, for the Royal Navy was then attempting to prevent contraband reaching Germany, whether carried in German or neutral ships. Even food had been declared contraband, and if considered excessive for neutral use its ultimate destination was considered to be Germany and so it was then confiscated. Furthermore, the Germans questioned the legality under International Law of British actions in mining the Straits of Dover, in that this minefield on an important international shipping route contravened the Hague Agreement of 1907.

The many attempts to clarify the rules of war at sea had culminated in the Declaration of London in 1911 which, *inter alia*, declared that private property at sea must be immune from capture. Paradoxically in view of the title of this Declaration it was the British government, at the insistence of the Admiralty, which refused to ratify this denial of the Royal Navy's traditional rights of search on the high seas. It was felt that the new rule would be flagrantly abused, with all kinds of munitions of war being listed as the private property of some neutral company, and therefore immune from seizure. It had not been forgotten that in 1812 Britain had actually gone to war with the United States over the right to examine neutral ships for contraband.

Nevertheless under International Law a submarine was bound by the same rules as a surface ship when stopping an enemy merchant ship or even seeking to inspect the papers of a neutral. It was to be this factor more than any other that was to dominate the drift to unrestricted submarine warfare. Thus a submarine must not torpedo the merhant ship without warning but was obliged first to order her to heave to and then send a party onboard to inspect the ship's papers. Before sinking an enemy ship adequate provision had to be made for the crew's safety, while a 'suspect' neutral could only be sent into harbour with a prize crew on board. There were obvious difficulties. The submarine had to surface, thereby losing its best form of defence; also because she had no boat of her own, the submarine had either to go alongside the merchant ship or rely on the other ship's boats. Another problem peculiar to the submarine was the lack of space on board for either enemy survivors or even additional men to form prize crews.

This, then, was the background against which Cromie and his fellow Commanding Officers were sent to sea to attack German shipping plying between neutral Sweden and the German Baltic ports. Whereas Feldkirchner had sunk the *Glitra* almost by accident, now Admiral Kanin ordered the attack on commerce as the primary object of the patrols of the three submarines, though of course attacks on any warships that happened to be met would always take precedence.

For Cromie and his crew it was to be their first patrol since arriving in Russia and the excitement in the *E19* was intense. One can imagine therefore the feelings of those in the control room as Cromie's First Lieutenant, George Sharp, came down the ladder from the bridge to report to his Captain that the submarine was ready for sea. Dressed for the expected cold and wet passage to their patrol area he squeezed his large frame, made even bigger by sweater and waterproof coat, through the hatch and jumped the last few rungs to the deck below him. There to receive his size twelve seaboots was the last basket of eggs to be brought aboard, and not yet stowed away! Taking the indescribable mess of broken eggs as omen of what they would do to the Germans the submarine was soon on its way. There was to be one incident to mar their first departure for patrol for Cromie mistook his bearings in the dark and took the *E19* over the net of the inner defences instead of through the gate. There was no damage and with only a short delay they were out into the open sea, a few quick flashes of the dimmed signal lantern marking their meeting with *E18* which was returning to Revel.

Cromie took the *E19* first to an area southwest of the island of Bornholm, while Goodhart and the *E8* went further east and operated off the Pomeranian coast. It was Cromie who was to have the first success in what was to be one of the most momentous patrols of the whole war by a British submarine, probably exceeded only by those of Lieutenant-Commanders Boyle and Nasmith in the submarines *E14* and *E11* in the Sea of Marmora. Yet Cromie's patrol started inauspiciously.

In the early morning light of 2 October Cromie sighted what he took to be either an armed merchant ship or a transport, but as he had not made the sighting early enough in the bad light to make an attack he decided to follow, hoping that the enemy would alter course and give him a second chance. Suddenly the *E19* was entangled in an anti-submarine net. Rudder and hydroplanes were all caught in the steel mesh and any attempt to go ahead or astern resulted in the most alarming alterations of trim, the sound of wires scraping along the hull, and nerve-shattering small sharp explosions. Cromie tried going astern and blowing large amounts of ballast but to no avail. Twice the *E19* broke surface like a giant wounded whale — to the astonishment of the Germans onboard the patrol ship *Silvania*, Cromie's erstwhile target, who promptly opened fire on the trapped submarine, luckily without effect.

With the struggle to escape apparently hopeless, Cromie's thoughts were for the crew whom he had led into this trouble. He told them that if all else failed he would try and surface to enable them to get clear while he stayed onboard to light the fuses on the demolition charges. A typical gesture of this man; considerate for his crew, but dramatic and heroic. It was the sort of action that made him so beloved by his crew that they would have followed him anywhere. Luckily it was not needed. One final effort and the *E19* slipped clear of the clutches of the deadly steel net after two hours of exhausting struggle, and crept away to fight again.

The following day passed quietly enough until at 5.30 p.m.

111

the *Svionia* of 2,500 tons — Cromie thought she was bigger — was sighted through the periscope. Unaware that she was being watched the German sailed on until the *E19* came to the surface in a cascade of foam and signalled her to stop, an order that had to be emphasised by opening fire with the small 2-pounder gun with which the *E19* was then fitted. The second round hit the German but did little damage. While the crew abandoned ship the *E19* drew closer to her victim and then put five more shells into her hull. With such a small gun it was soon obvious that it would take a long time to sink her in this way, so it was decided to use a torpedo. Yet even now the Gods were hardly on Cromie's side for the first torpedo failed to run, and the second passed under the target. With the light of the early winter's day failing fast and the wind rising, the *Svionia* was left on a lee shore in the hope that nature would complete what man's own weapons could not.

It is whimsical to note that with the daily casualties in the fighting on both the Eastern and Western Fronts being total-led in thousands rather than hundreds, and with so many ships being sunk as a result of the war, Lloyd's Daily List for 6 October still had space to record the loss of this enemy ship. It stated that some of the crew were landed at Kolliger Ort while the Master and remainder were on their way to Sassnitz further along the coast, that their ship had been torpedoed (*sic*), and that the British ship had first worn false colours before opening fire without warning. Although quite a legiti-mate *ruse de guerre*, providing one's own colours are hoisted before opening fire, there is no mention in Cromie's own report of his having hoisted a German ensign, nor in the circum-stances does it seem a likely tactic for Cromie to have used.

Meanwhile what of Goodhart further east along the coast? After seeing a number of small coasters which he had not attacked, hoping for something larger to come along, it was the early afternoon of 1 October when he sighted four ships in line ahead coming from the west. Surely these were not mer-chant ships, but looked more like naval auxiliaries? Goodhart prepared to attack and with little difficulty was able to fire his single bow torpedo at the second ship in the line. As had happened all too frequently the torpedo missed while the Germans fired haphazardly in the general direction of Goodhart's periscope and continued onwards towards Danzig. It was an area where there had been no submarine activity before this and the Germans were caught unprepared by an attack that deserved better success. The German ships were the four auxiliary minelayers *Kaiser*, *Odin*, *Hertha* and *Hugen*, and within a week were busy laying a total of 680 mines in new minefields between the Gulf of Riga and the coast of Gotland.

For the next few days Goodhart and the crew of the *E8* fought the elements rather than the Germans while enemy coastal shipping stayed in harbour for shelter. Thus it was not until midday on the 5th that the next ship was sighted by the *E8*, the small *Margarethe*, of only 400 tons. The *E8* was surfaced and the German signalled to stop, an order that had to be emphasised, as in the case of the *Svionia*, by a shot from the submarine's puny 6-pounder gun fired across the German's bows. Because they were only two miles off the coast Goodhart was worried that enemy ships would arrive to help the *Margarethe* and that the *E8* would be forced to dive in a hurry and perhaps have to abandon any boarding party that had been put aboard the coaster. Instead, once the small German crew had taken to their boats he began to shell the ship to sink her. As Cromie had already found out this was no easy task with such a small gun, but Able Seaman Doug Savory — the gunlayer — persevered. He not only fired the gun but also had to aim the weapon with its shoulder piece damaged in the recent bad weather. Within two hours of first sighting the deed was done and the *Margarethe* sank slowly by the bow.

Goodhart then intended to bombard the nearby Stilo lighthouse and adjacent barracks but was deterred because the damaged gun made accurate fire impossible in the sea conditions at that time. It was this action that caused more comment than his success in sinking the *Margarethe* when Goodhart's report reached the Admiralty. It was feared that if the lighthouse was bombarded then the Germans might retaliate, in which case the Allies had more to lose than the Germans if the habit spread. It is amusing to note the lengthy procedure required by protocol

113

to warn the commanding officers of submarines in Russia of their Lordships' concern: first there was a letter to the Foreign Office, then a telegram to the Ambassador in Petrograd, the Ambassador had to call on the Russian Minister of Marine who in turn had to send a mesage to his Commander-in-Chief who finally told the commanding officers of the ban.

The *Margarethe* was to be Goodhart's sole success before he returned to Revel on the 7th. Meanwhile Cromie continued with his patrol, though the bad weather which he had hoped would finish off the *Svionia* now prevented him from attacking any new targets. The sea was too rough to surface and examine the several merchantmen he saw and often heavy rain reduced visibility to such an extent that ships could pass his patrol position unobserved. It was to be Sunday the 10th before Cromie could claim his next victim. Like the previous days the early morning had been rough with frequent rain squalls, the weather slowly improving as the day wore on. In mid-afternoon he surfaced and ordered the *Lulea* (2,250 tons) to stop. There, just outside Danish waters and with the white cliffs of Moen island showing clearly, not much more than 50 miles from her final destination in Lubeck, the crew abandoned ship and Cromie made ready to sink her with a torpedo. To his chagrin the first torpedo had a gyro failure and circled round missing the *E19*'s own stern by only 15 yards while the second hit the stern of the *Lulea* and failed to explode. The third ran deep and passed under the target while the fourth missed ahead! With the sea too rough to put men on the submarine's casing to use the gun the *Lulea* had to be left to drift on to a reef where the Germans were soon able to salve her. Cromie took the *E19* off towards Bornholm and then on to the southern end of the island of Gotland while his report fails to record his comments on the performance of his torpedoes.

The next victim was sighted after breakfast the following morning and the *Walter Leonhardt* was soon stopped and the crew ordered to abandon ship. By now the sea was much calmer and Cromie was able to take the submarine alongside and to put a boarding party on to the German, for with harsh memories of his attempts to sink his first two prizes he determined to scuttle this one. It was intended to explode a guncotton charge in the after hold while at the same time opening the seacocks, but even now events did not go as planned for the fuse was damp and failed to explode the charge. After a new fuse was fitted and the charge exploded the ship sank stern first three minutes later, taking with her a cargo of iron ore.

While this had been going on the Swedish steamer *Fernebo* had been directed to stop and pick up the crew of the *Walter Leonhardt* from their two boats: 15 men and two women. According to an account of the incident given by the Swedish Captain the boats were well provisioned and the Germans, who had been given 15 minutes to leave their ship, had even managed to take many of their belongings with them. Onboard the *E19* Cromie had taken the ship's papers and also the German's new chronometer. The crew of the *Walter Leonhardt* were later transferred to the German destroyer *S113* when the Swedish ship met with her in The Sound.

Hardly had the *Walter Leonhardt* disappeared beneath the waves when another German ship came in sight running the gauntlet of the open sea between Swedish waters at the southern end of the island of Gotland and those on the mainland coast. This proved to be the *Germania* (9,000 tons), bound for Stettin with iron ore. Disregarding both Cromie's signal to heave to and a shot across her bows she continued on her way, and in her anxiety to reach the safety of Swedish waters as quickly as possible, ran aground on some shallows about two miles from the coast. The *E19* was taken alongside the stranded German vessel which by then had been abandoned by her crew. Cromie spent an hour trying to tow her off so that she could be scuttled in deep water, but failed to move her. After taking the ship's papers and some meat to supplement his own rations Cromie left the scene.

But the story of the *Germania* did not end there. For in stranding only two miles off the Swedish coast the German ship was then in Swedish waters and safe from attack by a warship of a belligerent nation. A fierce three-sided diplomatic storm soon broke out. The Germans claimed that the *Germania* had been fired at up to the moment of stranding, that she had then been boarded and an attempt made to scuttle her by exploding a charge in the engine room. On the other hand the British claimed that shots had been fired at the ship but only to warn of her danger and that practice ammunition had had to be used as blank was not carried on the submarine. The explosion was due, so the British diplomats argued, not to a deliberate attempt to scuttle the ship where she could so easily be salved but to a boiler explosion. The Swedish govenment protested about the flagrant breach of their neutrality. The diplomatic notes passed to and fro for weeks and the matter was never resolved to everyone's satisfaction, while the ship herself was soon towed away by a salvage tug and taken back to Germany for repairs.

Unaware of the diplomatic storm which he had caused Cromie started after his third victim for the day, the *Gutrune* (3,000 tons). Obeying the signal to stop, the German Master sent a boat over with the ship's papers, returning to the *Gutrune* with the submarine's boarding party. Opening all the watertight doors in the ship the engineers removed the main inlet valve before returning to the submarine. Three shots into the hold along the waterline and the ship sank stern first taking with her to the bottom more valuable iron ore. The crew, who had taken to the boats, were towed by the *E19* towards a Swedish ship which rescued them.

Next to be stopped was the Swedish *Nyland* whose papers showed her to be taking ore to Rotterdam, and she was allowed to proceed. While this inspection was taking place the German *Director Reppenhagen* (1,700 tons) was stopped and then like the *Gutrune* scuttled taking more precious iron ore to the bottom of the Baltic. But this hectic day was not yet over for while the last German ship was still sinking the Swedish *Martha* was stopped. As she had a cargo for Newcastle Cromie was only too pleased to release her while at the same time putting the crew of the *Director Reppenhagen* onboard.

As night was falling operations for the day were concluded by bringing the *Nicomedia* (4,400 tons) to with a shot across the bows. While the crew pulled ashore in the boats a boarding party from the submarine scuttled her and her cargo of more

Admiral Kanin, the Russian Commander-in-Chief, decorating the crews of HMS *E8* and *E9* with the Cross of St George. (*Photo: Imperial War Museum*)

A Russian submarine (Bars class) seen leaving Revel. Note the externally mounted torpedoes. (*Photo: Submarine Museum*)

An externally fitted torpedo, a standard fitting on Russian submarines but also tested experimentally on the British boats. This is probably the *E8* with Lieutenant A.B. Grieg, the First Lieutenant. (*Photo: Submarine Museum*)

The *Dvina* with submarines alongside in Revel, autumn 1916.
(*Photo: Submarine Museum*)

Officers and Seamen of HMS *E19* in 1916. Cromie seated in the centre – note the two Russian Telegraphists. The sailors all wear the HMS *Maidstone* cap ribbon. (*Photo: L.W. Benson*)

'C' Class submarine on its barge in a floating dock being made ready for the voyage down the River Dvina from Archangel, 1916. (*Photo: Author's collection*)

ore. The Germans claimed that this ship too had been scuttled in Swedish waters and made her the subject of yet another protest. This time the claim was rejected by the Swedes as they said there was no proof that the position where she sank was in their waters.

As soon as it was light the next morning, Tuesday, Cromie began to seek out the enemy's shipping, hoping that it would be as busy a day as the one before. First he chased a ship that was southbound and found her to be Swedish, then going north again he found two more Swedish ships — small ferries heading for Visby on the west coast of Gotland — then yet another Swede going south. Where were the Germans? This last Swede was halted and Cromie took the *E19* alongside to look at the ship's papers. The ship was the *Nike* (1,800 tons) and originally built in Southampton in 1883 as the *Caledonia* for a Cardiff-based company, but now Swedish owned. More important, she was found to be bound for the German port of Stettin with a cargo of iron ore. Although a neutral vessel it was considered that this indeed was contraband and should not be allowed to reach the Germans. Lieutenant Mee with two armed sailors, all that could be spared from the submarine, scrambled aboard with instructions for the *Nike* to follow the *E19* to Revel for further investigation. Before long another Swede was stopped, the *August*, but found to be carrying timber for England and was naturally allowed to proceed unhampered, though not before the friendly Swedish crew passed some newly-baked bread across to the submarine. Manna indeed to submariners after two weeks on patrol!

Early next morning, the 13th, a Russian torpedo boat, the *Dostoini*, was met and the *Nike* handed over to her charge, while Mee and his men re-embarked in the *E19*. Captain Anderson of the *Nike* had been formal and not unfriendly despite the seizure of his ship, and had told Mee that Cromie's activities had already had far-reaching results. Already there were many German ships held up in Swedish ports fearing to sail in case of interception by the English submarine. Luckily, too, the crew had been friendly, for on returning on board the submarine it was found that the boarding party had taken the wrong ammunition with them for their rifles, and would not have been able to fire them if the need had arisen!

So Cromie returned to Revel leaving behind him the coastal trade between Sweden and Germany in disarray, even if only temporarily. But the reverberations were to continue for many weeks, especially in the case of the *Nike*. The Germans claimed that under the 1909 Declaration of London (which it will be remembered had not been ratified by Britain) ores could not be declared contraband. The Russians did not want to upset the Swedes, who as neutrals resented having their ships involved by the warring nations. Finally, as there was no British Prize Court in Revel to adjudicate in this case it was decided that it would be politic to hand the matter over to the Russians. Not wishing to offend the Swedes the Russians in their turn promptly released the ship. An interesting corollary was the German reluctance, throughout the war, to interfere with the thriving Swedish timber trade with Britain, possibly for fear of antagonising the Swedes and resulting in a curtailment of the important iron ore traffic with Germany.

But of more importance was the immediate result of Cromie's foray. The Swedes made an attempt to protect their ships by having them sailed in convoy and escorted by Swedish warships. Prince Henry, the German Commander-in-Chief in the Baltic, did not consider it advisable to introduce convoys for German shipping, as he was being pressed to do by the German shipping companies. Apparently he felt that convoys would offer the submarine a better target than single ships and that there was a danger that if escorted the ships might be torpedoed without warning, an argument that was to be used by the British Admiralty in 1917. Nevertheless, even a single warship in the vicinity of the merchant ships would have prevented the submarines from carrying out their task, bearing in mind the strict observance of the law that was imposed upon their activities. Instead, German shipping was halted for many days whilst additional patrols were organised, necessitating the withdrawal of destroyers and torpedo boats from the High Seas Fleet and causing the postponement of some operations planned for the North Sea.

THE ATTACKS ON GERMAN SHIPPING
OCTOBER - DECEMBER 1915

One other tactic was tried as a result of this attack on shipping. A steamer was manned by a naval crew and used to tow the *U-66* which was submerged. If the former was stopped the submarine would be informed by a telephone and could then slip the tow and proceed to attack the other submarine. This was a ruse already used by the British in the North Sea earlier in 1915 when eight 'C' class submarines had been paired with trawlers to attack U-boats preying on fishing boats in the Dogger Bank area. HMS *C24* with the trawler *Taranaki* had in this way sunk the *U-40* in June, the *C27* with the *Princess Louise* had sunk the *U-23* the following month while in August the *C27* had been unable to fire when a third U-boat, the *U-17*, attacked the trawler *Ratapiko*. By this time the ruse had become known to the Germans and it was abandoned. It was to be tried again in the Adriatic with French trawlers towing a British submarine and, as will be seen, also in the Baltic when Russian trawlers were used with British submarines. None of these other attempts was successful.

An indication of the jumpy state of the German defences is shown by the attack on the Swedish submarine *Hvalen* by the German patrol boat *Meteor*, south of Ystad in south Sweden. Although one of the submarine's crew was killed in this incident the Germans made a prompt apology for their hasty action and offered compensation, so that what could have been yet another diplomatic wrangle was soon smoothed over.

While Cromie was having these successes off the Swedish coast Halahan in the *E18* was sent to keep watch off the port of Libau. His short patrol was hampered by poor weather conditions in which the visibility was seldom more than a few miles, frequently much less. He had one chance on 11 October when the old pre-Dreadnought battleship *Braunschweig* was attacked, but when only 800 yards off his target and ready to fire he was unable to open his bow caps.

Horton took the *E9* to sea on the 17th to carry on where Cromie had left off, his orders being to act against the traffic of German vessels proceeding up and down the Swedish coast. The following afternoon he stopped his first vessel, the Danish *Karla*, which was bound for Stockholm and carrying, literally, coals from Newcastle. While onboard the Master had time to joke with Horton's boarding officer, 'First the Germans in The Sound, now the British. I am suddenly very popular'. He also reported seeing another German warship only a few hours previously. That evening Horton stopped the German *Soderhamn* (1,500 tons) with a cargo of wood which, though destined for Holland, was still a legal prize as it was carried in a German ship. While the German crew abandoned ship a boarding party from the submarine prepared her for destruction. A small charge was exploded against the bulkhead against the ship's side at the after end of the engine room and all the sea cocks were opened. Strangely the ship did not sink but drifted on to the rocks in Norrkoping Bay where she was eventually salvaged.

Collecting his boarding party in a hurry from the *Soderhamn* Horton gave chase to another vessel which was the German *Pernambuco*. The Germans hastily abandoned ship in the gathering darkness and were soon lost to sight, but Horton once again put his boarding party on to the German ship to carry out the same routine to scuttle the ship as before. He then stood by to watch her sink with her valuable iron ore cargo. Two hours later she was low in the water but did not seem to be sinking further! Not wishing to remain in the vicinity any longer Horton decided to finish her with a torpedo. In the excitement Horton's usually well-trained crew fired the first torpedo too early, mistaking the order 'Stop' to the motors for the 'Fire!' However, they made amends and the second torpedo struck the *Pernambuco* amidships sinking her almost immediately.

In the early dawn of the 19th the *Johannes Russ* was stopped and small charges used to blow out the sea cocks to sink her. Then after a short chase the *Dal Alfoen* was stopped. Before a boarding party could be put over a destroyer was sighted closing the submarine and her prize at speed. One torpedo was fired at the *Dal Alfoen* to finish the matter quickly, but it failed to start and sank on leaving the tube, while a second one swerved to starboard for 40 yards and then straightened onto its original course, just enough to cause it to miss the stern of the merchant ship by a few feet. But 'a miss by a few feet is as good as a mile' and the *Dal Alfoen* was left afloat and Horton

had to dive to avoid the destroyer. While the latter was collecting the crew of the *Dal Alfoen* from their boats Horton was
relieved to see the blue and yellow ensign of the Swedish Navy
flying and he recognised her as the *Wale*. Again Horton surfaced to complete his task but the Swede intervened with a
laborious exchange of signals.

Wale: You are in Swedish waters.
E9: I make myself six miles from land.
Wale: I make you five.
E9: Neutral limit is three miles.* Please stand clear while I
sink this ship.

Horton then fired his stern tube and running true before the
Swedish audience the torpedo struck the *Dal Alfoen* amidships, sinking her in two minutes.

Two more German ships were sighted that day but they
escaped into neutral waters before they could be stopped,
while the next day only Swedish ships were in sight. No more
German ships were sighted before Horton left his patrol to
return to Revel on the 25th.

At this time the Russians extended the area of operations
against German shipping into the Gulf of Bothnia. Their
submarines the *Kaiman* and *Drakon* went on patrol on the 20th
with the *Krokodil*, *Makrel*, the old *Som* and *Alligator* following shortly afterwards. The *Alligator* had the first success on
the 24th, chasing two steamers; one escaped but the *Garda
Vith* was taken as a prize into a Finnish port. Later the
Kaiman captured the *Stahleck* while some torpedo boats took
a third prize. It was in 1918, when the crews of these three
ships returned home to Germany, that it was established that
at least one of them had been taken while in neutral Swedish
waters, a fact unknown until then to either side.

While Horton and then the Russian submarines had continued the pressure on German trade off the Swedish coast
Goodhart had taken the *E8* down to keep watch on Libau.

*Sweden claimed a territorial limit of four miles, but this was not recog-
nised by either side in the war.

122

There on a bright sunny morning, 23 October, with a light southerly breeze and only a small swell, smoke was observed on the horizon to the east of the submerged submarine. Soon a three-funnelled German cruiser was in sight coming towards the *E8* from Libau. The enemy was in fact the *Prinz Adalbert*, only recently returned to operations after repairs following Horton's attack on her in July, and now escorted by the two destroyers *S142* and *S143*. Goodhart had little to do to reach an attacking position, and passing under the port wing escort he was 1,300 yards on the beam of the cruiser. 'Fire!' With the familiar *choom* the torpedo left the bow tube. It seemed an interminable wait to Goodhart watching through the periscope, and then there was the vivid flash of an explosion on the waterline. The ship was hidden by a huge column of smoke and the sound of an enormous explosion reached those waiting in the submarine as the cruiser's magazine exploded. Large portions of the ship could be seen falling back into the water, some even near the submarine, and Goodhart decided it was prudent to take the boat down to 40 feet. From the cruiser the destroyers were able to pick up only three survivors.

The *E19* next went to sea at the end of October, although Cromie himself was far from well, suffering from a bout of 'flu, and conducting operations for the first few days from his bunk. Apart from having to dive rapidly on the first day out for a suspected U-boat, all was quiet. Reaching the area between the southern ends of the islands of Gotland and Oland, where on his previous patrol he had caused so much damage to German trade, he found the seas deserted apart from a few Swedish vessels. For once the weather was calm and clear, though the temperature had fallen low enough to warn that winter was not far away and that there could not be many more patrols before the ice forced them into winter's inactivity. On 2 November he moved further south into the area between Sweden and Bornhom, and was rewarded that afternoon with the *Suomi* trying her luck to reach Germany, before she was surprised and stopped with a shot across her bows. Taking the *E19* alongside he found the ship was carrying a cargo of timber. The Master, philosophical about the fate of his ship, followed his crew into the boats, while a boarding party made ready to explode a charge under the ship's main inlet and to set fire to the cargo. When last seen from the submarine as she left the area the *Suomi* was burning brightly, had a list to port and was down by the stern.

By the 7th Cromie had moved west of Bornholm where he suspected that train ferries frequently crossed from Germany. Sure enough after stopping a small lonely Swede which was allowed to proceed, a ferry was sighted in mid-morning. In the midst of the chase a light cruiser and two destroyers arrived in the area, and although it was not then possible to attack, Cromie lay low, suspecting that they would return to the area and perhaps give him a better opportunity. Tantalisingly, several ferries came in sight during the morning but grimly Cromie waited for the return of the warships. Eventually they were sighted again in the early afternoon. Diving he found that he hardly had to manoeuvre the *E19* in order to get into an ideal attacking position; just wait for the *Undine* — such was the identity of the enemy cruiser — to come to him. Twenty-five minutes later he fired a torpedo from a beam tube at a range of 1,100 yards and for once the torpedo ran true and hit amidships. The track of the torpedo had been seen by the Germans but too late for them to take any avoiding action. The cruiser swung round in her tracks and halted.

Aboard the *Undine* it was soon clear that she was mortally hit and the destroyer *V154* was called alongside to take off first the wounded and then the other survivors. Meanwhile Cromie had taken the *E19* around the doomed ship's stern and had fired a second torpedo at her which struck just aft of the main mast. There was a large explosion which threw quantities of debris and smoke into the air and the cruiser rapidly sank. A large ferry came up and joined the destroyer in rescuing the remaining crew, and despite the rough sea and cold the majority of the cruiser's crew were picked up, only 24 being killed or missing.

Cromie took the *E19* back to Revel in rapidly worsening winter weather, arriving back there on the 8th having added another 1,500 miles to his total distance travelled. In his official report Cromie gave due credit to his subordinate,

Lieutenant Sharp, who had been the Officer of the Watch when the *Undine* had been sighted, saying that 'only his sound judgement and prompt action had made the attack possible under the existing weather conditions'. Shortly afterwards the Tsar himself was in Revel to inspect the fortifications and Cromie was among those sent for to be decorated being given the Order of St George* — the highest Russian decoration for bravery — while five of his crew received the Silver Cross of the same Order. That evening he was honoured by being included with those dining with the Tsar in the Royal train. Cromie described the whole incident in a letter to his mother.

. . . We sat down 28 at one table and still left room for waiting. Nearly all spoke English and said all sorts of nice polite things, and I sneaked a menu card, but had not the cheek to ask for signatures. It was a very hard frost during the Emperor's inspection, and all were very much surprised to see us without greatcoats, but the cold is so dry here that one does not feel it so long as one moves about. The place is lovely under snow . . .

Both Goodhart and Horton were also at sea in the early days of November, the former being sent in the *E8* down the coast to attack the enemy on the Libau and Memel routes, while the *E9* went looking for enemy ships off the Swedish coast. Both suffered from the miseries of the weather with severe gales and increasing cold. Goodhart did have the chance to attack the light cruiser *Lubeck* escorted by a destroyer but the submarine was rolling so badly in the heavy seas — even at periscope depth — that the torpedo fired from a beam tube could well have missed by passing under the target. Later he had the mortification to hit the naval collier *John Sauber* with a torpedo that failed to explode. To add to Goodhart's frustration the *E8* was in collision in the dark with the Russian submarine

*He had already received the Order of St Vladimir for his entry into the Baltic and the Order of St Anne for his previous patrol against German merchant shipping. His DSO for these feats was not gazetted until 31 May 1916.

Gepard, the one entering and the other leaving Revel. The damage meant that the *E8* had to spend several weeks in dock while the damage was repaired. Horton on the Swedish coast saw no suitable targets: on one day a small Swedish convoy, on another a German patrol too far off to attack, on another small neutral merchant ships.

So the year dragged to a close with worsening weather making life in the submarines a continual battle to attain just a small degree of comfort and warmth while waiting to meet an enemy who seemed to keep to harbour. Cromie himself had one more success on 4 December while operating west of Bornholm. Then he stopped the *Friesenburg*, managed to go alongside in the heavy swell to transfer a boarding party, and sank her after the crew had left by blowing out the main inlet valves in the engine room. This was the last success of the year, although Halahan managed to take the *E18* to sea for a final (and uneventful) patrol in the early days of January 1916 before the ice closed in and prevented further patrols.

Excepting the *E13*, which had been lost in exceptional circumstances while entering the Baltic, and the Russian *Akula* which had been lost in late November while on an experimental minelaying mission, no Allied submarines had been lost to enemy action in the Baltic. Yet during the last few months of the year they had been extraordinarily successful, virtually bringing to a halt the German trade with Sweden, at least in German shipping, as well as damaging, and then in another attack, sinking the *Prinz Adalbert*, damaging the *Moltke* and sinking the *Undine*. How much more impressive this list would appear but for the faulty running of some of the torpedoes, particularly earlier in the year when Horton and Laurence were on their own. Even so the German Fleet was forced on to the defensive by the end of the year. The Russians themselves had not been idle, their boats had carried out many attacks but of the 50 torpedoes fired none had found a target. So, in high spirits on account of their success, the British submariners settled down to another cold and bleak winter far from home, but looking forward to being able to carry on their good work in the summer months to come.

IX

After Success — Frustration

Christmas 1915 came and went, the second of this 'over-by-Christmas' war, and the winter weather once more brought operations to a close for the small party of British sailors isolated far from home in Russia. For some of them it was to be their second winter in this harsh and forbidding climate, whilst those who had arrived during the summer were to learn that all the stories of its severity were not exaggerated. The five submarines lay motionless and ice-covered in Revel harbour, while the sea itself froze solid all the way across to Helsingfors in Finland.

The summer of 1915 had not been a successful one for the German Baltic Fleet who had failed to force an entry into the Gulf of Riga and had finally been thrown on to the defensive to protect their merchant shipping from submarine attack. But on land it had been a different story and it was the Russians who had had a disastrous summer, losing ground all the way along the front to the Germans and their Austrian allies. In the north the Russians had been pushed back from Memel to the gates of Riga, where they had held the city and even regained a few miles. Elsewhere massive attacks had given the enemy huge territorial gains including all of Poland, so that the front ran roughly north and south from Riga to the Rumanian border. All this had been achieved at a cost of nearly a million and a half Russian killed and wounded and another million as

127

prisoners of war. It was, as the Minister of War said, 'only the immeasurable distances, impassable roads and the mercy of St Nicholas, patron of Holy Russia, that had staved off defeat'; a situation not unsimilar to that of the French invading army in 1812 and the Germans again in 1941.

Damaging though the casualties were to the Russians it was their actual loss of ground that was to be of more importance to their future war effort. With the capture by the Germans of all the industrialised area of Poland the Russians lost a large proportion of their total railway mileage and rolling stock leaving the remaining network hopelessly inadequate for the task of supporting a country at war. It also meant the loss of many factories and a major part of the chemical and mining industries. With conscription taking too many skilled workers from their necessary jobs to swell the ranks of an army which was ill-prepared to take them, the moribund Russian industrial machine became less and less capable of coping with the demands of modern war.

To add to the problems there was rampant inflation. Wages had indeed risen during 1915 but only at less than half the rate of the cost of living. The number of strikes rose dramatically during the year and as the news from the battle fronts became increasingly worse so discontent grew. Government and the bureaucracy grew more inefficient and stultified as time went by, suffering from a lack of leadership from the Tsar himself who in turn grew more detached from the situation and the feelings of his people, while remaining firmly influenced by his haughty and autocratic Empress. It was, perhaps, only a portent of the future that the general discontent should have shown itself in the more inactive units of the Fleet, those units which had spent much of their time in idleness in harbour rather than on active operations. For, when in November 1915 a sortie was planned for the battleships a mutiny broke out in one of them — the *Gangut*. As in 1905 the cause was ostensibly over food, but to this complaint other demands were soon added, including the replacement of some of the officers. Although 50 seamen were arrested and later imprisoned this mutiny was followed a few days later by a similar outbreak in the *Imperator Pavel*. This again was soon quelled. In the circumstances it is perhaps unfortunate that when the battleships did finally put to sea they did not meet with the enemy.

For the British sailor living close by his Russian counterpart in the *Dvina*, Russian discipline seemed at once both harsh and lacking in any humanity. The yawning chasm between officers and ratings was noticeable even in an age when the Royal Navy was much more class conscious than today. The Russian rating was required to use the obsequious expression 'Excellency' or 'High Born' when addressing an officer and had to remain at the salute throughout the entire meeting. Ashore they were required to step off the pavement and to remain at the salute whenever an officer was met in the street, while certain restaurants, theatres and cinemas were barred to the Russian rating (even if he could afford the prices charged). Food was little in quantity and basic in quality, which perhaps explains why the mutinies of both 1905 and 1915 had their origins in complaints about food. Pay was low and there was little chance for most of the sailors to travel the long distances to visit their families. There was little in the way of organised sport so beloved by the British sailor. Punishments for even minor misdemeanours were severe by Royal Navy standards.

Against this it must be remembered that while it was all strange and rather disturbing to the British ratings to be in the midst of such discipline it was not considered unusual in a country where there was such disparity between the upper and lower classes. Again, the Russian ratings were largely uneducated and were conscripted. In a country where life was hard everywhere, conditions in the Navy were simply the same.

When Laurence and Horton had first arrived in Russia in October 1914 they had been welcomed enthusiastically by the Russians of the Baltic Fleet, but by the winter of 1915/16 this friendly attitude had steadily deteriorated. The successes enjoyed by the British submariners contrasted with the poor results by the Russians and led to the development of an

129

unhealthy jealousy. This attitude, which was bad enough in its effects on individual relationships among men who were supposed to be working together, was not confined to the Russian submarine flotilla but became prevalent throughout the Baltic Fleet. During the forthcoming summer of 1916 it was to have an unfortunate operational effect.

The change of attitude became manifest in a number of different ways. Complaints began to be made about the behaviour of the British sailors, not so much that they had become ill-disciplined but more because given their comparative freedom they suffered none of the 'off limits' problems of the Russians as long as they behaved themselves and the fact was not understood and resented by the Russian officers who were in a mood to be critical. Their presence in places normally reserved only for these officers was one cause of friction, while their better pay and more fraternal relationships with their own officers highlighted the differences with the Russian regime and added to the mounting resentment.

Aside from the official complaints which tended to emphasise events out of their true importance, two incidents serve as examples of the relationship between the two allies, due in part to different standards and in part to the jealousy already referred to. One day Halahan had the mortification of having his salute returned by a Russian officer who at the same time deliberately turned his head away and spat over his shoulder. Telegraphist Benson, of the *E19*, suffered even more. While on the way to deliver a signal to the Russian Admiral he met another senior officer on the ladder leading up the ship's side and stood aside to let him pass, and was then soundly abused for his pains. According to Russian standards he should have gone back down to the bottom and waited. In this case the incident was seen by Cromie who demanded — and received — an apology. It was not a happy relationship! Yet even in such an atmosphere the British kept many personal friendships alive.

The opportunity was taken during these winter months to rearm many of the Russian cruisers and destroyers with heavier and more numerous guns, while other ships of the

1912 Programme were at last completing and joining the Fleet. The Russians had also made arrangements to purchase more submarines abroad and these were to enter service during the coming summer of 1916. The submarines were built in sections in Canada to an American design, shipped across the Pacific to Vladivostok and then taken across Russia by rail to be finally assembled at the Baltic Shipbuilding Works at Petrograd or, in the case of the boats destined to join the Black Sea Fleet, at Nickolaev.

The design was essentially the same as that of the ten boats of the British 'H' class which had been built at Montreal and were then the first submarines to cross the Atlantic. Subsequently, HMS *H1* was one of those which successfully penetrated the Dardanelles and operated with such devastating effect against the Turks in the Sea of Marmora. In the Russian Navy they were designated the 'AG' class, AG standing for *Amerikansky-Golland*, or American-Holland type. These boats were an improvement on the British 'E' class as they were capable of a bow salvo of four torpedoes at any one time; a big advantage with the somewhat unreliable torpedoes of the day and with only the small warhead of the 18 inch torpedo. Smaller than the new Russian *Bars* class (see page 102) they were 151 feet in length overall, had a displacement of 356/434 tons and were capable of a speed of 12 knots on the surface or 8 knots dived. They had a crew of 30. Easily manoeuvrable, they would be potentially useful additions to the Russian submarine flotillas.

The British boats themselves were in need of a lot of maintenance during the winter and the engineers rigged up a primitive form of steam heating which was led through each of the boats to counter the worst of the winter's cold. The *E1* and the *E9* were in the worst mechanical state because they were older and also because they had been away from proper base facilities for over a year.

Inevitably there were changes in personnel, the most notable being the return home of both Laurence and Horton. Probably as a result of a personal disagreement with his senior officer Horton had applied to return home for a new appointment. Horton was never one to refrain from speaking his mind, especially if he considered that it was for the good of the Service, but his criticisms of other officers at this time were inexcusable and can perhaps be explained in part by the stresses of the previous 15 months operating in an alien environment far from home and with shortages of stores, weapons and facilities. Laurence too, uncharacteristically, let the petty differences with some of the Russian officers on board the *Dvina* overcome his usual tact, and he wrote on this subject to the Commander-in-Chief. Rear Admiral R. F. Phillimore, CB, MVO, the British Liaison Officer at Imperial Headquarters, was called to Revel by Admiral Kanin to investigate and smooth things over. Although some Russian officers were replaced it was decided that Laurence ought to go too.

The Russians asked that Horton should stay to be the Senior Officer of the Flotilla, but the Admiralty decided that both officers should return for re-appointing. Commenting on the Admiralty file the Second Sea Lord, who was responsible for officers' appointments, wrote 'I understand Commander Horton is something of a pirate and not at all fitted for the position of SNO [Senior Naval Officer] in the Baltic'. Strong words, and perhaps partly due to some of Horton's escapades as a junior officer, and also perhaps to an incident earlier in the war following the sinking of the German cruiser *Hela*. On that occasion when Horton returned to Harwich he flew the Jolly Roger from the *E9*'s periscope* to signify his success. Obviously senior officers in the Admiralty had long memories.

Even in 1920 Their Lordships had still not quite forgotten this flouting of convention by Horton for a letter was sent to him concerning his actions against the German merchant ships carrying the iron ore from Sweden and wishing to ensure that no more of his piratical actions had taken place. It has already been narrated how he, and Cromie, had acted quite legally against this shipping, yet obviously a doubt remained.

---

*A custom perpetuated during the Second World War by all successful British and Allied submarines on their return to harbour.

The Secretary
Admiralty, S.W.1.
10th September 1920

Captain Max K. Horton, D.S.O., R.N.,
H.M.S. Dolphin,
c/o G.P.O.

With reference to the affidavits which were made by you regarding the capture and sinking of certain enemy merchant vessels by H.M. Submarine E.9 in the Baltic Sea in 1915, I am to inform you that it is desired to ascertain whether or not due warning was given to all the unarmed merchant ships which were dealt with by the vessel under your Command before any offensive action was taken against them.

By Command of their Lordships,
(Signed) V. W. BADDELEY.

Horton replied:

From: Captain Max K. Horton, D.S.O., R.N.,
To: Secretary of the Admiralty.
Date: 13th September 1920

Submitted,
With reference to your letter of 10th September 1920, due and proper warning was given in every case in which submarine E.9 was concerned. Moreover careful search of each vessel sunk was made to ensure that there was none of the enemy crew remaining on board. Ample time was allowed for placing personal gear, food and water in the boats and in no case was the weather unsuitable for small boats or the distance to the nearest shore more than fifteen miles.

I was informed by Russian Intelligence Department that no casualties occurred or were reported in Sweden where enemy crews landed.

(Signed) Max Horton
Captain.

Horton was the first to go home. He had endeared himself to the Russians not only for his prowess as a submariner but also because of those traits in his character which were so Russian — his love of gambling, at which he was undoubtedly lucky, combined with his ability to drink the best of them under the table. After a full-scale banquet in his honour he was escorted to the train by many of the Russian officers, all the British officers in the Flotilla, the Commander-in-Chief's band and the submariners' concert party. Young Ashmore — now a Lieutenant and moved from the *E18* to become the First Lieutenant of the *E1* — recalls an impersonation of Charlie Chaplin clinging to the top of a lamp-post and waving a bowler hat as the train pulled out, and with Horton on the step of his coach, swaying gently and blissfully from side to side, with a benign smile on his usually severe face.

Laurence left soon afterwards to take command of the new large submarine, the *J1*. Cromie, who with Goodhart had been promoted Commander at the end of 1915, was now the senior officer. Two new Commanding Officers had arrived: Lieutenant-Commander Hubert Vaughan-Jones for the *E9* and Lieutenant-Commander Athelstan Fenner for the *E1*. The former had joined submarines in 1906, Fenner a year later. Despite many weary months on patrol during 1915 in the Heligoland Bight, where they had each commanded a 'D' class submarine, neither had had the luck to sink an enemy warship. Indeed it was seldom during those long months that they had even seen the enemy. Vaughan-Jones was described as a conscientious commanding officer, a strict disciplinarian and a good seaman, yet somehow remained remote from his men. Fenner too was a competent submariner with a cheerful and calm manner which never became ruffled however difficult the situation. He was no stranger to taking a submarine many miles from home for in early 1911 he had commanded the *C37*, one of three submarines which had made the 10,000 miles trip to Hong Kong in only two and a half months. In conditions which had varied from sultry calm to full gale, from the cold of an English winter to the heat of the tropics, Fenner as Commanding Officer had had to stand watch and watch with only one other officer. Now his urbane manner would be tested to the full in taking over Laurence's lame duck *E1*, with all the frustrations and engineering defects added to the new problems of operating in the Baltic Sea.

Cromie, in his role of senior officer, was soon involved with the social side of his duties, a matter which he carried out with the same panache that he gave to commanding a submarine. With six of his officers he paid a four-day visit to Moscow at the request of the British Consul, Bruce Lockhart, and the British Club. The finale of the visit was a supper in honour of the British submariners given by the artists' and actors' club during which the visitors met and saw the best of Moscow's ballerinas, actors and singers perform. But it was Cromie who stole the show with a very brief impromptu speech of thanks which delighted his hosts.

Ladies and Gentlemen. You are all artists — musicians, poets, novelists, painters, composers. You are creators. What you create will live long after you. We are simple sailors. We destroy. But we can say truthfully that in this war we destroy in order that your works may live.

Once more the tedium of winter was brought to an end with the arrival of spring, the thaw beginning earlier than usual. At the end of March the ice-breakers were able to begin clearing a passage out of Revel along the coast to the open waters, a route taken on 1 April by the minelayer *Amur*. As in 1914 and 1915 minelaying operations were to have a high priority in the Russian operational plans. Minefields which had been depleted by the winter gales and then the ice had to be topped-up and then strengthened. The minefields protecting the Irben Straits and the Gulf of Riga were particularly important, for the defence of the Gulf was once again considered to be of such importance that it was assessed that if the Straits were forced by the German Fleet, then the entire right flank of the Russian Army could be endangered. To the north of the Gulf the spring thaw enabled work to continue on strengthening the defences of Moon Sound where extra coastal batteries were mounted. Mining was an early priority with the Germans too in the spring of 1916 with nearly 4,000 mines being laid in April to prevent any sortie by the Russian capital ships into the central or southern Baltic.

Aircraft were to play an increasingly active part in the naval war of 1916 and it is noteworthy that they scored the first success of the year. On 27th April the battleship *Slava*, so staunch in the defence of the Gulf of Riga in 1915, had the distinction of being the first capital ship to be hit by aircraft bombs. Three seaplanes carried to the area in the specially converted seaplane carrier *Santa Elena*, a converted freighter, dropped 31 bombs on the veteran ship and scored three hits without loss to themselves. The *Slava* was left in urgent need of repair having earlier received two hits from the *Moltke*'s 11-inch shells in addition to damage and casualties from shrapnel fired at her from ashore. To avoid exposing the damaged ship to the chance of German attack if she returned to the Gulf of Finland through the Irben Straits, it meant taking her through Moon Sound. But the maximum depth of water there was only 15 feet, not enough for a ship of the *Slava*'s size in normal circumstances, let alone a ship in a damaged state. For once the problem was tackled energetically and a force of 40 dredgers was soon hard at work. Initially a channel was dredged to a depth of 30 feet; later this was increased by an additional 10 feet. The new channel was deep enough to allow both the *Slava* to leave and for reinforcements to arrive.

Despite this early activity it was the end of April before the first British submarines left Revel. The *E18*, with Halahan proudly flying the broad pendant of Commodore N. L. Podgursky, the Russian Baltic Fleet submarine commander, and Fenner taking the *E1* to sea for the first time, and with an ice-breaker to help them through the still thick ice fields, they cautiously made their way into the Gulf of Riga and secured for the night alongside the *Slava*. Even in such surroundings they were not free from worry from the ice as the cold north wind caused the melting pack to drift down and threaten the two submarines. But the trip itself served little purpose other

136

than to show that spring was on its way and that the submarines could leave harbour, for after accompanying two destroyers on a short bombardment of the German trenches in front of Riga — hardly, it would be thought, a duty for two submarines — they returned to Revel.

Fearful of a repeat of the success by the British submarines against the Swedish iron ore trade, the Germans made arrangements early in 1916 to protect their merchant shipping. Masters were given strict instructions to remain inside Swedish territorial waters, sailings were controlled so that patrols were at sea to protect the merchant ships forced by geography to cross the open sea, and increased use was made of Swedish registered ships. It will be remembered that the Swedish *Nike*, having been taken as a prize by Cromie, was then released for political reasons. Hopefully the Russians planned once more to halt the flow of vital German supplies and the *E9*, the *E19* and the Russian *Volk* were sent out on 14 and 15 May. The *Volk*, operating in the Bay of Norrkoping, was given a free hand while on the other hand the two British boats, the *E9* between the Pomeranian and Swedish coasts and the *E19* off Libau, were ordered to attack only cruisers and larger ships.

On the 17th the *Volk* sank three German steamers, the *Hera*, *Kolga* and *Bianca*, a success by any Russian submarine which was not to be exceeded until 1945 when Commander Marinesko in the *S13* sank the liners *Wilhelm Gustloff* and *General Steuben* within ten days. The *E9* saw a number of small ships but was unable to get within range of the only worthwhile target seen during a relatively uneventful patrol.

Cromie's patrol in the *E19* off Libau was also fruitless, but with his boundless energy it was by no means uneventful. He soon realised that there was small chance of a target — despite the fact that he soon established that there were five enemy cruisers lying in Libau harbour — so he began a careful and detailed reconnaissance of the approach channels. Hour by hour as the days went by he added to the information. Landmarks were sighted through the periscope and checked against those shown on the chart and additional information added.

Carefully the movements of the trawlers and destroyers patrolling off the port were watched and plotted so that gradually a picture about the passages through the minefields could be drawn. For much of the time the weather was bad, which added to the difficulties in obtaining the information. High winds whipped up the sea making depth keeping difficult and with the added danger that as the periscope had to be raised higher to be able to see above the wave tops so the risk of it being observed by a watchful patrol increased. In between the storms calm and heavy rain made life no more pleasant.

It was during one of these periods of calm that the inattention of one officer nearly ended this story prematurely and tragically. With the sea like a sheet of glass the periscope must be exposed by only a few inches, the speed of the submarine must be the absolute minimum to reduce the amount of 'feather' to be seen by an enemy, and the periscope can only be up for a matter of seconds to reduce the chance of its detection. It takes an alert and experienced officer of the watch to keep a careful lookout under such conditions. On such a day Cromie was called to the Control Room by the officer of the watch, his RNR navigating officer Lieutenant Mee, the same officer who had taken the *Nike* in prize to Revel. Now he reported a ship in sight. When Cromie raised the periscope to assess the situation he found not one but two trawlers less than a mile away. It later transpired that Mee hadn't taken a look for some 25 minutes and then had had the periscope up for three minutes before he had seen the trawlers. It was fortunate that the enemy too had not been alert for it was soon obvious that the submarine had not been sighted. Because they were too close inshore and in rather shallow water Cromie was restricted in the manoeuvres available to evade and there was just one way out. He took it, and at the submarine's full underwater speed he went to seaward of the two trawlers and into deeper water. The trawlers, still without depth charges, spread a net with explosive charges attached hoping to catch the submarine, an exercise Cromie was able to watch in safety for the next two hours, thankful that he had got clear in time.

After his return to Revel on 22nd he wrote in his report:

I am convinced that the passage west of Libau is at least two miles wide and quite clear of mines and having dived in it at varying depths to 40 feet I am sure that there are no electric or observation mines. The trawlers are such a useful mark that they should not be attacked.

Such was his faith in his own reconnaissance!

On the return of these three submarines five more left Revel on the 25th to attack any German merchant ships or large warships to be found over a large part of the eastern Baltic. The *E8* and *E18* were to operate between Memel and Libau, the *E1* off the Pomeranian coast while the Russian *Gepard* and *Bars* were sent to the Swedish coast.

The two Russian boats had unsuccessful patrols and were lucky to return. In an attempt to attack a convoy the *Gepard* was rammed amidships by a German auxiliary ship — a merchant ship taken over as a temporary convoy escort and similar to the British Q-ships. Although the Germans thought they had sunk a submarine the *Gepard* managed to return to Revel with damaged superstructure and a buckled gun. The *Bars* too was attacked by another auxiliary vessel and again the ecstatic Germans claimed a kill while the shaken *Bars* returned to Revel.

The *E1* made one unsuccessful attack on an ex-British steamer, the *Winterton*, which had been caught in a German port on the outbreak of war and taken for service with the enemy. The *E1* had been fitted with a Russian device so that two torpedoes could be carried slung outside the hull and fired from there, supplementing the single internal bow tube with which she was fitted. Poor Fenner fired a salvo of three torpedoes at this tempting target which was escorted by a destroyer, all three running straight towards the *Winterton*. Alas, the two Russian torpedoes ran on the surface giving the Germans ample time to alter course and avoid them all!

Later the same day the *E1* was bombed by an aircraft, a new experience for the British submariners, and one which was to occur more and more frequently during this frustrating. year. Fenner had run dived from the area of his attack on the *Winterton*, and then late in the afternoon had surfaced to recharge his batteries. Hardly had they reached the surface when a lookout gave the alarm as the aircraft turned towards them. As the submarine was disappearing beneath the surface so four small bombs exploded around them, close but quite accurate enough; far enough away that no damage was done, but near enough to give Fenner and the crew of the *E1* a nasty moment or two. Warily they surfaced again an hour later; once more they were forced to dive with three bombs exploding in the sea above them as they levelled off at 50 feet. In the calm clear waters of the Baltic the shape of a submarine was still visible to the German airmen, at times even when they were as deep as 90 feet, and provided a good aiming mark for the small aircraft bombs.

After his return from this patrol Cromie arranged for Fenner to go up in a Russian seaplane from Revel and take note of how easy it was to see Goodhart's *E8* which was exercising off the port. As a result proposals were made to repaint the British submarines avoiding the strikingly obvious bright red of the underwater anti-fouling paint among other innovations.

But it was to be Halahan's *E18* which was to claim the glory, and to mark the occasion with tragedy. She had sailed south with the *E8*, the two boats parting company the day after sailing. During the afternoon of the 26th Goodhart, in the *E8*, sighted an enemy force of five destroyers and another larger ship which he thought might be one of the new German seaplane carriers, but was unable to get close enough to attack. Halahan was more lucky. At 4.42 p.m. when 30 miles to seaward of Libau he made a brilliant attack in which a torpedo blew the bows off the new German destroyer *V100*. With 12 men killed the destroyer was lucky not to sink and in fact, thanks partly to the calm weather at the time, the Germans were able to tow her back to Libau for repairs. Meanwhile Halahan went looking for new targets.

It was almost the last that was heard of the *E18*. Two days

140

later the Germans reported her as being seen off Memel, but nothing else. It is believed that she was lost during her return to Revel, most probably through striking a mine. Young Ashmore who had made the journey out from Harwich in the *E18* with Halahan recalled his Commanding Officer's last lingering look at the coast of England as if sensing that he would never see his homeland again. He also recalled how they anxiously waited for the overdue submarine, hoping against hope that somehow she would turn up. How on a Sunday morning the Chaplain from the Embassy in Petrograd came to Revel to conduct the service for the British on the quarterdeck of the depot ship, *Dvina*. How, near the end of the service, the congregation heard a submarine come alongside and rushed to see whether it was the missing boat, hoping to see their missing friends, only to return shamefaced to their places, for it was only the *E1* returning from engine trials.

The Tsar sent Cromie a letter of sympathy for the loss of the submarine, awarded Halahan the Cross of St George, the other two officers the Order of St Vladimir and a medal for each of the crew. It was a welcome gesture if unusual, for the rules of the Orders did not allow for their posthumous award.

So the summer campaign of 1916 opened, though without the trade-stopping successes of the previous autumn. Indeed Cromie felt that his boats were being misused, as a letter to Commodore Hall shows, the frustration being scarcely concealed by his enthusiasm to get out of harbour and on patrol:

We are all in full swing once more, but oh the begging and 'weeping' I have had to get the staff to move, and the lies they keep putting me off with, with what idea I never discovered. Now I am doing my best to persuade them to keep at least two boats always at sea in two positions having direct offensive bearings on any naval movement against Riga, viz, Libau and Steinort. I reconnoitred these positions last trip and located the swept channels, patrols and courses used, and went right up to Libau, counting five cruisers inside, but they never stirred out.

Or again later:

There is very little for us to do at present beyond the eternal 'stand by', as I have failed to persuade them to let us hunt Fritz off the entrance to the Gulf.

Both the *E9* and *E19* were sent out on 9 June. The next day Cromie, like Fenner, was harassed by an aircraft. In the space of five hours he was attacked four times, each time the bombs dropped clear but near enough to shake the submarine. Two days later he was again attacked, a total of no less than 34 bombs being dropped on the *E19* during the two days. On this occasion he engaged one of the aircraft involved with his gun, but after the eighth round the aircraft kept astern where the gun could not bear. Not that it made much difference for the gun was as ineffective as the aircraft bombs. Of 1897 vintage its bore was by then quite smooth and Cromie claimed to be able to see the shells tumbling through the air. After this he vowed to try and get a Russian 47 mm gun fitted during the next winter's lay-off.

These attacks on the *E19* were kept up until 9.30 p.m. after which Cromie was able to steam away from the area as quickly as possible expecting surface ships to appear and take up the hunt. He reported the incident by wireless, and it says much for the Russian Intelligence Department that within a very short time he was told that destroyers were at sea looking for him *and that they had instructions to search till daylight.*

These two patrols by the *E9* and *E19* were made to cover a sweep by a force of cruisers and destroyers seeking German shipping along the Swedish coast, the submarines being placed to catch the German ships should they have left Libau to give battle. The Russians claimed five ships destroyed, but German records only show the loss of another of their auxiliary ships of the type which earlier had given the *Bars* and *Gepard* such a hard time. A second anti-shipping sweep by Russian cruisers and destroyers at the end of June also met with no success though on this occasion there was a sharp but inconclusive action with German destroyers. In early July the

Russian submarines moved north into the Gulf of Bothnia where the steamer *Dorita* was sunk by gunfire by the *Volk*, while the *Vepr* torpedoed the *Syria*. The latter was just inside Swedish waters when she sank and the incident led to a burst of inconsequential diplomatic activity. This was followed by the capture of two more steamers in the same area by destroyers. Meanwhile the British boats had maintained a watch off the Irben Straits and off Libau.

Cromie was not only the Commanding Officer of the *E19*, he was also the Senior Officer of all the British submarines operating in the Baltic. The lack of success of the *E19* and the other boats during the opening months of the summer of 1916 was just one problem that Cromie had to face. Fighting the war at sea was something for which he had trained for many years though the problems met were not always those which he had expected; the other battle had to be fought in harbour back in Revel. It was a battle fought against the Russian staff and Russian officialdom and inefficiency, a battle fought at long range with the British Admiralty and its many departments back in England. It was a battle that took not only his courage but his tact, forethought and patience.

In 1914 Laurence and Horton had dealt directly with the Commander-in-Chief, Admiral von Essen, who appreciated their efforts and the capability of their boats. Admiral Kanin, besides lacking the ability of his predecessor, did not get on with Laurence or, later, Cromie. He mistrusted his allies and failed to realise the opportunities their presence in the Baltic gave him and he ignored, or was unaware of, the respect with which the British submariners were held by the Germans. Obsessed with the fear of a successful German attack on the Gulf of Riga he tended to keep the British boats back from routine operations ready to oppose such an attack, or to expend their patrols on routine watches off Libau. It was a frustrating experience for those professional submariners so far from their home, the more so since the expected German offensive never developed during 1916.

Stores were a never-ending problem. Small parties of men could be brought overland through neutral Norway and

Sweden, but stores had to go the long way by sea. There were only two ports in north Russia that could be used: Port Romanoff or Murmansk on the Kola Inlet, and Archangel at the mouth of the Dvina river on the White Sea. Murmansk was 1,200 miles from Lerwick in the Shetlands, the nearest British port, or five days steaming at even a modest ten knots — Archangel being another 450 miles. But there were more fundamental differences between the two ports.

In 1914 Archangel was a town of 50,000 people, with extensive quays and warehouses and a prewar trade of over half a million tons annually. A single-track railway led south from the port for over 350 miles to connect with the rest of the Russian railway system at Vologda. In contrast Murmansk was a much smaller town, consisting mainly of a number of log houses, some official buildings also of wood and a rather impressive church. It was virtually undeveloped as a port. The railway south to Petrograd had been started just before the outbreak of war but even in 1916 was still unfinished, being finally opened on 1 January 1917. Yet Murmansk had one great advantage over its big sister, for the waters around the North Cape were warmed by the Gulf Stream and the port remained ice-free throughout the year. Archangel is closed by ice for long periods; generally speaking navigation is suspended from December to May, while in 1916 the port was not declared open until 9 June.

During those early months of 1916 stores arriving at Murmansk had to be taken south first by sledge until they met the railhead when they could be transhipped to the railway. But before starting their journey they first had to clear the bureaucracy of Customs and then be identified as consigned to Revel as opposed to the British forces in north Russia. It seems that despite frequent pleas the store depots in England were unable to appreciate the problems and difficulties involved. All too often advice from Cromie about the correct address for stores went unheeded or forgotten. Stores were addressed to the SBNO (Senior British Naval Officer) Archangel when the port was closed, and so waited for summer and the port to open so that they could be delivered.

144

On other occasions the stores were addressed to the SBNO's ship, the old cruiser HMS *Iphigenia*, with more delays while they waited for the ship to return from patrol. It could be said that he was a SBNO in Russia, and that Revel was in Russia too, but there was no appreciation of the distances and lack of communications over those distances. One batch of torpedoes actually ended up in Sevastopol, though it might be expected that this was not entirely the fault of the stores organisation in England!

Three times I have had to send a Russian officer to Archangel to trace the gear from that end. I would suggest that complete details of every shipment be sent here and that every case be clearly addressed Senior British Naval Officer, Revel and numbered to correspond with the advice note. It is necessary to put the address in Russian as well. This sounds a tremendous business, but I assure you it is most necessary, you cannot compare things here with arrangements in England. It is nothing to lose a truck for six months in a siding.

It must not be forgotten that on top of all this the submarines were still, nominally, part of the 8th Flotilla based on HMS *Maidstone* in Harwich. This meant that all but the most minor requests had to be forwarded through the Flotilla, a process that was certain to add six weeks' delay to even the simplest problem. For some unknown reason private mail took even longer to reach the submarine crews. In May Cromie was complaining that they had only one parcel mail since Christmas, and that had arrived via Canada. Later two lots of letters arrived via Berlin! The mail ships had been intercepted by the Germans in the Gulf of Bothnia after the route for the mail had been announced in *The Times*.

Poor Cromie, no wonder he complained of having to do at least three hours paper work every day. When he was at sea this chore devolved on Goodhart with consequent lack of continuity — certainly not an ideal way of running the Flotilla.

No, the start of 1916 was not a good time. With all the high promise of the last months of 1915 behind them the British submariners waited in vain for their luck to change, waited with growing frustration for some success to crown their efforts, waited, seemingly forgotten, miles from home in an inhospitable land.

X

The End of an Era

Back in London early in 1916 the Admiralty had considered the possibility of sending more submarines into the Baltic. Two aspects of the problem were considered; first, whether a reasonable proportion of the submarines which made the attempt could succeed, and secondly what to do with the submarines which did reach the Baltic until the Russian ports were ice-free and available to receive them. The second part of the problem was never to be answered for after considering several ideas for passing more submarines through The Sound it was concluded that because of increased German defences the chances against a submarine getting through were at that time much greater than in either 1914 or 1915. The First Sea Lord thought that with good luck perhaps about half might get through, while in the worst case it was possible that all would be lost.

At the same time as the Admiralty decided against sending any more submarines to the Baltic it was stated that the best way remaining in which to help the Russians was not by offensive sweeps into the Kattegat towards The Sound, which could lead to unacceptable losses by the cruisers taking part and which would certainly be beyond the effective range of the coal-hungry destroyers. Instead they should ensure that the submarines in the Baltic were 'in the pink of condition' to begin operations as soon as the melting ice allowed. Fine words, but the writer did not elaborate on how this was to be achieved with the submarines in a Russian dockyard and at the end of a long, slow and dubious supply line through the north Russian ports.

One final suggestion was made. If no more British submarines could enter the Baltic then perhaps — with Russian consent — some good crews could be sent overland through neutral Norway and Sweden, or north through Archangel, to man some of the Russian submarines. It is not known if such a proposal was ever made to the Russians, but if it were it would hardly have done anything to help the already strained relations that existed between the two allies in Revel.

There the matter appeared to end. No more 'E' class were to attempt the passage through The Sound and the campaign of 1916 would have to be fought with the five British boats already there together with the increasing number of new Russian boats. And indeed, as has been described in the last chapter, this was the case in the months immediately following the spring thaw. But in July the question was again before the Admiralty Board for consideration as a new plan had been put forward. The idea was that four of the small old 'C' class submarines would be towed to Archangel — it was too far for them to go on their own — and then be taken on barges down through the rivers and canals to Petrograd and the Baltic. There they would once again be readied for service. It sounds simple but it involved a journey of nearly 4,000 miles from the dockyard at Chatham where it was all to begin.

Unfortunately the papers still available do not reveal just when this plan began to be considered, but it must surely have been soon after it had been decided that no more boats could pass safely through The Sound. On this occasion considerable planning had taken place, for the state of the rivers and locks in the Russian waterways system had all been taken into account, as had the availability of suitable transit barges. Perhaps the pity of it was that all this planning did not allow greater warning to be given to the submarine crews and to

'C' Class submarine in dock. Note the bow cap of the starboard torpedo tube is open. (*Photo: Author's collection*)

HMS *C32* at sea, a photograph taken pre-war. (*Photo: Author's collection*)

Lieutenants Stanley (left) and Ashmore aboard the *Pamiat Azova*. (*Photo: Imperial War Museum*)

Crowds of revolutionary Russian sailors on the jetty alongside the *Dvina*, Easter 1917. (*Photo: Submarine Museum*)

Cromie talking to delegates from the Duma. (*Photo: Submarine Museum*)

ПРОПУСКЪ

Данъ сей отъ Штаба Начальника Дивизіи подводныхъ лодокъ

Балтійскаго моря *Матросу Анг*

скоЙ службы Джонс

на право свободнаго прохода по улицамъ Г. Ревеля послѣ

ДЕСЯТИ часовъ вечера.

Что подписью съ приложеніемъ казенной печати удо-

стовѣряется. " 1 Ноября .....1917 года

Старшій Флагъ-Офицеръ

Штаба Дивизіи под.лодокъ *Поручикъ графъ*

Pass issued to Able Seaman Jeffries of HMS *E1* in November 1917 allowing him free passage through the streets of the City of Revel after ten o'clock at night.

those who had to prepare the boats themselves for this momentous project.

No sooner had the Admiralty Board agreed to this plan than Commodore Hall nominated the *C26* (Lieutenant Eric Tod), *C27* (Lieutenant Douglas Sealy), *C32* (Lieutenant Christopher Satow) and *C35* (Lieutenant Edward Stanley) as being in the best condition to make the trip. The four boats were sent to Chatham to be prepared for the tow while the *C28* and *C30* had to be sent to Dover to replace them.* By this time only two weeks remained before they were due to leave for Russia, two weeks in which the dockyard had much to do. The boats had to be docked, scraped and painted, while at the same time removing the periscopes and blanking the resulting holes in the hull, removing the bow hydroplanes, and then locking in the amidships position both the rudder and the after hydroplanes. Internally the batteries, which were to travel separately, were removed and extra ballast was added for the ocean voyage. Meanwhile other gangs of workmen were busy rectifying as many defects as possible.

The 'C' class boats were already obsolete in 1916 but these four boats were chosen as being the largest that it would be possible to take through the rivers and canals. They had all been completed by 1910, were driven on the surface by a single petrol engine, and had only two torpedo tubes. Nevertheless it was thought that they would be able to carry out short patrols in defence of the Gulf of Riga quite adequately, releasing the larger 'E' class boats for more distant offensive patrols.

By 1 August all was ready but then departure was delayed by the late arrival of one of the tugs because of fog. All four of the tugs carried a certain amount of the submarines' fittings and stores, the main bulk being in the *Racia*. In each case too the coxswain and one junior rating were also in the tug towing their submarine. The submarine batteries, because of their

---

*These two boats had been intended to go from the Humber to Portsmouth to relieve the *B1* and *B5*, the former to pay off and the latter to go to Ardrossan.

weight and bulk, had to be shipped separately and were to go in the *Slavonic*, a freighter taking other stores and supplies for the Russian armies.

The tugs with their submarines in tow finally sailed on the 3rd and the first stage of the journey took them to Lerwick in the Shetland Islands where they had to call for the tugs to top up with fuel. As with the departure of the submarines for Russia in 1914 and again in 1915 great secrecy surrounded the identity of the destination of these four boats, so that it was quite by chance that Sir Frederic Brock, KCMG, CB, the Vice-Admiral Commanding Orkneys and Shetlands, on a visit to Lerwick found them there with their tugs, the centre of attraction for 22 neutral merchant ships also present in the anchorage. It was not difficult to see that the submarines and tugs were in company so that it was all the more unfortunate that the large cases on the tugs were all marked 'Archangel' in large letters. So much for security!* There was little the Admiral could do at this stage except ensure that none of the merchant ships sailed within 24 hours of the submarines' departure.

Almost immediately the tugs and their charges ran into bad weather, despite the time of year. Slowly the eight vessels battled north towards the North Cape where they would turn east towards Archangel. Even when the wind dropped there was a nasty long swell to make conditions unpleasant for those on board the little group of ships. They were in the latitudes of the 'midnight sun' and though it was now after midsummer it seemed that there was no such thing as a night watch, just a short period of twilight followed the sunset before the sun rose again. However short the night it was a strange experience for all onboard to look at the sun in the northern quadrant of the compass.

Soon after rounding the North Cape trouble arose for the tugs and the submarines. First, when off Kola Bay, not far

---

*Similar tales are told concerning ships preparing for Malta or the Russian convoys during the Second World War, being loaded with their stores in crates boldly marked with the destination.

150

PASSAGE OF 'C' CLASS SUBMARINES
FROM NORTHERN RUSSIA TO THE
BALTIC

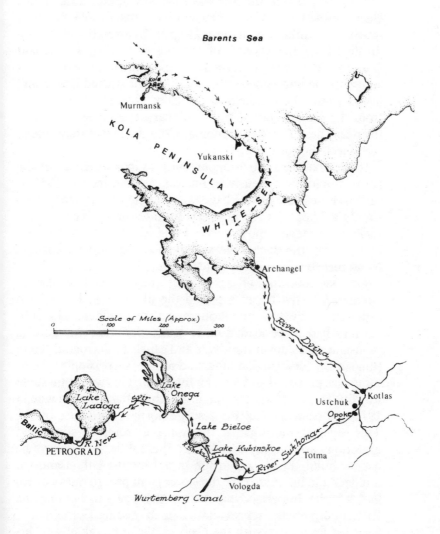

from Murmansk, the *C35* broke adrift when the towing slip broke loose. Although close to a lee shore and with a heavy sea running the tug managed to pass a new tow. Later approaching the Yukanski anchorage, nearly 200 miles south east of Murmansk, both the *C26* and *C27* also broke adrift. In the case of the *C26* the tow was soon recovered, but a link of chain on the *C27*'s towing pendant had broken, making this a much more difficult situation. Despite the superb seamanship displayed by the captain of the tug *Hampden*, Lieutenant Lucy, RNR, it was at first found impossible to get a fresh tow across to the unmanned submarine. As she drifted nearer and nearer to the shore Able Seaman 'Algy' Steel pluckily jumped from the tug and boarded the submarine, no mean feat with the heavy seas that were running. Only then were they able to reconnect the tow.

If they had had much opportunity to look at the coast the crews would have seen what one officer described in 1919 as the 'most desolate place I have ever seen; no towns of any sort, simply a Lapp settlement every 30 miles or so. The coast is rock, occasionally moss covered and about 200 to 400 feet high.' Even the anchorage at Yukanski brought no change, being merely a stretch of water sheltered by some islands.

On the morning of 21 August they arrived at last at Archangel. Now began a period the like of which has been experienced by few submariners, before or since. The submarines had to be loaded on to barges for their voyage of a thousand miles down the rivers and canals to Petrograd. Here some of the forward planning paid off for, surprisingly, everything was prepared and waiting for them. This was in no small way due to the efforts of Captain Roschakoffsky, a man who in 1915 had been sent to this desolate northern province by the Tsar especially to organise the transport south of stores and munitions arriving by sea. Where there were no railways he had to build them, and in the meantime used thousands of reindeer and horses to take the stores from port to railroad. He had left the Imperial Navy before the war and became the Russian diplomatic representative in an obscure German city. Recalled for service with the Navy on the outbreak of war, his boundless energy was devoted to his unglamorous but essential task. The submariners were now to have good cause to be thankful for his presence. This notorious eccentric appeared to be the very model of what many believed to be the typical Russian of the time: tall, stately, bearded and smothered in medals. With a booming voice it was said that his choice of language at times bore little trace of the usage so preferred in his other profession; he was feared by most of his subordinates and cordially disliked by higher officials.

By the time the submarines arrived in Archangel Roschakoffsky had the first barge ready to take its submarine. It was lashed down on the bottom of a floating dock, ballasted with chain cable and stones and with a side plank removed to ensure that it filled with water when the dock flooded. With the docking blocks, which had been brought to Russia in the tugs, placed onboard the barge the floating dock was flooded down. The *C26* was edged gently into the dock and with only inches to spare was secured over the barge. When the dock was then carefully raised the submarine settled on to her blocks. The ballast was then removed from the barge and the side plank replaced. When the dock was once more flooded the barge floated out bearing its unusual load.

On the evening of the 22nd, less than 36 hours after arrival, the *C27* too had been floated on to a barge and all was ready for the next stage of the journey. At 10 o'clock that evening the two barges were towed away upstream by the large river paddlesteamer *Sealnia*, the paddler also being used to accommodate most of the British party while one member of the submarines' crew and ten Russian soldiers were housed in a hut erected on each barge. The *C32* and *C35* followed on their barges the next morning accompanied by Captain Roschakoffsky himself.

It was thought that at certain places up river the depth of water would be less than the 3 feet 1 inch draught of the laden barges, and this strange flotilla had been increased by two large pontoons towed behind the leading barge. If necessary they would be secured alongside the barge and would decrease the draught by about six inches. However, the spring

153

and early summer of 1916 had seen much rainfall near the headwaters of the River Dvina which was now flowing much deeper than usual for the time of year and it soon became obvious that the pontoons were not needed and could be left behind.

As the flotilla travelled inland the rise in temperature was one of the most surprising things for the British party. Even in summer the White Sea is quite cool, while the town of Archangel only a few miles up river is noticeably warmer. As the submariners travelled further inland so the warmth of the land under the summer sun gained ascendancy and the temperatures rose rapidly to the upper 70s F. Indeed when British forces were operating in north Russia in the summer of 1919 it was not unusual to see tropical white uniform being worn by some officers and men!

For a few days after leaving Archangel they travelled up the broad Dvina with its flat sandy banks to Kotlas, then to Ustchuk where the Sukhona joins the Dvina. Occasionally they met some busy dredgers keeping the channel clear of the sand which was continually being washed from the banks. Towns were generally small and far between. At Ustchuk the *Sealnia* was replaced by a smaller paddle steamer of shallower draft for the next stage.

The following day, when they were just past the small town of Opoke, they reached the shallowest part of the whole river which occurred on a steep bend. Three tugs were required to help each barge in turn over this difficult stretch. Then on to Totma where the tugs were again changed as the river became narrower. Just before reaching the main railway junction of Vologda, where the line south from Archangel joined the east-west line from Petrograd, the river turned sharply to the north taking the submarines into Lake Kubinskoe, and on 1 September from there into the Würtemberg Canal.

The Würtemberg Canal was built in the nineteenth century to connect the Sukhona and Sheksna rivers, even then part of an important network of waterways connecting the north and south of European Russia with the Baltic Sea. Entering one of the dozen locks on this stretch the barge carrying the *C35* could not be slowed in time and rammed the gate at the far end, fortunately without damage to the gate but leaving the barge leaking badly. There was only one solution and with Captain Roschakoffsky energetically conducting operations the whole lock was drained into an instant dry dock for the necessary repairs to be made. Nearby a pitiful group of some 3,000 Austrian POWs, who were being made to dig new locks, watched this unusual operation with apathetic stoicism.

With the help of other canals the four submarines skirted Lake Bieloe, then Lake Onega and Lake Ladoga and finally on 9 September entered the River Neva, passing under the first of the many bridges in Petrograd three hours later, just 17 days from Archangel. What an achievement! What must the citizens of Petrograd have thought seeing these strange craft coming down the river and into the city proudly flying the White Ensign!

From Petrograd there was one more stage. The barges with their precious cargo were towed across to the great naval fortress on the island of Kronstadt to be unloaded, and then the submarines returned to the Baltic Works in Petrograd to be made ready for operations. Items removed in England had to be replaced, while other work carried out included making the boats more habitable for the Russian Winter.

Despite the comparative ease with which this difficult journey had been carried out so far there was to be just one hitch that would prevent these four boats becoming involved in operations in the coming weeks — the safe arrival of their batteries. These batteries had been sent out from England in the merchant ship *Slavonic*, but had been badly packed with the result that many of the cells were unusable.* Even so, it was the 20th of the month when the cells arrived in Petrograd and the damage was discovered. Two out of every three containers were found to be cracked and useless.

---

*Contrary to many accounts which lay the blame for the late arrival of the batteries to the loss of this ship. She did in fact arrive safely in north Russia.

With the batteries in some of the four 'E' class already beginning to show their age and require replacement this was just one more worry for Cromie wrestling with the problems of keeping the submarines ready for operations. He was to write to Commodore Hall:

> You will have heard all about the mess up with the C batteries. It seems almost incredible that anyone would pack heavy plates into containers for transit. The whole thing was undoubtedly aggravated by the cases being stowed loose on top of the coal in the ship, but that cannot excuse the persons responsible for packing. I have sent up all the spare containers from here (Revel) so as to finish off one boat in October at least. I am very anxious that the C's should show their metal (*sic*) this season. If the (new) containers are not here in one month I shall use those out of *E.8* as soon as the new battery is ready to go into her. This will delay the programme of battery refits, but it cannot be helped as it is important to get the C's going.
>
> The *E.8* has begun battery trouble again so the new battery is being prepared for her, and we expect to shift batteries if we lay her up for ten days only. The new battery for *E.8* will be prepared with the old positives of *E.8* ready to slip into *E.9* when the opportunity occurs.
>
> From *E.9*'s battery we hope to have ample material to do anything necessary for *E.1*, and by starting this repair work for all three early in the winter it will relieve a very congested battery shed for the winter rush of battery work.

A daunting programme if carried out in a British dockyard; all the more so when thousands of miles away from home and with the urgent need to keep the submarines at readiness and trying to prepare the Cs for operations before the onset of winter rendered the task nugatory.

The first boat, Stanley's *C35*, finally left for Revel nearly a month later on 18 October with Satow's *C32* a week later still. Less than two months of open water could be expected by then, after which the winter would be upon them, and with the sea freezing another season's campaigning would be over.

Even at the end of November the little flotilla was still not at full strength with Cromie reporting that the *C26* was at Kronstadt with her main motor being repaired, and the *C27* was having to be towed from Petrograd to escape being iced in on the Neva for her battery was still not complete. Worse, some of the torpedoes for these four new arrivals had gone astray having been wrongly addressed and were 'somewhere in Russia'.

The reinforcement of the British flotilla meant that more accommodation was required in the old *Dvina*. Perhaps in this respect it was fortunate that the four 'C' boats were delayed for so long in Petrograd for it took Cromie many weeks to persuade the Russians that not only was the accommodation necessary but also that they must get the work done. Eventually extra cabins were constructed, and even four extra bathrooms, while for the sailors additional messdecks were formed by taking over some of the ship's workshops. As a penalty the British submariners became even more dependant on the shore-side facilities of Revel dockyard.

The arrival of the boats had two other benefits for Cromie. The first was the news that from 1 August the flotilla was to be made an independent command for Cromie, freeing him from the necessity of referring all decisions back to the *Maidstone* in Harwich. In addition it meant that he was to be sent an Assistant Paymaster — Percy Haywood — to help with many of the administrative chores. Cromie returned from a patrol in the *E19* to hear this unexpected news, though incredibly he was kept unaware of the reason, and believed that it was the result at long last of something which he had advocated all year in his reports back to Commodore Hall. It wasn't until Haywood arrived a week later that he was given the news that his flotilla was to consist not of four boats but eight. It was then that he learnt that the four reinforcements were already on their way! Even so Haywood had few details to give his new Commanding Officer and Cromie was left largely in the dark and unable to check any of the arrangements.

While Cromie and the rest of the submarine crews waited for the arrival of their new companions there were changes on the Russian side too. On 20 September the weak and vacillating Admiral Kanin was relieved by Vice-Admiral A. J. Nepenin, a man with much more ability and drive. Among the Russians the news was well received, while Cromie was to report home:

> ... we have a new C in C, Admiral Nepenin, whom I count as a personal friend and has always been very much in favour of us. He was in charge of their excellent intelligence office; in fact he created it, and there we were always in touch with him. My official call was of a most satisfactory and even flattering nature, and he raised great hopes that we shall once more get a move on, and that we shall be under the C in C's personal direction. As far as we are concerned it is a most fortunate appointment, as I think it is for the Baltic Fleet in general, and it meets with general approval among all grades of Russian officers.

Mention has already been made of the speed of some of the intelligence given by the Russians which in no small way was due to the efforts of Admiral Nepenin in the early months of the war, when he was chief of this branch of the Baltic Fleet. As Captain Nepenin he had been in charge of the Fleet's communications on the outbreak of war and had assumed the intelligence role as a natural secondary role. His big chance came on 26 August 1914 when the German cruiser *Magdeburg* went aground in foggy weather on the island of Odensholm at the entrance to the Gulf of Finland. Unable to refloat his ship the German captain ordered the forward magazine to be blown up after most of his crew had been taken off in a destroyer. Alerted by the nearby lighthouse keeper who had heard German voices in the fog Nepenin hastened to the scene with two Russian destroyers, and sent a boarding party across to the wreck. The German captain and the five remaining crew were sent across to the Russian ships while the boarding party set about searching the German vessel. A great prize

158

lay amidst a confused mass of stores, wreckage and personal belongings on the upper deck — the German secret signal book. Later, divers found a second copy of the same book on the body of one of the crew lying on the seabed near the wreck. One of these books was forwarded to the British who, like their Russian allies, found it invaluable throughout the war. For though the Germans changed and developed their codes as the war progressed, this original capture remained the key which enabled the codes to be broken so quickly and regularly.

Another change brought Captain D. N. Verderevsky to command all the Russian submarines in the Baltic. He too was someone who shared the same offensive spirit as Cromie; like his Commander-in-Chief a man of considerable ability and boundless energy.

Nepenin soon made proposals for more active participation by the Fleet in the war, rather than Kanin's obsession in having it always on hand in case of any offensive action by the Germans, particularly in the Gulf of Riga. Nepenin proposed a twofold assault on the German ore traffic from Sweden; first by extensive use of his increased Russian and British submarine flotillas, and second by further minelaying operations along the shipping routes. To his chagrin, action by the submarines was vetoed by the Supreme War Council, and despite Cromie's high hopes their pattern of ineffectual operations continued for the rest of the year. As a consequence little else was achieved during the remaining patrols carried out before winter set in once more. Even the German *Desterro*, captured by the *Krokodil* on 18 August, had to be released after diplomatic pressure from the Swedes, adding to the sense of frustration of the submariners.

Cromie himself saw the enemy but twice and on neither occasion was he able to damage or sink him. In mid-October he wrote home 'I nearly rammed Fritz on the surface one night on my last trip'. A slight exaggeration, for his official report implies that the *E19*, travelling at speed on the surface, was as surprised as the U-boat when the two submarines passed a mere 50 yards from each other. A month later off Steinort he made an attack on an empty transport steering a steady course at only eight knots. Both torpedoes went under the target in the rough sea and the German sailed on in blissful ignorance of his lucky escape.

Operating from the advance base at Rogekul, in Moon Sound, the *C32* and *C35* managed only one short patrol apiece before the worsening winter weather put an end to operations once again. All the planning and hard work which had on this occasion resulted in the swift passage of the four submarines from England to the Baltic via Archangel had been wasted by the disaster to the boats' batteries and the subsequent delays in getting even two of the four operational. But how much better if the passage could have been made in June or even May rather than August.

Rogekul had few facilities, even as late as 1916, and only one advantage in that it was much nearer the potential theatre of operations. Before the war it had boasted little more than a pier to which destroyers could secure from time to time. With the emphasis on the defence of the Gulf of Riga in the fighting of 1915 and 1916 it had been developed as an advanced base for the forces defending the Gulf and for the huge flotilla of dredgers employed on deepening the channel through Moon Sound. Ashore there were no sports grounds or canteens so beloved by the British sailor to while away his off-duty hours, only a bleak landscape, a few pitiful houses and supplies of fuel and ammunition to support the ships based there. It was an unlovely spot.

Despite the lack of success by either the British or Russian submarines no account of the naval war in the Baltic in 1916 would be complete without mention of the actions of a German squadron in early November. Patrols by U-boats towards the Gulf of Finland had led the German Command to believe that the Russian minefields of 1915 were now neither so extensive or effective as they had previously thought. On 10 November a German force of eleven new destroyers of the 10th Torpedoboat Flotilla sailed from Libau to harass shipping north of Dagerort and towards the Gulf of Finland. Early that evening, when north of Cape Tachkona, the *V75* was disabled by a mine, and while the *S57* was alongside taking off her crew she hit a second and sank. The *S57* was damaged by the explosion of this second mine and after hitting a third she had to be scuttled, the survivors of the two crews being taken onboard the *G89*.

Surprised to find no shipping in the area — once again the Russians had been warned of the presence of the German ships through intercepted wireless transmissions — the Flotilla Commander decided to bombard Port Baltic expecting that shipping would be sheltering in the port. However the harbour was empty and the German ships had to be satisfied with firing at the harbour installations, with scant success and few casualties to civilians in the area. Looking for new targets the German ships were soon in the middle of another minefield and in the three hours before dawn on the 11th lost another five destroyers — the *V72*, *G90*, *S58*, *S59* and *V76*. Only four ships returned to harbour and of them the leader, *S56*, had damaged machinery and required the aid of the other three — *V77*, V78 and *G89*. Remarkably these ships brought back over 400 survivors and despite the magnitude of the disaster there were few casualties. During this calamatous night two light cruisers and a further flotilla of destroyers cruised to seaward in case the Russians put to sea, but they returned to harbour having seen no sign of their enemy but the flash of a number of explosions as their inshore comrades met their fate. It may be said that this incident was at the time, and still remains, one of the most cogent arguments in naval history in favour of a policy of defensive minefields.

So the year's operations by both sides came to an end. So far as the British were concerned the only success was the torpedoing of a destroyer by the unfortunate *E18*. For the Russians it was a year which had seen their fleet extensively reinforced with new ships but nevertheless they had failed to achieve any worthwhile results. Although a few merchant ships had been seized by submarines and destroyers the iron ore trade from Sweden to Germany had remained largely uninterrupted. Nor could the Germans look at the year's results with any satisfaction; they had failed to breach the defences of the Gulf of Riga, leaving their army outside this lynchpin of the Russian northern defences.

On land the summer had seen the usual series of defeats for the Russian Army coupled with mounting evidence of a serious decline in the morale of the troops. There were incidents of their troops' openly fraternising with the enemy or deserting in large numbers, either to their own rear or to the comparative safety of German and Austrian POW cages. By the time General Brusilov's offensive on the southwestern front petered out in the mud of the autumnal rains the army's losses since the outbreak of war exceeded four and a half million men with over two more million languishing in prison camps. Front line units were under strength and it seemed that even the legendary Russian reserves of manpower were becoming exhausted.

Worse was to follow. In October 1916 the first signs of a serious drop in military morale appeared in the capital, Petrograd, far behind the front line, and in regiments which had not been decimated by enemy action or suffered the miseries of the front line. Yet, when two regiments of the garrison were ordered to open fire on rioting strikers they turned their rifles on the police. It was a mutiny which was soon dealt with on this occasion, but it was a sign of things to come.

Among the civilian population too there was a mood of growing dissatisfaction with the war. Food shortages were becoming more widespread, especially in urban areas. Wages in 1916 did not increase as fast as the rise in prices. Shortages of labour as more and more men were called to the front did nothing to help to raise industrial output, while a general feeling of despair coupled with a steady rise in the number of strikes added to the general decline.

The government, weak and lacking the trust of nearly all sections of public opinion, was incapable of giving the country the lead it required. All levels of the Duma (Parliament) were affected by the situation, while a barrier had fallen between them and the Tsar so that he remained aloof from the advice of the few able men in the country.

The Fleet, having had much the better war than the Army,

was less liable to be affected by the general discontent, but the sailors could not fail to be aware of the situation, nor indeed could they remain unaffected by the general mood of the country as a whole. This was particularly true of the crews of the battleships and some of the cruisers which had yet to meet the enemy and had spent so many monotonous months in harbour.

Lurking behind the scenes there remained the presence of Rasputin. Tall, dirty and unkempt, his peasant manners were a strange contrast in a court renowned for its splendour and to people accustomed to the best things of life. Stories of his drunkenness and debauchery are legion, but form no part of this tale. More relevant is the sway he exercised over the Empress. For all his vices it does seem that he had a remarkable soothing way with both children and animals, and had some miraculous power to control the Tsarevich's haemophilia — on one occasion, reputedly, while far removed from his patient. For this, if for no other reason, the Tsarina kept him constantly at court, would listen to no criticism of him and relied more and more on his advice. This dangerous liaison, added to the suspicions caused by the Tsarina's German background, did nothing to help political stability or strength for she came to rely on Rasputin's advice outside the realm of her son's health. If he advised that a Government Minister or someone else at court should be replaced, then the Tsarina passed this advice, as coming from her, to her husband. The Tsar, often away for long periods at his military HQ, listened to the Tsarina and, ignoring all other advice and warning, acted accordingly. Thus critics of the monk, like the Grand Duke Nicholas earlier, found that it was they and not he who were banished from court and power.

So in one of the last acts of this last year of the Russian Empire this enigmatic man was killed by a group of young nobles led by Prince Yusopoff. It took cyanide cakes, several pistol shots and finally drowning under the ice of the frozen Neva to dispose of this man. In a meeting with the Tsar shortly before his death Rasputin is reported as having warned the Tsar 'nobody in your family will remain alive for more than two years. They will all be killed by the Russian people'. Despite his reputation for prophecy the eventual truth of this can hardly be surprising in the circumstances of Russia at the end of 1916.

So, as the winter ice began to close in and the fighting began to die away once more, all the signs — political, military and economic — pointed to a crisis approaching which would be of unprecedented proportions, and would at the very least shake the foundations of the Empire.

XI

Revolution

While the Russian Empire simmered with discontent and edged towards the greatest social upheaval of all time the British submariners were spending another winter ice-bound in Revel. Inevitably changes took place among the flotilla personnel. In the new year the familiar figure of Commander Goodhart, the popular and successful commander of the *E8*, returned home to England with what was becoming the habitual send off from the station with a Russian naval band and the British submariners' Concert Party competing for honours with a noisy crowd of well-wishers.

The new Commanding Officer for the *E8* was Lieutenant Thomas Kerr who had travelled out via Bergen, Stockholm and Petrograd to reach Russia before Christmas. He was a tall, slim, dark haired man of 29 years; a submariner since May 1909 whose experience had already been tempered by wartime command of the submarines *B5* and *C23*, although he had yet to meet the enemy. His quiet manner was that of a reliable and capable Commanding Officer well suited to the difficult task ahead. Later in life, as a retired officer, he was to be recalled for service in the Second World War and given command of the Coastal Forces base at Felixstowe where even among the slightly unconventional but dedicated officers of the MTBs and MGBs he was regarded as a well-loved man whom they would have followed anywhere.

Poor Goodhart, fate was not to be kind to him. Having survived all the hazards of operating in the Baltic and suffered the frustrations of working with the Russians in 1916 he returned home to be given an exciting new command, that of the submarine *K14* then building at the Govan shipyard on the Clyde. The 'K' class were enormous boats compared to the *E8*; nearly twice as long and displacing 1,980 tons on the surface, they carried three guns and were fitted with ten 18-inch torpedo tubes, while steam turbines gave them a surface speed of 24 knots. Some senior naval officers had an obsession, not shared by most submariners, that submarines should be capable of working as units of the Fleet, and this in turn meant speeds in excess of 21 knots and steam engines as the only means of achieving this.

When the *K13*, commanded by Goodhart's friend Commander Godfrey Herbert, sailed from the Govan yard for her final trials on 29 January 1917 it was natural that Goodhart should go with them to gain some experience in handling this novel craft. All went well during the morning despite some trouble with the boiler room ventilators, and a final dive was to be made after lunch before the submarine was accepted from the builders. During this dive the boiler room flooded and the submarine, unable to surface, sank stern first to the bottom of the Gareloch.

Later Goodhart volunteered to make a daring escape from the submarine, through the conning tower hatch, carrying details of the predicament of the submarine and the surviving members of the crew. Unfortunately the plan went wrong, and Herbert, who was assisting and had intended to return to the submarine's control room after Goodhart's escape, was himself shot to the surface in a bubble of air while Goodhart became trapped and was drowned. For this final act of bravery he was to receive the posthumous award of the Albert Medal.

To Cromie and the other British submariners in Revel the mood of intense dissatisfaction which prevailed among the Russian middle and working class was only too obvious. Equally obvious was the fact that the government must make changes or else the unrest would become worse. Yet because the city was detached from the political activity and unrest of the capital they found it difficult to gauge the extent of the trouble to come and to estimate just when the storm would break.

On 26 February small-scale disturbances broke out in Petrograd where a high proportion of the Russian war industry was situated and where as many as one-fifth of all the 250,000 workers were employed in only five factories. On that day crowds of up to 500 people gathered to march through the streets. Shop windows were — inevitably — broken while the crowds sang the revolutionary *Marseillaise* and shouted slogans. As the days went by so the crowds grew larger as more and more workers went on strike. In these early days it was significant that it was the problems of daily life that were foremost in driving the people into action rather than any political dogma. One spectator recalls looking from the windows upon an unusually quiet city with no trams running and the streets almost deserted. Then, at a major junction groups of women began assembling, with mounted police trying to disperse them by riding into the crowd and using the flat of their swords. Cursing the police the crowd would part, only to reassemble behind them.

By 8 March the shortage of food in the capital led to the outbreak of serious rioting with several bakeries and food stores being broken into and looted. The Cossacks, in the past firm stanchions of authority, were called in to disperse the crowds but it was noticeable that they performed their duties without their usual zealous thoroughness. On the 10th the Tsar ordered the Garrison Commander, General Khabalov, to suppress the demonstrations with all the force at his command. Yet the General was aware that he could rely less and less on his own troops; a fact that was borne out over the next two days as regiment after regiment mutinied until the whole garrison of some 17,000 men had joined the crowds on the streets.

March 12, the 27th day of February by the Russian calendar, is the day generally regarded as the day of the Revolution. There was no bread and no transport in the capital while the temperature dropped below zero degrees Fahrenheit. The police were unable to restore order and the troops had mutinied. The President of the Duma, Rodzyanko, had telegraphed the Tsar the day before begging him to form a new government in which the country would have greater confidence. His appeal was contemptuously ignored and the Duma was prorogued on the 12th.

What were the members of the Duma to do in such a situation? In the end, urged on by delegations of soldiers and workers, they took power from the government and formed a new provisional government under Prince Lvov. Rodzyanko wrote that they acted to try to curb the growing anarchy, while the new government itself proclaimed an amnesty and undertook not to victimise the Petrograd troops. Within four days the Tsar had abdicated and, with his family, was taken into a form of protective custody while his future was decided.

Russian sailors of the Baltic Fleet had not been standing idly by while law and order had been breaking down and the foundations of the Russian Empire had been cracking. Sailors in shore establishments around the capital, with little to do over the winter months and with officers who were more interested in their own welfare than that of their sailors, soon travelled into the city and joined the rioters. The captain of the cruiser *Aurora*, refitting in a nearby shipyard, was shot and killed in a senseless act of violence while remonstrating with a mob of demonstrators who had boarded the ship.

At the great naval base of Kronstadt there were thousands of sailors in various stages of recruit training or undergoing courses. There were also a number of prison hulks and detention centres and additionally the base tended to have a high proportion of men whom the Fleet had sought to rid themselves of as being undesirable. In the circumstances the great base only 20 miles across the water from the capital was ripe for trouble.

When the Revolution broke out in Petrograd Cromie had just arrived there for some well deserved leave and was staying at the Astoria hotel. It was a military hotel catering for visiting foreign officers as well as Russians on leave with their families. By chance, also staying there at this time was Commander Oliver Locker Lampson, RNVR, also MP for North Huntingdonshire, who commanded another unit of the Royal Navy fighting alongside the Russians — the Royal Naval Armoured Car Division. Both men recorded their impressions of the Revolution in letters home, both stressing that at this stage it was something affecting the Russians themselves, and how foreigners, particularly the British, were not maltreated. A particularly detailed account was sent by Cromie to Admiral Phillimore, who had by then returned home to England.

I arrived in Petrograd on Monday (12th March) with Miss Buchanan, who had been staying near Revel. Colonel Knox [British Military Attaché in Petrograd] met us, and considered the disorders as quite minor affairs. There were no trams or ishvoshnicks, and many people were chartering ordinary sledges to get away on. That morning the people went to the Duma and asked Protopopoff [Minister of the Interior] to meet their delegates. Of course he refused. The matter was placed very seriously before the Emperor, who replied by closing the Duma. They expressed their regrets and closed immediately, meeting again in the name of the people to restore order in the city. Troops ordered to fire on the people immediately sided with the people, disarming or killing their officers. Desultory firing broke out all over the town, the worst being the Nicholai Station, Shpalernia, around the Duma, and the Lutenia (arsenal) — and of course the Nevski. Only two regiments and the police could be relied on by the Government. That afternoon the mob burnt the Palais de Justice and most of the prisons, freeing all prisoners, criminal as well as political. Government troops still held certain areas in fairly good order, but many casualties occurred on both sides. About one a.m. trouble began round the 'Astoria'; Eady [Commander RNVR, Assistant Naval Attaché] went down to see what was the matter and was met by a Russian officer who wept on his neck, beseeching him to save him. Eady collected every one, and all the foreign officers, headed by General Poole

[Head of the Military Supply Mission], collected in the vestibule, and sent the Russians upstairs out of the way. When the yelling mob came in they were quite put off their stroke on being met by smiling faces. I think they were quite disappointed, and so surprised that they listened to reason, and after searching one or two rooms they returned peacefully.

The effect of this was to put us away up top with the crowd and with the officers. Ladies were seven deep round each Englishman, clamouring for protection. Neither Gilbert nor Sullivan dreamed of such situations.

About 10 a.m. Tuesday 13th some fool policemen, who were now being hunted by everyone, started to fire from the roof of the 'Astoria' on the crowd below. In two seconds they were howling inside firing at everything. Some very foolish Russian officers rushed out with pocket pistols and added to the general melee. One old General was killed and a lady shot in the neck. Several officers were marched off by sailors. Several rooms were ransacked, and poor Eady's new case of whiskey emptied and my sword stolen. They were persuaded to destroy 3,000 bottles of wine but, of course, not without a few 'drunks'.

Thornhill [Lieutenant-Colonel, Assistant Military Attaché] saved one General's life by jerking aside a hooligan's rifle (many soldiers had given their arms to the civilians when they got tired). Poor Thornhill was, and is, ill, and had 15 refugees in his room. The sailors soon took charge and placed sentries on every landing, keeping out all who did not possess keys. But it was a pitiable sight to see the poor old Generals, who ran the hotel, being 'told off for duty' by the sailors.

All Russian officers were made to give up their swords and fire-arms; those who resisted were killed; many of those who gave them up killed themselves. Some regiments killed many of their officers, and the Duma orders seemed to be quite ineffective. There seemed to be no leaders for troops or Government; Rodzyanko was far too weak for the situation. Colonel Knox was sent to the Duma to get in touch with someone responsible and could get no satisfaction whatever.

Englishmen were well treated everywhere, and when their swords were taken by mistake they were immediately restored. I have never seen better-tempered people — both troops and mob — they always seemed sorry to kill, and very jovial over any little jest. Commodore Kemp and I got caught in a hot corner by the Admiralty for five minutes. I was told Ivanoff [a Russian general; had earlier commanded the armies in Galicia] had been appointed Dictator and was coming to suppress the rising with an Army Corps, so I decided to clear out if I could as I had no news from Revel.

It was obvious to Cromie that in times like this his duty lay with the boats of the flotilla in Revel and that he had no option but to cancel his well deserved leave and to return. If he could. Conditions in Petrograd were naturally chaotic and few trains were leaving the city. Collecting a small party together, including Count Keller who commanded one of the Russian submarine divisions, his wife and a young Baroness who had become a friend of many of the British submarine officers, he made his way on foot the two miles to the railway station. They had to avoid indiscriminate machine-gun fire and aimless mobs, but eventually arrived safely to find the station packed with sailors from the Kronstadt base arriving to join the Revolution. Despite their recent violence at the base Cromie found that they seemed good natured and did their best to make way for the small party led by the British officers.

Another small group of British sailors had arrived in Petrograd on the afternoon of the 15th, having travelled the long route to Murmansk from Liverpool by steamer and then on by rail. Among them was a young able seaman from Suffolk, destined to join the *E1*, whose diary has fortunately survived. There he too records the chaos that existed in the city and of the friendly feelings that were still present towards the British.

171

Snowing fairly heavily. We made some tea whilst waiting for our baggage to be taken away, and had to go underneath the station to get the water. What a sight! Everything was smashed up, evidently there had been a large food store there. We loaded our gear in motor lorries, and were driven to the British Embassy. Our lorries were stopped by the crowd, and didn't they cheer when they knew who we were. It made one proud that we were Britishers. We had only a few hours wait in Petrograd, I should have liked to stop longer, but under the circumstances it was not advisable to let us stay. All shops were closed except the bakers, outside which people were formed in long queues. Occasional shots were still being fired. We left the Embassy and were driven to the Baltic Station where we waited for four hours, being the centre of attraction all the time. Just before our train left some excitement was caused by the machine guns opening fire just outside the station, as also did several hundred soldiers who were entraining. It appears that a police spy was seen on the roof of a house, and they meant to make sure of him, anyhow. During the 'action' the belt of one of the machine guns jammed, and there was not a soldier there who knew what was the matter with it. One of our petty officers set it going again!

Predictably the garrison on Kronstadt mutinied as soon as the news reached them of events in the capital. Poor Admiral Viren was horribly mutilated and killed, his wife and daughter also dying, while almost every officer was either killed or imprisoned. Anarchy soon reigned as the poorest quality sailors sought to excel each other in proving their commitment to the Revolution.

The trouble soon spread to the Fleet at Helsingfors. Unfortunately Admiral Nepenin was unable to take the one course of action that might have brought some degree of calm to the situation — the winter ice preventing him taking the Fleet to sea. Instead the crews of the battleships *Andrei Pervozvanny* and *Imperator Pavel I*, who had seldom been to sea since the outbreak of war, led the slide to mutiny by butchering many

172

of their officers. Other ships followed their example with varying degrees of ferocity and willingness. Nepenin himself was shot in the back while on his way to meet a delegation from Petrograd, some say by an agent of the Germans but more probably by a single disgruntled sailor. Other officers were killed, many imprisoned, while the remainder were divested of their authority, leaving the ships in the hands of elected committees.

Nepenin was succeeded as Commander-in-Chief by Admiral Maximoff. Maximoff had already tried to take over on the outbreak of revolution when he had persuaded some of the sailors to elect him to the post, had then donned a red tie and driven to see Nepenin. Naturally Nepenin dismissed such opportunism and told him that only the new Provisional Government, which had already been recognised by Nepenin, could change the appointment of Commander-in-Chief. Now with Nepenin dead it was to be not the least of Cromie's difficulties that such a weak self-seeking man was to direct the activities of a demoralised Fleet.

Revel was relatively quiet when Cromie eventually managed to return to the city, though seething with rumour of events elsewhere. However, on the 15th two members of the Duma arrived to talk to the sailors and soldiers in the port and to tell them of the events in Petrograd.

Of course no work was done this day, and after dinner the red flag crowds came down to the pier preaching rank anarchy and demanding a Republic. Our Russians were fallen in to go ashore . . . Off they went midst much cheering. First thing was to release all prisoners and to burn the prisons. The old Strand Port was soon ablaze. When the crowd collected there Gerashimoff [Military Governor of Revel] drove up alone in a car and spoke to the people reminding them of the new Goverment's desire for order, but made the fatal mistake, when they would not disperse, of threatening them with troops. 'Where will you call them from?' shouted the crowd. 'Who can protect you?' and set to beat him. They very soon smashed in his face, and killed the Governor of the prison and set fire to the whole show. I am glad to say Admiral Gerashimoff is out of danger and progressing now.

The prison opposite Gerard's [British Consul in Revel] was also opened, much to Mrs G.'s alarm. They then set fire to the old prison behind the Governor's Palace. Veryofkin [Civil Governor of Revel] was persuaded not to talk to the crowd. I brought up a hundred men to save his furniture, but he would not let us move anything but the silver and his old mother until the day following when the fire got very bad. Of course, we were careful to avoid all contact with the crowd.

Matters now reached an unpleasant state onboard. The men came aft and disarmed the officers, and would not permit any officer to leave or enter the ship until their Committee (headed by the man who gets my bath ready every morning) decided what to do with certain officers.

I sent over to the *Peter Valiki* [an old battleship, then used as the Gunnery School], who had a better crowd of men, and they sent deputies who persuaded the men to return the arms. This was done, and I persuaded Captain Nikitin [Commanding Officer of the *Dvina*] to once more give the arms to the men and place the onus of the officers' protection on the more sane of the sailors. This too was done, and calmed things sufficiently to get a few hours rest.

Next morning I had some argument as to my rights to receive Russian officers onboard. I obtained this on the understanding that they did not discuss current matters with the Ship's officers.

This set the pattern of Cromie's actions in the difficult months to come: his willingness to try and give discreet help to those in trouble with the mobs, even to using British sailors; his refusal to allow the political situation or the revolutionaries to interfere with his sailors, his actions or the British submarines; while at the same time giving sensible advice to many Russian officers helping them to ride the storm. He was even able to retain his authority over the Russian liaison officers and telegraphists that had operated with the flotilla. Indeed, as Cromie himself said at the time he had become something of a Scarlet Pimpernel, what with saving furniture, posting sentries to prevent the homes of friends being looted, persuading crowds to break wine instead of drinking it, getting places on trains for people to get away and even storing jewels and money.

The next crisis again showed Cromie's determination not to be dictated to by the mutineers. They had decided to arrest a number of officers in the *Dvina*, among them Lieutenant Boris Miller and Sub-Lieutenant Makaroff, two of the Russian liaison officers. With no hesitation Cromie faced the crowd of truculent armed Russian sailors and made it quite clear to them that the two officers were serving under his command and that if they had any complaints against them they should be put in writing and he would deal with the matter. Taking advantage of the respite both officers were got out of the ship and sent on leave. Miller was to survive the revolution and finally emigrated to Australia, and during the Second World War joined the Royal Australian Air Force. In 1944, as a Wing Commander, he even returned to Moscow and acted as an interpreter during Churchill's visit to Stalin!

Another officer whose life was undoubtedly saved by Cromie's actions was Commander Darmaross, the *Dvina*'s paymaster. During the preceding years he had given every assistance to the British submariners and had been awarded a British DSC, but was, like many other paymasters before and since, unpopular with the sailors. Fearing that the poor man might be summarily executed Cromie argued with the ship's committee saying that he did not wish to interfere but he could not stand by and see the officer murdered. Darmaross was sent to the Central Committee, Centrobalt, to be tried and escaped with a month's imprisonment.

Of all the Russian telegraphists serving with the flotilla only one of them gave any trouble. This one, serving in the *E1* like Boris Miller, began agitating and trying to prevent the other telegraphists going on board their boats. He defied Cromie to take any action against him, but he had not reckoned on the strength of Cromie's determination not to allow the Revolution to affect the life and discipline of the British flotilla. As the rating was serving in the *E1* he was under Royal Navy discipline and Cromie was able to summarily dismiss him, forfeiting the DSM which he had been awarded together with his bounty and share of prize money. It was a course of action that was applauded by the other Russians in the flotilla, and thereafter there were always more volunteers for service in the British submarines than there were vacancies.

There was one other factor working against Cromie, for the crew of the *Dvina* was probably the most disaffected of all the ships in Revel. Even the previous summer Cromie had not been impressed with the state of affairs whereby the depot ship for the British submarines had a Russian crew, a crew moreover which even in 1916 was showing signs of the disaffection and ill-discipline to come. He had then proposed that the *Dvina* be taken over as a ship of the Royal Navy and be totally British manned. It was a proposal that was to be repeated just before the Revolution broke out, and one to which the Russians agreed but which was turned down by the Admiralty in London! Despite this Cromie had held back some of the submariners due to return home on relief, and had asked for some other crew to be sent down from HMS *Glory* in Archangel. Now with the outbreak of revolution it was a plan that was clearly impracticable, and Cromie was forced to make the best of the situation.

On the Russian Easter Day great crowds of sailors and civilians gathered around the *Dvina*. As the bands played the old ship resumed her original and honoured name of *Pamiat Azova* — an earlier ship called *Azova* had been the Russian flagship at the Battle of Navarino in 1827 and had been honoured for her part in the action. It was this name which had been taken away from the present ship by direct order of the Tsar after the mutiny onboard in 1906, and which was now proudly restored by the revolutionaries. After this there was no further chance for Cromie's idea of taking over the ship for the sole use of the British.

It was also at this time that Cromie needed all the tact and determination that he could muster, for the crew of the newly renamed ship decided to make an example of the old boatswain. This elderly and able warrant officer was a great favourite with the British sailors but the charge against him was simply that he had been on board the ship at the time of the previous mutiny and had taken no part in it. He was sent to the Centrobalt for trial who, to the disgust of the more extreme ship's soviet, acquitted him and sent him to another ship. In defiance of the central committee he was dragged back to face another trial on board, disrated and sentenced to imprisonment in Kronstadt. His shoulder badges were ripped from him and dressed as a sailor he was subjected to much abuse. At this stage Cromie had to step in for fear of a serious confrontation between British and Russian sailors, the former not willing to stand by and see the old man lynched. Again, by force of argument and the strength of his own determination Cromie had the boatswain sent back to the Centrobalt to decide his case — and they had already acquitted him. Nothing more was seen of the boatswain until, to Ashmore's surprise, in 1919 when he was entering the Tsarist Consulate in London there should be the old sailor acting as the doorman!

It is interesting to note that while so many of the Russian officers had suffered physically or been degraded and abused, like the old boatswain in the *Pamiat Azova*, the sailors' Revolutionary Committees were at pains to continue to respect the British and wished them no harm. Cromie himself records one instance of this, and tells how one of his officers was insulted by a Russian sailor while out walking with a lady friend. The sailor was dragged away by his friends but when released returned and struck both the officer and the lady. Once again he was dragged away by the Russians. The next day he was brought on board and made to apologise publicly on his knees for his actions before being removed to face a sentence of banishment for 12 years in Siberia. Characteristically Cromie stepped in to try to get this harsh sentence reduced.

The Provisional Government continued to plan to carry on the war against Germany, blissfully believing that a mutinous army and navy controlled by committees, and with the officers virtually powerless, could ever hold off the disciplined and experienced forces of the enemy. It was the minority of Bolsheviks, not yet in power, who were preaching peace. After the excesses of the Revolution there was no possibility of the battleships fighting again, but there was hope for the smaller ships — including the submarines — where all discipline had not yet been completely destroyed. As for the Germans, they were not anxious to re-open a full-scale offensive, hoping that the Russians would ask for peace, yet action by the Germans was the one thing that Cromie hoped for, believing that with their Homeland threatened the Russian Army and Navy would again show some discipline and fighting spirit. These then were the conditions under which Cromie waited for the ice to melt, hoping that he could then leave the politics of revolution behind and get on with fighting the war against Germany.

But spring was late in 1917.

XII

~~~~~~

The Last Battles

The winter of 1916–17 was particularly severe and it was later than usual before the ice broke to allow naval operations to begin. As had been the case in the previous years of the war, the Germans were the first to go to sea in early May with their minelayers to freshen up the minefields after the winter storms and with the U-boats to watch the ice-limits and also to lay even more mines.

For the Russian submariners, who were the first of their Fleet to venture out, it was unfortunate that on top of all else that had happened during the winter their commander, Rear-Admiral Verderevsky, was replaced by Captain Vladislavoff. Whereas the former was energetic, informed about submarine operations and a popular figure, the latter had been commanding the battleship *Sevastopol* and apart from having had little operational war experience he knew nothing about submarines. Verderevsky became Chief of Staff to the Commander-in-Chief, giving the Russians a good man to support the vacillating Maximoff. In fact in July, with Maximoff out of favour with the Provisional Government he was to become Commander-in-Chief, but not before a mutually destructive fight in Helsingfors harbour between battleships supporting the respective claims of the two admirals had been narrowly avoided. If the situation had not been so serious it could have been regarded as farce.

This, then, was the situation on 19 May when the *Bars*, *Gepard*, *Vepr* and *Volk* left Revel to operate against German shipping along the Swedish coast. With all the experience of 1916 behind them the Germans had their shipping well organised and protected so that targets were few and the four submarines had no success. On the debit side the *Bars* did not return from patrol. A second group of Russian submarines sailed from Revel in early June to continue the offensive policy against the German shipping. Again the Russians had no success, while the Germans could be well satisfied with their defence of their merchant ships. On the 14th the *Pantera* was attacked by an airship, damaged, and forced to return. The *Lvitza*,* like the *Bars*, failed to return.

The Russians had to wait for the 8th August for their first success of the year, when the *Vepr* sank the *Friedrich Carow* in the north of the Gulf of Bothnia, south of the iron-ore port of Lulea. A week later the *Tigr*, on patrol south of Oland, tried a long shot at an escorted merchantman but was foiled when one of the torpedoes broke surface giving the enemy enough time to evade. In another episode south of Oland in September the *Gepard* attacked a small convoy while she was on outward passage to patrol. She had the mortification of seeing the two wing torpedoes of a fan salvo of three pass ahead and astern of the target while the centre torpedo misfired and did not leave the tube. The submarine was then heavily counter-attacked for four hours, after which though she had suffered no real damage the crew decided that they had had enough and forced the captain to return to Hango. The *Volk* was sent out in her place but she had gone only about 20 miles when she returned with a damaged main bearing, a defect the captain was convinced had been deliberately caused following discussion of the *Gepard*'s experiences. Such was the state

---

*Graf records that the *E19* came across parts of a torpedo which was floating upright and which they were able to identify as being from the *Lvitza*, and suggested that the Russian boat had been torpedoed. Also, that shortly afterwards the *E19* too avoided a torpedo fired at her. There is nothing in either the *E19*'s reports or German records to support this story. The *Lvitza* probably fell foul of a mine.

British submarine officers on board the *Pamiat Azova* 20 May 1917.

From left to right—

Back Row: Baldwin (*E8*), Ashmore (*E1*), Mr Wilton, Stokes (*C26*), Berg (Russian LO *E8*), Mr Kent

Standing: Jackson, Haywood, Upton (*E1*), Skulsky (Russian LO *E9*), Stanley (*C35*), Fersen (Russian LO *E19*), Tod (*C26*), Mr Williams (*E19*), Gibower (*C26*), Sealy (*C27*), Downie (*E9*) and Smith (*E19*).

Seated: Hale, Fenner (*E1*), Vaughan-Jones (*E9*), Cromie, Lombard (Embassy Chaplain), Kerr (*E8*), Sharp (*E19*) and Zabeilo (Russian LO *C32*)

In front: Marnevitch (Russian LO), Cotter (*E19*), St John (*E9*), Bawlby (*C35*), Kershaw (*C32*) and White (*C27*)

(Photo: Imperial War Museum)

N° 40

Available for this journey only.

By His Britannic Majesty's Ambassador Extraordinary and Plenipotentiary to ~~His~~ Majesty the Emperor of ~~All the Russias~~ &c &c &c

These are to request and require in the Name of His Majesty all those whom it may concern, to allow

Frederick Asker Esq. proceeding to England

to pass freely without let or hindrance and to afford him every assistance and protection of which he may stand in need.

George W. Buchanan

Given at St Petersburg, the 24ᵉ day of April 1917

Age of Bearer:
Years.
Profession of Bearer

Signature of Bearer.

Head
Consul Secretary

A passport issued to Mr Asker, a Warrant Artificer, to return to England via Norway and Sweden. Note the amendments made necessary by the fall of the Tsar.

Kerensky with a crowd of revolutionary sailors and deputies from the Duma. (*Photo: Submarine Museum*)

Three 'C' Class submarines in Helsingfors being prepared for scuttling. (*Photo: Submarine Museum*)

Some of the Russian doctors and nurses in Revel who looked after the British sailors. (*Photo: Submarine Museum*)

of morale by September, even among the more efficient submarines.

At this stage it is worth recording the misfortunes of two other Russian submarines in the opening months of the 1917 campaign. In July the *AG15*, recently completed in Petrograd from parts shipped across from Canada, was lost when she dived with a hatch open. Eight of the crew were saved but there were 18 casualties. The boat was subsequently salved and refitted. More important was the loss of the *AG14*, probably the most efficient of the Russian boats, which became overdue on 3 October. It is believed that she was mined when returning from a patrol off Libau. This was a particularly poignant loss for Cromie and the British submariners, for the *AG14* had been commanded by Lieutenant-Commander Otto von Essen, the only son of the Russian Commander-in-Chief in the early months of the war, and himself for many months the liaison officer of Horton's *E9*, where he had been awarded the British DSC.

As a submariner Cromie must have felt more than a pang of sorrow when the trying circumstances of the situation were at last recognised by the Admiralty and he gave up command of the *E19*. Now he was able to devote all his energy and talent to commanding the flotilla without being diverted every time the *E19* went off on patrol; the Revolution meant that even more than in 1916 he would have to try to cajole the depressed and pessimistic Russian staff officers into implementing an offensive forward policy for the British submarines, whilst domestically he would have to ensure that on the one hand his sailors kept apart from the ill-disciplined revolutionaries with whom they were forced to live, and on the other hand that the politics of the Revolution did not interfere with his submarines and the British sailors. For George Sharp it meant that at long last he had the chance to command his own submarine.

The first few months of 1917 gave the British submariners few opportunities to attack the enemy. The large 'E' class boats were used to keep watch off the port of Libau or to seaward of the Irben Straits, for, as in 1916, the main fear of the Russian staff was a German attack on the Gulf of Riga.

The small 'C' class boats were used in support of the Russian ships actually in the Gulf of Riga and were based at Rogekul. It was a disappointing time for the British officers and men who fretted and wished they could be taking a more active part in the war.

There was worry too over the safety of the base at Revel, with doubts of the ability of the Russian Army to hold Riga or even prevent a German advance up the coast on Revel. Not wishing to move to Helsingfors with its unpleasant atmosphere of extreme revolution Cromie proposed that the submarines operate from Hango in southwest Finland at the mouth of the Gulf. Even so, it was the end of August before the *Pamiat Azova* and the submarines with their spare torpedoes and stores were moved across the Gulf to their new base.

While down off Libau watching for any German movement or build-up of forces both the *E8* and *E19* had chances to attack the enemy. On 6 August Sharp fired two torpedoes at a 3,000 ton transport leaving the port unescorted. Both torpedoes missed, perhaps because the transport was riding high in the water — in any case the German sailed on blissfully unaware of his lucky escape. Later, Kerr refrained from attacking two steamers although, as he stated in his report, he was in a perfect position to do so. He considered that the military advantage in doing so seemed not so great as the unhampered observation of Libau. The value of this watch on the port is shown by the fact that when on his return from this patrol he was able to report the lack of German activity in the area, confirming Sharp's earlier report, the Russian staff were much relieved and concurred in his decision not to attack the enemy on this occasion. At that time the Russians had been much concerned over reports from spies and rumours of forces gathering there.

The *E9* made a rare visit to the Pomeranian coast in September. There, on the 12th, Vaughan-Jones made an attack on two merchant ships escorted by six trawlers. He fired two torpedoes at the leading ship at a range of 800 yards when he himself was only just ahead of the leading trawler.

Both torpedoes missed. Strangely it was a full 20 minutes before the first depth charges were dropped — not very accurately. Two hours later the escort had been joined by more trawlers and 19 of them, obviously fitted with hydrophones for detecting the noise of a submarine's propellers, began sweeping the area. Wisely Vaughan-Jones crept away and headed for the south of Oland where the following day he made another unsuccessful attack, this time on a single escorted steamer.

The *E19* did carry out one long-distance patrol at the end of August, going to an area between Bornholm and the Danish coast where the British submarines had spent so much time in 1914 and 1915. But now in 1917 the sea was virtually devoid of any shipping, and what there was for Sharp to see was neutral. The entire Swedish coast from Lulea at the northern end of the Gulf of Bothnia to the south of the island of Oland had the three-mile limit buoyed, and ships could navigate safely within the area. Neutrals passed direct across the Hano Bight to the south while the Germans hugged the coast except when under strong escort. With the increased number of German warships in the area it was not possible in 1917, as in 1915, to surface and order a neutral ship to heave-to so that her cargo could be checked and the ship then scuttled or taken in prize if necessary.

The end of September found Sharp on patrol again off the port of Libau. For day after day the rain and rough seas prevented him from approaching close enough to the port to see into the harbour and observe any German build-up of forces. On the 30th the weather suddenly cleared and he was able to see two *Deutschland* class battleships, a light cruiser and some transports. It was a significant increase in forces, especially the presence of two battleships, but it was apparently unappreciated by the Russian staff when Sharp reported this on his return to harbour.

On the way back to Hango the *E19* came upon a small open boat and they were able to pick up the two occupants who were nearly dead from exposure and lack of food and water. They had an extraordinary story to tell.

One of the two men was a private soldier of the 33rd

Siberian Rifle Regiment while the other had been a quarter-master aboard the merchant ship *Suchan*. Both had escaped from a POW camp near Danzig in June. The quartermaster related how he had taken two months to reach the coast near Colberg with a view to taking a boat and crossing to Bornholm. After a 15-day wait for a favourable wind they set sail but during the night a gale sprang up and they drifted for four days. They were picked up some 250 miles from their starting position.

The quartermaster had been a member of the crew of the *Suchan*, 3,781 tons, which had been captured in September 1916 by the *U-48* near the North Cape while on passage to Archangel with a cargo of ammunition from America. All the ship's officers were put aboard the submarine while a German prize crew directed the Russians to follow to Wilhelmshaven. Later they met up with a Swedish ship (probably the *Tuva*, 2,270 tons) which had also been stopped by U-boats. The Swedish crew were all transferred to the *Suchan* before their ship was sunk. Unbelievably the Swedes showed no resentment for this treatment and even suggested to the Germans that the Russian ship be repainted in Swedish colours, and that if they were stopped by the British they would take over the ship while the Germans hid below. An escape attempt by the Russians was even betrayed by their fellow 'prisoners'.

With these two interesting passengers the *E19* returned to Hango, but not without further excitement. Following the narrow passage between the islands leading to the base they found that many of the spar buoys were missing or broken, the product of neglect and the recent bad weather. On the way in the *E19* grounded, as the *E9* had the day before, and both submarines were required to go to Revel to be docked for repairs. As it turned out it was a most unfortunate time for them to be away.

For the 'C' class in the Gulf of Riga the summer had been a time of endless patrols from Rogekul without the merest glimpse of the enemy. Yet these four old submarines won the approbation of the Russians with their determination to carry out their tasks under the most difficult conditions. With minimal support from their allies and inadequate intelligence they navigated with extreme care around the numerous mine-fields to keep watch on the defences of the Irben Straits. Their only respite was an infrequent visit to Hango or Revel for a brief call on their colleagues or for repairs in the dockyard.

It was on just such an occasion that the *C32*, commanded by Lieutenant Satow, became the centre of a bizarre accident. The submarine had broken down and had to be towed to Revel for repairs. Though it was then midsummer the Russians assigned their latest ice-breaker rather than a tug for this task and escorted the two vessels with 12 trawlers. All went well until the force had arrived within sight of the breakwater at Revel, when the ice-breaker suddenly disintegrated with a shattering explosion, immediately followed by a second as one of the trawlers also exploded. The whole force had been navigated into the middle of a Russian minefield. Fortunately the submarine had a full battery and safety was not far away so that Satow was able to manoeuvre away from the scene on his electric motor. With all the crew on deck, with the exception of Lieutenant C. A. Kershaw his First Lieutenant who stayed below to work the motor, they crept away from the scene expecting to hit another mine at any moment. Their luck held and they survived to reach Revel without further mishap.

There were two more attempted revolutions during the summer to disturb the already doubtful efficiency of both the Russian Army and Navy. In July the Bolsheviks attempted to seize power. They failed but only just. The government instructed the Commander-in-Chief, Verderevsky, to send some trustworthy destroyers to the capital to provide backing for the government. He eventually acceded to this request, but some of his actions were considered suspect and afterwards he was arrested and imprisoned on the direct orders of the Minister of War, Kerensky. For three days the situation was tense and then the Bolsheviks surrendered. Lenin fled, Prince Lvov resigned and Kerensky took over the government. Verderevsky was released from prison to become Minister of Marine! The new Commander-in-Chief was Rosvosoff, only recently promoted to Rear-Admiral and previously the senior officer in the Gulf of Riga. Rosvosoff was described by Cromie as 'charming and friendly; a man who commands great respect — a practical man'. In another of his letters to Admiral Phillimore Cromie summed up the abortive coup as 'a conspiracy to throw out the government with the aid of Kronstadt sailors and Bolsheviks. Fortunately for all of us the government troops got the upper hand or I believe the Terror would have started'.

In September it was the turn of the more conservative elements. This rising was led by General Kornilov, a Siberian Cossack who had risen from the ranks through sheer martial ability and courage — no mean feat in Tsarist times. But his political acumen did not match his other attributes for he had hopelessly misjudged both the situation and the strength of his support and the revolt was put down without a shot being fired.

Reaction to this affair inevitably spread to the Baltic Fleet where it was represented that this was a case of the officers trying to reassert old ideals and institutions. The sailors' committees demanded that all officers should sign a declaration that they would obey the orders of the Centrobalt rather than those of the Commander-in-Chief in any dispute. Aboard the ultra-revolutionary battleship *Petropavlovsk* four young officers gallantly refused pointing out that the Commander-in-Chief was appointed by the provisional government and only acted as they instructed him. The four were arrested, taken ashore and brutally murdered.

Aboard the *Pamiat Azova* Cromie's influence once more prevailed and the potentially dangerous situation passed in a relatively calm manner. When the orders from the Centrobalt arrived for all Russian officers to sign a similar declaration he insisted that as far as the liaison officers on board the British submarines were concerned he was the final authority as they were under British discipline. He made it quite clear that he would work with the Centrobalt but that he did not recognise their authority over the Commander-in-Chief under whose sole orders he had been placed by the British Admiralty. He insisted that politics would not be allowed to stand in the way of his ensuring that the British submarines were available for action against their common enemy, the Germans. Somehow his charm and unflinching determination took the passion and bitterness from the meeting with the revolutionary sailors.

Meanwhile the Germans had struck. In the early hours of 1 September German artillery fired gas shells on the Russian positions on the east bank of the River Dvina some 75 miles south of Riga in an area held by the least reliable of the Russian troops. The Germans were quickly across the river and by the 4th had eliminated the Russian bridgehead to the west of Riga and captured the city itself. After recovering from the shock of the initial débâcle some of the Russians fought back and were able to stabilise the situation to the northeast of the city, limiting the German gains and forcing the offensive to a halt.

To seaward of the Irben Straits the Germans had become more and more contemptuous of the Russian forces in the Gulf of Riga and their minesweepers more and more active both in the Straits and off the islands of Dago and Osel to the north. German aircraft had complete command of the air. During a visit to Hango in the *C27* Lieutenant Sealy described to Cromie how as many as 200 bombs were being dropped in one night on the Russian forts on the islands. The German aircraft were so confident that they would taxi in on the surface and then only at the last moment take off to fly over their targets at about 300 feet. Few shots were fired at them from the ground and the Russian air force was outclassed. Yet these forts were vital if the Russians were to hold on to the islands guarding the Gulf and their base at Moon Sound.

During one night attack on a recently completed battery of four 30.5 cm (12 in) guns a bomb hit a munitions dump, which exploded killing and wounding over 100 of the garrison. This battery at the south end of the island of Osel was one which had been harassing the German minesweepers operating in the Straits; thus the fortuitous result of this attack was a big bonus for the Germans preparing their attack on the Gulf.

In addition to bombing the Russian batteries the German

aircraft also indulged in minelaying — at least 70 mines being laid in this way in the three months from the end of June. One of them accounted for the destroyer *Ochobnik*, the first ship to be sunk by an aerial-laid mine.

Within days of the fall of Riga the two German minelaying submarines *UC-57* and *UC-78* had arrived there prior to beginning operations in the Gulf. Both the *C26* and *C27* made daring reconnaissances in the minefields off Riga and along the coast to the west of the city towards the Straits, the information that they brought back being received with acclaim by the Russian staff. In thick mist and heavy rain Lieutenant Tod took the *C26* up the channel, which in places was not much wider than 150 yards, almost up to Riga itself, noting the channel marks still in place and the new ones placed there by the Germans, all the time checking the mine-free channels used by the enemy. He even attempted an attack on a small steamer in the approaches to the port which if successful might have blocked the channel for a time. He was thwarted when the vessel disappeared into the mist.

The Commanding Officers of both these submarines commented that it should have been possible for the Russians to intercept and attack the small German craft that were slipping through the Straits, inshore of the minefields, and creeping along the coast in the dark to enter Riga with much needed supplies for the army. But it was not to be.

This was Tod's final patrol. He was relieved by Lieutenant Downie and returned to England. He had the unpleasant task of having to escort a British sailor who had been sentenced to 90 days detention. His crime was that of interfering with a Russian sentry and attempting to strike and disarm another Russian on duty in the *Pamiat Azova*. An unfortunate occurrence, but one which as Crombie had feared was becoming more frequent. It was symptomatic of the difficult times in which the British submariners were living, being aggravated by the growing contempt felt by the British sailors for the Russians and the insolence of the latter.

The long-awaited German attack on the islands to the north of the Irben Straits was launched in the early hours of

AREA OF GERMAN ATTACK ON THE

GULF OF RIGA

OCTOBER 1917

GULF OF BOTHNIA

SWEDEN

FINLAND

AALAND
ISLANDS

Lapvik

Hango

GULF OF FINLAND

Revel

ESTONIA

Dago
I.

Rogekul

Osel I.

Moon Sound

Pernau

Irben Straits

Gulf
of
Riga

GOTLAND

BALTIC SEA

Windau

RIGA

Steinort

Libau

```
50            0            50            100
Miles                                      Miles
```

Memel

12 October — Operation 'Albion'. The German orders for the operation laid down that the islands of Osel and Moon were to be taken by a joint land-sea attack and the Great Moon Sound denied to the Russian Navy. Naval forces allocated were the battlecruiser *Moltke*, ten battleships, eight small cruisers, 55 destroyers, six submarines and numerous minesweepers, torpedo boats and anti-submarine trawlers. Air support was provided by six zeppelins and over 100 aircraft. The landing force consisted of a total of 23,000 men, 5,000 horses, 1,400 vehicles and 54 guns together with ammunition and supplies for 30 days.*

To defend the islands and the Irben Straits it is believed that the Russians had a theoretical strength of about 14,000 men, but widespread desertions and absence for other reasons left many units with little over half their effective strength. Naval forces in the Gulf were led by the old battleship *Slava*, which had fought there so valiantly in 1915 and early 1916, with her sistership the *Tsarevitch* (now known as the *Grazhdanin*). There were only two submarines in the Gulf when the Germans launched their attack — both British: the *C27* and the *C32*.

The attack on the islands had been expected all summer, and indeed, throughout the previous year. The fear of this attack had been the main reason for not employing the British 'E' class submarines constantly on Baltic-wide operations against German warships and the iron-ore trade. Yet little progress had been made in extending or improving the coastal batteries, the general political situation in 1917 in no small way militating against much reinforcement. Again, the Russian staff had been aware for some time of the German intentions, for the *E19* and other submarines on patrol off Libau had reported the increase in the number of German ships in the port. Yet the actual assault seems to have caught the Russians by surprise, and worse, came at an inopportune time for the British submarines.

*Figures taken from Vice-Admiral Schmidt's despatch to the Kaiser, in which he describes the whole operation.

At Hango there were only the *E9* and *C26* with the *E1* which had just returned from patrol with, as usual, engine trouble and needing repair. Apart from the two boats in the Gulf the remainder of the British flotilla were at Revel for repairs. The Russians were in little better position. New boats were still being completed but had done little to increase the overall numbers available for operations. The *Edinorg* had run aground returning from patrol; her bows on the bottom in six fathoms of water, her periscope standards awash and her stern afloat. The *Tur,* arriving from the builder's yard, damaged herself and the *Tigr* when going alongside. The *Ugor* was left damaged and partially flooded having been hit by a destroyer's propeller. One of the British officers took passage to Hango from Revel in the newly built *Ruis* and had a frightening tale of low standards that hardly gave confidence in the ability of an operational crew. He found that the crew had dismissed all the boat's engineers and had decided to do without replacements. Whenever it became necessary to start the diesel engines there was a furious discussion as to how this should be done, and the result was rarely kind to the engines. The man with the most know-how was the boat's cook!

There was a feeling among the British that when the Russian submarines did go to sea they frequently broke down, ensuring their quick return to harbour, and that the crews were more concerned with a safe and speedy return than with operations against the enemy. At the time of the German attack on the islands there were nominally only eight Russian boats ready for sea, but their value was doubtful.

The German attack, delayed for 13 days by bad weather, opened at three o'clock on the morning of 12 October when the Germans arrived off Taggalaklet Bay on the northwest coast of the island of Osel. Before the troops were landed the battleships bombarded the Russian positions during which both the *Bayern* and the *Grosser Kurfürst* struck mines but were able to carry on with their tasks. The shore batteries were soon silenced and the troops were established ashore by eight o'clock.

191

Briefly, the land battle went all the way of the Germans. On Osel the Germans spread out from their bridgehead southwards towards the Sworbe peninsula and the batteries at Tzerel which dominated the Irben Straits. There the dispirited Russian soldiers quickly surrendered after only a short fight. The way into the Gulf of Riga was open. Within days the islands of Moon and Dago were also in German hands, the last Russian troops being evacuated from Dago on the 19th, whilst the surviving Russian ships passed through Moon Sound northwards towards their bases in the Gulf of Finland, leaving the *Amur* to lay even more mines behind them. Even the base at Rogekul had to be abandoned. Easy though the operation had been for the German Army it had been an altogether different and tougher seven days for the Navy. They had had to cope with extensive minefields, skirmishes with the Russian forces and keeping a wary eye for submarine attacks.

When the news of the German attack was received the *E9* and *C26* were at sea off Hango carrying out torpedo practice attacks on each other. Both Vaughan-Jones and Downie were recalled to prepare for immediate operations against the enemy. Downie was instructed to proceed into the Gulf of Riga, via Moon Sound, while the *E9* was sent down the coast off the Filsand Light Ship off the west coast of Osel, but returned on the 16th reporting that the weather was too bad to do anything much. He had made one attack on two large escorted steamers but once again Vaughan-Jones had missed. Two Russian boats, *Tigr* and *Tur*, were then sent to the same area but by then it was too late, the Germans had succeeded in taking Osel. Downie on the other hand had a much more exciting time.

Having worked his way down towards the Irben Straits Downie was able to see the smoke of the German ships outside the Sworbe peninsula as well as the smoke and fires ashore, the result of the German bombardment. The following evening he was lucky enough to see more smoke, this time from German ships which had already forced their way into the Gulf. They were so far away that he risked surfacing to give chase and though hindered by the presence of an airship he persisted for more than two hours before his lack of speed forced him to give up the attempt to gain an attacking position.

On the 17th he was south of Moon island when he saw two *König* class battleships, three light cruisers and a large number of destroyers and other ships. The water was shallow and far from ideal for an attacking submarine, but Downie unhesitatingly made towards the enemy. Before he reached his firing position he went hard aground. Unable to break free by going astern on his motor he had to lighten the boat and promptly bobbed to the surface in full view of the enemy. Managing to dive again before he could be hit by any of the shells that were immediately fired in his direction, or even rammed by any of the eager destroyers, Downie had to sit on the bottom with barely enough water to cover the conning tower while the Germans systematically hunted him for over two hours, and of course while the battleships passed well beyond his reach. With a lull in the remorseless attacks Downie once again surfaced and made a dash for deeper water with the startled Germans all too soon in pursuit. Trying to dive again he found the hydroplanes had jammed, but somehow managed to reach the safety of the bottom, fouling his propellor in an anti-submarine net in the process. He was hunted until darkness forced the Germans to leave the area.

Once more on the surface, Downie found himself in the unenviable position of commanding an unseaworthy submarine in waters which seemed dominated by the enemy. He was in no state to try to break out through the Irben Straits while to the north large fires and the recent enemy activity indicated that Moon Sound offered no relief. Barely able to keep afloat the *C26* was taken through the extensive minefields into the port of Pernau in the northeast corner of the Gulf, her ship's company hoping for time to make the submarine ready for sea again before any German advance up the coast robbed them of their last safe haven.

Sealy, in the *C27*, also went south from Moon Sound to the area off the Irben Straits. There, at sunset on the 16th, he sighted the German Fleet entering the Gulf and at once closed to attack. In the van were two large transports escorted by destroyers, then four battleships with more destroyers, while three more transports brought up the rear of the German line. It was the dream-come-to-life of every submariner and Sealy turned to make a submerged run towards the leading battleship, the *König*. In a text-book manner he passed under the destroyers of the screen and came to periscope depth for a final look before firing. To his horror he had underestimated the speed of the battleships and the *König* was now only 300 yards away, filling the whole of his field of vision through his periscope. It was too good a chance to miss — right on the port beam of the great ship — and he fired both his torpedoes and watched their tracks run straight and true towards their target. But he was too close and 300 yards was not a great enough run to allow the torpedoes to settle to their correct depth, and both passed underneath the target. Despite the fact that the *C27* momentarily broke surface on firing the attack brought no reaction from the Germans* and Sealy was able to speed up and flood tanks to take his boat to a safe depth. While thus unsighted Sealy heard a loud explosion which he hoped was one of his torpedoes hitting a destroyer on the far side of the *König*. This was not so.

Sealy remained deep taking the *C27* under the line of ships and using the time to reload his torpedo tubes, intending to make another attack from the other side of the ships. By the time he was ready the battleships had passed but looming in the gloom was a large transport with two or three torpedo boats as an escort. He fired one torpedo at a range of 800 yards and had the satisfaction of hitting the ship amidships. His last view of the target was of red Verey lights being fired from the bridge as she settled in the water. Sealy took the *C27* away from the scene to the east as the Germans ineffectually dropped a number of depth charges at the scene. His target had been

*The attack is not mentioned in Admiral Schmidt's despatch though he does mention the *König* being missed by two torpedoes on the 14th while bombarding the Russian batteries on the Sworbe peninsula from the west. No allied submarines were in that position at the time.

the *Indianola*, so often the target of the British submarines in 1914 and 1915 and now acting as the parent ship for a minesweeping flotilla.

When it was fully dark Sealy brought the *C27* to the surface as he appeared to have left the hunt for him behind, but on reaching his bridge he was horrified to find himself in the midst of another German fleet. Signal lamps winked and illuminating searchlights were everywhere, he could even distinguish German voices! Scrambling down below and slamming the hatch shut behind him he took his boat hurriedly to the bottom. He had not escaped detection and once more the *C27* became the target for German depth charges. Once more his crew could do no more than stick out this nerve-racking ordeal; as the depth charges exploded around him so the water spurted in through an increasing number of leaks. Eventually the hunt was called off and Sealy was able to surface his battered submarine to take stock of the situation and charge his batteries. The first task was to begin to repair the damage that had been inflicted.

The big problem facing Sealy was what to do next. He had one torpedo left, German ships swarmed over the Gulf of Riga whilst it seemed likely that they controlled the approaches to Moon Sound as well. To Sealy there was only one possible way out — through the Irben Straits with all the mines laid by both Germans and Russians of which Sealy had only scant knowledge. By strange chance he found an ally to help him make this dangerous passage, his target of the day before. The *Indianola* was still afloat though low in the water and probably kept that way only by the four ships that had been lashed alongside to help her make the journey south to Libau for repairs. Resisting the temptation to use his remaining torpedo against her he decided to follow her down the swept channels towards the open sea, when he would be able to turn north, surface to charge his exhausted batteries and then head for Hango and safety.

Yet this resourceful young Commanding Officer was still not safe. As he approached the Finnish coast with its profusion of small islands and shoals thick fog came down and he only narrowly avoided running ashore. When the fog cleared he found himself in the midst of a Russian minefield. His luck held and he navigated clear and arrived at Hango nearly exhausted in the late afternoon of the 19th. As Cromie summed up his exploit when forwarding the details to the Admiralty, Sealy had shown excellent judgement and great courage.

The *C32* was also at Rogekul when the Germans began their Operation 'Albion', and Satow sailed at once. His orders were to go first to an area inside the Irben Straits and to the west of Riga. That afternoon a German submarine (probably the *UC-57*) came to the surface on his quarter and opened fire with his 88mm deck gun. Satow dived before he was hit and the German followed suit, neither submarine then being able to attack the other, and nothing more was seen of this dangerous adversary.

It was the following evening when Satow next sighted the Germans, but they were the wrong side of a minefield and he was unable to attack. Anticipating that the enemy were moving against the Moon Sound position he too moved north across the Gulf. Again he sighted the enemy and began to attack a four-funneled cruiser (probably the *Strassburg*) but shortly before firing was startled by a succession of explosions which were all too close for comfort. In the calm clear water the *C32* had been spotted by a German seaplane and at a crucial moment Satow was forced to go deeper for his own safety, breaking off his attack on the German cruiser. Later he fired a torpedo at a transport but failed to hit.

On the 20th he sighted a large transport escorted by three trawlers and once more began an attack on the enemy. Despite the flat calm sea he was able to close the small group undetected and fire two torpedoes at 600 yards range on the starboard quarter of the transport. One of the trawlers was very close — Satow claimed that he could almost see the faces of the crew — and the track of his first torpedo passed right under this ship. As he fired the second torpedo he was seen and had to take the *C32* down to 60 feet to avoid being rammed. He heard two explosions at about the right interval after firing and assumed that he had hit the enemy.* Then the depth charges began to explode around him. The lights went out, several leaks were started and, worst of all, the compass was damaged.

Several hours later when darkness had fallen and he was able to surface attempts were made to repair the compass. To no avail. Without a compass Satow had no hope of navigating through the many minefields to safety through the Irben Straits. He believed that the Germans would also block his way out through Moon Sound and that by that time the Germans would have also occupied all the remaining ports around the Gulf. On this basis he decided that he would have to get his crew ashore so as to make their way overland through the German lines to Revel and that the *C32* would have to be scuttled.

Satow can have had few thoughts of Nelson's glorious victory as in the cold early morning light the *C32* was beached in Vaist Bay to the west of the port of Pernau. By the time the crew had been ferried ashore they found that the coast was still in Russian hands, and learnt that not only was the port still held by them but that the *C26* was sheltering there! Poor Satow's feelings can only be imagined especially when it was found that the only tug in the port was not powerful enough to tow him off. The submarine was destroyed by charges placed strategically within the hull. Cromie was far from pleased.

It was an unsatisfactory ending to the battle. However, it must be remembered that apart from one attack by Vaughan-Jones in the *E9* the brunt of the battle was borne by three old 'C' class submarines with the least experienced commanding officers. Cromie himself summed up his feelings in a report to Commodore Hall:

> I regret that the C's did not accomplish more, but my job finished with putting them in the right spot; as it is we claim a transport and an aeroplane carrier. Outside the Gulf it is not my fault, my forecasts there proved to be more or less

---

*His target was the netlayer *Eskimo*, which was undamaged. The attack is not mentioned in Admiral Schmidt's report.

accurate; but who could foresee that the forts at Tzerel and Takhona would never fire a shot, or that a crew would blow up their ship? The whole thing is beyond belief, and one's best efforts are paralysed. I feel sick of these people, and long for a clean chance instead of fighting in this strain.

For the crews of the three 'C' class submarines there was an even sorrier postscript. With the withdrawal of the last Russian forces from the Gulf and the abandonment of the base at Rogekul the crew of the vessel used by the British crews for accommodation all deserted. When they left they looted as many personal belongings and stores as they could carry away.

By then winter was fast approaching and though it was considered that the Germans would be unlikely to launch a further offensive the remaining submarines, including the *C35*, were deployed to defend the approaches to the Gulf of Finland. The Russian *Gepard* sailed for her turn at this duty on 22 October going to the west of Osel but failed to return. A submarine was reported by the Germans on the 29th north-west of Windau, and it may be that the *Gepard* was lost in one of the many minefields in that area.

Once again the fighting petered out. There was little to show for the summer's work; while on the debit side there was the loss of the *C32* as well as the loss of five Russian boats. For the Germans, they had at last taken Riga, and gained control of the Gulf of Riga but had failed to follow up their advantage. Overall there was the dominating factor of the Revolution with politics taking over from discipline and making the successful prosecution of the war only a secondary matter for most Russian officers.

XIII

The Final Scenes

By the end of the German offensive in the Gulf of Riga even more responsibility had fallen on Cromie. In the early days of the battle the Russian submarine commander, Vladislavoff, disappeared and was later believed to have committed suicide, leaving Cromie to run the operations of all submarines, both Russian and British, until another Russian officer could be found for the post. Meanwhile Cromie himself was promoted and given the rank of acting Captain, Admiralty's tardy recognition of the great responsibility resting on his shoulders in the turmoil of revolutionary Russia. Certainly the promotion was of great help to him in carrying out his many duties, the Russians being readier to deal with a Captain than a Commander.

It has already been related how after the battle the submarines were only involved in watching for any renewed German offensive against the defences of the Gulf of Finland, and how the Russian *Gepard* was lost in a minefield. The only other operational matter affecting the British submarines in the remaining weeks of 1917, before ice once again forced them into inactivity in their winter berths, was how to recover Downie and his damaged *C26* from Pernau. On the other hand it was recognised that the *C32* was beyond salvage, and for a while Cromie hoped that one of the Russian 'AG' class could be made available for Satow's crew, but, like so many other schemes, nought came of it.

A team of British engineering ratings went to Pernau and worked for days to get the *C26* ready for sea, working in a desperate race against the clock in the daily expectation of a German advance from Riga towards the port. Twice Downie took his battered submarine out to sea only to return for still more work to be carried out. On the second occasion the makeshift repairs failed and gave rise to a raging petrol fire in the engine room. The crew scrambled up from below, shut the hatch and allowed the fire to burn itself out when all the oxygen in the boat was exhausted. For the crew it was a daunting experience with the submarine only a few miles from the enemy, the boat helpless and themselves exposed to the elements on a bitterly cold November day at the beginning of winter and unable to snatch any warm clothing before they had to rush on deck. With the fire eventually out and his crew suffering from exposure Downie took his boat back once more to Pernau.

A third attempt in December was more successful and the submarine escaped back to Hango arriving on the 13th like a seagoing sieve kept going with some 'Heath-Robinson' devices and even some parts salvaged from the *C32*. Her main petrol pump was driven by a hand-made wooden pulley. It was a magnificent achievement demanding both great courage and determination from the young Commanding Officer and his crew. Cromie reported that it had called forth the admiration of the demoralised Russian Fleet. Yet it was a success story that was nearly still-born; the Centrobalt fearing that it would upset the armistice talks in progress with the Germans tried to stop her sailing from Pernau. Cromie himself had to persuade the Committee to agree but then only on condition that Downie took no offensive action. Downie was awarded the DSC for his efforts.

As the year had started so it ended with another revolution. On the night of 6/7 November (24/25 October by the Russian calendar) the Bolsheviks, organised by Lenin and Trotsky, went into action, and almost without bloodshed occupied all the key points in Petrograd including banks, railway stations, bridges and the telephone exchange. Kerensky had not only hopelessly underestimated the power of the Bolsheviks but overestimated the strength of active support for his own government. Three destroyers were sent to Petrograd by the Centrobalt to support the Bolsheviks against the Provisional government. Ironically these destroyers which went to the capital against the orders of the Commander-in-Chief were commanded by their original Tsarist officers onboard. In Petrograd the cruiser *Aurora* made her historic appearance when she landed some of her crew to support the Red Guards and in the course of fragmentary fighting she fired a few rounds of blank ammunition to bring about the surrender of the members of the Provisional government conferring in the Winter Palace. Kerensky himself was outside the city at the time vainly trying to drum up support. He escaped to France disguised as a seaman.

The Revolution in March had been more of a collapse of the Tsarist government brought about by its own inefficiency and popular dissatisfaction. Events followed no preconceived plan. In contrast, this latest upheaval was deliberately engineered by the Bolsheviks as a positive seizure of power by armed force. The Bolsheviks did promise elections for a Constituent Assembly — Lenin even promised to abide by the result — voting starting on 25 November. The Assembly convened on 18 January with the Bolsheviks having polled about a quarter of the total vote. The first day's meeting was a farce dominated by the Bolshevik-inspired disorder which led to the Soviet decreeing the Assembly dissolved. Civil war was then inevitable.

The success of the Bolshevik Revolution had one important effect for Cromie: the future of the British submarine flotilla in Russia was immediately in doubt. Within weeks the new government was negotiating an armistice with the Germans which was to lead to the Treaty of Brest Litovsk in March 1918. It was obvious that the Russians lacked the will, let alone the resources, to fight on and with the Bolsheviks wishing to devote all their efforts to consolidating the success of the Revolution such overtures to the Germans were only to be expected however unpalatable to the Allies.

During these peace talks there was some personal contact between the Russian and German delegates. Cromie was able to write back to London with an account of one meeting between the Russian Admiral Altfata and Admiral Hoppman, the latter having been the Captain of the *Prinz Adlebert* in June 1915 when that ship had only just been able to limp back into harbour after being hit by two torpedoes from Horton's *E9*.

... Admiral Hoppman told him in private conversation that the English flotilla was a constant anxiety to them in the Baltic, in fact the only one, and the Huns had organised and constantly kept at sea a special force to deal with the 'pests'.

Altfata said that they refused to commence pourparlers before they had guarantees that the English boats had ceased hostilities.

The course of the negotiations at Brest Litovsk is outside the scope of this story though the outcome is of importance. The Bolsheviks were in no position to bargain though they tried to and used every trick in the book to prolong the talks as long as possible. Finally the Germans and their Austrian allies lost patience and on 2 March resumed their offensive. The Red Army was not able to offer effective resistance, the front collapsed and two weeks later the Bolsheviks capitulated. Besides ceding large tracts of territory the treaty included a clause which specifically included the surrender of the British submarines in the Baltic.

With the possibility that Russia would make a separate peace with Germany there was the problem for the Admiralty of what to do with the submarines and their crews once the fighting died down for the winter. If nothing else the boats themselves were in a critical state. The 'E' class were long overdue for a major refit whilst the remaining 'C' class too were old, out of date, and unreliable for anything other than short periods at sea. The *E1* was in the worst state; Fenner himself was in no illusions about his submarine and had even mentioned it in a letter to his father:

My boat is an awful anxiety. She is quite unfit for a long trip. I have only been out twice this year without a bust up, and one of these days shall find myself trying to make the Swedish coast under sail.

Even before the Bolshevik *coup*, or the German attack on the Gulf of Riga, the matter had been under consideration in London for in October Cromie was to write to Commodore Hall:

Anyway, it is time to consider what you wish done with our boats in the event of peace or utter defeat at sea. In the meantime I will continue to order the necessary stores etc. to keep us a going concern, but I saw in a letter to Jackson [Engineer Lieutenant Stanley Jackson, the Flotilla Engineer Officer] that you had said no engine room reliefs were to be sent out; does this mean you think of abandoning the Russians and bringing us all home? We are the Russians' main hope in blue water.

A strange way, to say the least, for Cromie to have heard of major policy decisions under consideration, or even of the cessation of reliefs for his engine room ratings.

Meanwhile Cromie thought it wise to seek instructions from Rear-Admiral Victor Stanley, British Naval Liaison Officer in Russia, as to what should be done with the flotilla in the case of extreme necessity. Admiral Stanley wrote back that the 'C' class boats were to be destroyed should it become impossible for the British flotilla to work from a Russian base. The 'Es' were to make every endeavour to get out of the Baltic, making use of Swedish territorial waters. If this were not possible then he considered they should be interned in Sweden rather than destroyed. He recognised that these could only be general directions and that in the event Cromie and the individual Commanding Officers must have the last say since the situation was so fluid and that in the emergency which his directive was designed to cover there would be little opportunity for the two men to confer.

For the longer term there was still the coming winter to consider. Where were the boats to spend those long and tedious inactive months? How much work was to be carried out on them, or rather, how much repair work were the Russians capable of carrying out? In the event the Admiralty decided that the majority of the British submariners were to be brought home leaving only a small care and maintenance party in Russia. If the situation in the spring appeared more promising with the Russians showing some stability and willingness to fight on against the Germans then, so the Admiralty reasoned, additional crews could be sent back to Russia. This plan for the winter which had first been proposed to the Admiralty by Admiral Stanley and Cromie was one which appealed to the Russian Commander-in-Chief as being the most likely to be acceptable to the Centrobalt which was daily assuming more and more power. The submarines were to be laid up for the winter in Helsingfors though the already volatile revolutionary atmosphere there had been made even more difficult by the declaration of Finnish independence, accompanied by the demand for the withdrawal of all Russian forces.

At this time Cromie paid one of his periodic visits to Petrograd where he called on Sir George Buchanan. He was able to give him not only the latest news of the state of the British flotilla and the proposed plans for the winter, but also his own views on the state of the Russian Fleet. One idea that was discussed, and discarded, was a suggestion by the French Ambassador that two of the submarines should winter in Petrograd so as to supply guards for the two embassies. As usual he travelled both ways by train. His return journey was spent in a first class sleeping car shared with a Russian stoker. During the night Cromie was awakened by a man demanding to see his passport who, such was the state of Russia at the end of 1917, had no fears of the wrath of a British Captain but feared to waken the stoker and would have left him had not Cromie insisted that his papers too should be examined.

There remained one further incident involving the British submarines. Cromie had learnt that the sailors' committees were thinking of sailing the battleships to Kiel to fraternise with the Germans with hopes of spreading the Revolution. Such an idea was abhorrent to Cromie who saw that the only gain would be the accession of a number of ships to the German strength. He was determined to prevent it.

Ashmore recalled how all Commanding Officers were called to Cromie's cabin on board the *Pamiat Azova* and how, unusually, the door was then locked with an armed English sentry on the outside. Cromie then explained the situation and his plan of action which was in keeping with his fearless and forthright character. When the Russian sailing was imminent he intended to board the flagship with Jackson, his Engineer Officer, and confront the ship's committee. Either they were to allow Jackson to immobilise the ship's engines, or, at a prearranged signal the British submarines would torpedo the battleships one by one.

It is impossible to guess what would have been the reactions of the Russians if such a plan had been implemented, or how the British would have fared afterwards. Instead, Cromie made one of his dramatic appearances at a meeting of the Centrobalt and after an impassioned plea they decided to remain at Helsingfors. Not only that but he obtained the Committee's guarantee of safe conduct for the return home of the British crews.

Shortly afterwards Cromie had a final meeting with Rasvosoff, the Russian Commander-in-Chief, who had been dismissed by the government and his functions taken over by a group of 14 members of the Centrobalt. The two men had an emotional farewell and Cromie recalled that Rasvosoff feared that he had not much longer to live, a foreboding that was only too true. Soon afterwards he was shot. The day after their farewell Cromie received a short note from Rasvosoff that serves as a fitting epitaph for the whole operation.

Resigning [sic] my position as Commander-in-Chief of the Baltic Fleet, I consider it my duty to express to you, as Captain of the English Flotilla, my sincere admiration of the valiant war service and brilliant accomplishment of all war operations of the officers and men under your command.

Accept my deepest thanks for the great help given to us during the present war.

At last in early January it was announced that there was a train ready to take them to Murmansk. As a matter of pride the boats were cleaned until they sparkled before the crews finally left them. Lieutenant Downie, the hero of the *C26*'s exploits in the Gulf of Riga in October, was left in charge of the boats with three other officers and a small group of 22 sailors. They were to look after the submarines, guard them and watch over a vast amount of stores that had been accumulated. At the last moment there was one other officer left behind — Cromie himself. For some months he had heard rumours that he was to be appointed as the Naval Attaché and in his letters to Commodore Hall he had begged to be saved from this 'fate'. He had had enough of Russia and yearned to return home to see his wife and small daughter, neither of whom he had seen much of for years, having had only a short time in England on returning from Hong Kong in 1915 before going to Russia. But it was not to be. Benson, who had acted as Cromie's unofficial steward, recalls the look of utter sadness on Cromie's face after receiving the news as he instructed Benson to unpack his kit again.

At the station there was Cromie to say farewell. In uniform, wearing his distinctive greatcoat with astrakhan collar, the shoulder straps with the four stripes of his rank and his St George's Cross for all to see, his distinguished debonair figure passed down the train shaking hands with every man, taking time to have a few last words with many of them. As the train pulled out of Helsingfors station they in their turn waved a farewell to the solitary figure standing so sadly on the platform. It was their last view of this remarkable character.

At Petrograd the naval party saw the train that was to take Sir George Buchanan and most of the embassy staff to Sweden and then home. Even their departure did not save Cromie from his new duties, as he was required to stay on in Russia as one of the few people left in the embassy. Indeed, in the next few months he was to establish a commanding presence not only as the Naval Attaché, but come to be regarded by many as acting for the absent Ambassador.

For the British sailors the railway journey northwards to Murmansk was to be a feat of endurance. The coaches were heated against the worst of the winter cold, but there were no other amenities. The train was unlit except for a small stock of candles. There was a restaurant car, but no food or crockery was provided. The officers travelled two to a small compartment, the men in rather more large ones. Attached to the train were the luggage vans carrying not only their personal possessions but many stores and their food for the journey. In charge was a Russian commissar, an able seaman, who travelled in solitary splendour in a special first class coach.

With the adaptability of the British sailor and the ease of men used to working in the confines of a submarine it was no trouble to prepare their own food in the train's galley. What was more difficult was guarding their stores at all the frequent stops to allow the line to be cleared of snow. On these occasions while many of the sailors jumped down from the train to stretch their legs an armed guard would have to be placed on the luggage vans else they would have soon been stripped bare. At one such stop tragedy overtook the little black dog that had been adopted as the sailors' mascot some months before when it had arrived as a stray onboard the *Pamiat Azova*. It too left the train with many of the sailors at a stop, roamed off to follow one or other of the calls of nature, and could not be found when the train was ready to move. In vain the sailors pulled a broken communication cord to halt the train as the poor animal receded forlornly into the distance.

At another halt, to their surprise, they were greeted by a Russian soldier, the same one that had been picked up from an open boat by the *E19* off Libau. He was overjoyed to see his rescuers again. He had been guarding some of the thousands of German and Austrian POWs who had been building the railway. Now, with the coming of peace they were left largely to their own devices with starving and surly bands roaming the countryside in search of the necessities of life.

Every journey has its end. After ten monotonous and

depressing days the train drew into Murmansk. Waiting to take the submariners back to Greenock was the armed merchant cruiser HMS *Andes*, an ex-liner taken over by the Admiralty earlier in the war and given some armament. What the Admiralty had not given the ship was any protection against the Arctic cold for she was still fitted out for service in the tropics!

Of the men returning home it is tragic to note the fate of some. Fenner was killed within weeks. Like Goodhart before him he was appointed to command one of the new 'K' class steam-driven submarines. Like Goodhart he decided to go to sea in another boat to gain some experience, and joined his friend Commander D. de B. Stocks, DSO, RN, in the *K4*. On the night of 31 January 1918 in the Firth of Forth there occurred the biggest British submarine disaster of all time, sometimes known as the Battle of May Island. That night two flotillas of the 'K' class submarines left Rosyth in stormy conditions with other units of the Grand Fleet. Among them was the *K22*, as the recently salvaged *K13* was now known. Following a steering defect in one boat the *K4* was rammed and sunk with all hands, the *K17* was also sunk, while the *K14* and *K22* were both severely damaged.

Douglas Sealy, who had commanded the *C27* during the battles in the Gulf of Riga, survived the war only to be killed in March 1922 when his submarine, the *H42*, was cut in half by HMS *Versatile* during exercises off Gibraltar and sunk with all hands. On the other hand Leslie Ashmore returned to Russia in 1918, going with the British forces to the Crimea. He continued to serve in the Royal Navy and was to retire as a Vice-Admiral. He died in January 1974.

Back in Helsingfors Downie and his small party settled in to pass the winter and await developments in the spring. But life was not easy for them, now that the British party formed only a very small percentage of the ship's company of the *Pamiat Azova* making the Russians more truculent and aggressive in their attitude. Cromie was no longer present and although the Russians had not necessarily agreed with all that he stood for and had tried to do, they did respect his honesty and desire not to interfere with their Revolution as long as he had been able to get on with his main aim of fighting the Germans. Now it was up to Downie, still only a young Lieutenant with little over two years' seniority in the rank.

The first crisis occurred when the Russians demanded a share in the provisions which had been brought from England especially for the submariners. When Downie ignored the repeated demands of the ship's committee they became very abusive and threatened dire consequences unless the key to the storeroom was handed over. But Downie had not served under Cromie for nothing and he took a firm stand with the committee, adding a large element of bluff.

Watched with considerable interest by the Russian sailors, alarm clocks, fuses and explosive charges were taken on board the submarines. The committee were then informed that the clocks had been set and that unless the British were allowed on board from time to time to reset them the charges would explode the torpedoes on board the submarines and this would also blow up the *Pamiat Azova*. The bluff worked and the British were left largely to themselves. As an added precaution the handle of the storeroom door was electrified. At least one bellowing and cursing Russian sailor had to be loosed when the current was switched off!

The situation ashore was confused. Under the terms of the Russian-German armistice the Russians should have withdrawn their forces leaving Finland a neutral state. However, the Russian soldiers and sailors declared that they had a duty to stay and help the Finnish Reds assume control of the government, and so had no intention of leaving the country. Indeed, by then the Fleet was unable to do so because of the winter ice. After a battle in January the Finnish Whites left the city and with their departure control was in the hands of the Reds. This led indirectly to Downie's next major crisis. With the disruption of business he found that he could no longer cash his Navy Bills into Finnish money. Nothing daunted he felt that the situation was unusual enough for him to resort to rather unusual means. With the departure of the rest of the British he found himself the custodian of quantities of surplus clothing and tobacco. These he proceeded to sell at many times the official value on the black market, thereby keeping his sailors paid. What the Paymasters later made of his accounts has not been recorded!

At the end of March it became obvious that time was running out for Downie and his men. The Finnish Whites, unable to overcome the Reds who continued to enjoy the support of their Russian colleagues, sought the aid of the Germans. On 3 April Downie had official news that the Germans had landed at Hango and were advancing along the coast towards Helsingfors. He immediately began to take the necessary steps to destroy the seven submarines in his charge. At Hango the Russians had already scuttled their own 'AG' boats to prevent them falling into German hands. All the Russian officers who at one time or another had been attached to the British flotilla and who were then in Helsingfors came forward and offered to help Downie. Cromie was also there, having arrived from Petrograd the night before. The main trouble was persuading the Harbourmaster and the captain of the only available ice-breaker that the situation was serious and that they had to go to sea that day. When it became plain that talk would get them nowhere Downie once more resorted to bluff suggesting that he would have no alternative but to blow up the submarines and a large barge full of torpedoes where they lay. That the berths of these vessels was only some 50 yards from the house and office of the Harbourmaster may only be coincidental to the fact that the ice-breaker was promptly made available!

Downie went first in the *E1* followed by the *E9*, *E8* and *E19*, each in charge of one of the Russian officers. On board each submarine three charges had been placed; one forward, one amidships and one aft. Each consisted of two torpedo warheads with a 20-pound gun-cotton primer and wired to be fired electrically from an ordinary alarm clock. The *E1*, *E9* and *E19* were soon destroyed, but after a failure of the electrical circuits the *E8* had to be left in the ice overnight to allow the Russian vessel to return to harbour by nightfall.

Next morning, the 4th, the *C26* and *C35* were taken to sea with the ice-breaker towing the torpedo barge. The *C27* was left behind at Cromie's suggestion in case of any last-minute trouble with the Russians. Again electrical trouble delayed the proceedings. Finally, the *C26* and the *E8* were blown up together, but once more a submarine had to be left in the ice overnight with the torpedo barge while the ice-breaker returned to harbour.

On the 5th when Downie left to complete the work of destruction taking the *C27* with him the Germans were believed to be only 20 miles away. The two old submarines were soon sunk in 15 fathoms of water and the torpedo barge destroyed with a satisfying explosion, taking to the bottom many tons of other stores. Meanwhile a shore party had been destroying another stock of torpedoes aboard the Russian salvage ship *Volkoff*, as well as indulging in an orgy of smashing and burning the many tons of stores which there had not been time to load onto the barge.

There was to be a happier postscript to the story. Nearly forty years later the submarine HMS *Amphion* visited Helsinki to mark the centenary of the bombardment of Sveaborg in 1855 by a British Fleet, in which a previous ship of the name suffered the only British casualty. To mark the occasion the Finnish Navy presented to the submarine the name plate of the *E1*, whose salvage from the sea bottom in the approaches to Helsinki had just been completed.

It had been a distasteful job, but one which was well done and which was to earn Downie a letter of appreciation from Their Lordships at the Admiralty. But first, Downie and his small party had to get back to England. With the Germans giving active support to the Whites in Finland there was little option but to take the long route to Murmansk via Petrograd. Personal luggage was limited to what they could conveniently carry; a small case for each officer, a haversack for each rating and a couple of blankets each. The remainder of their personal belongings was left in the British Consulate in the hope that it could be sent back to England once the war was over. Each rating carried a rifle and officers carried revolvers. One Russian officer, Victor Geyseler, who had been Downie's liaison officer in the *C26*, also went with them to help smooth out the many difficulties they expected on the way.

The party arrived at the station in Helsingfors some time before the train was due to leave and found the whole place crowded with intending passengers. Dispensing with the formality of buying tickets since Downie considered that even had they done so it would have hardly improved their chances of travelling on the train, it was planned to rush one of the coaches and place sentries with fixed bayonets at each door to repel by force any attempt by other travellers to enter. The plan was successful, two Russian sailors were ejected and no one else seemed disposed to question their right to be there.

Cromie had originally intended to leave Russia with Downie and the last elements of the British submarine flotilla but about an hour before the train was due to leave he arrived at the station and told Downie that he considered that as Naval Attaché he ought to stay as there was still work for him to do, and that for the time being he would remain in Helsingfors. Downie tried to dissuade him but soon realised that it was a hopeless task. Cromie remained at the station until the train left, he talked to each of the ratings and shook hands with them all. Downie was only too well aware that Cromie had made many enemies, politically, and when the two came to bid each other farewell the young officer felt that it was probably the last time that he would meet his revered commander.

At Petrograd they had to wait three days for the train to take them north to Murmansk, during which time the party was accommodated in the almost deserted Embassy. Petrograd itself presented a picture of appalling desolation with shops either deserted or with little to sell, buildings with smashed windows, the streets littered with rubbish and the corpses of dead horses which no one troubled to move, and the population a pitiable sight insufficiently clad against the icy weather and on the verge of starvation. They were eager to leave this troubled city.

The journey to Murmansk took five days and was less eventful than they feared. Fellow passengers were the Belgian Minister and his wife, the Portuguese Minister and his family, the Greek Minister and the staffs of the three Legations plus a few influential or lucky refugees. On the third day a Commissar examined their papers at one of the many halts and decided that those of the British party were not in order and that they must return to Petrograd to arrange matters. Geyseler immediately stepped in and informed the Commissar that the party were armed and had no intention of returning to Petrograd. At this point it was decided that their papers were, after all, in order. One other incident disturbed the tedium of the journey. Not far short of Murmansk the train was brought to a halt by the railway lines having collapsed over a stretch of about half a mile. The party had to wait while another train was sent down from Murmansk and then walk with all their baggage from one train to the other.

Once in Murmansk they were again among friends. Soon they were onboard the transport *Huntsend* with their travelling companions from the Legation, the French Military Mission and a whole crowd of refugees and en route to Newcastle. Among the party was Geyseler who took the opportunity to leave his native land and accompanied Downie all the way to London and then, without further ado, vanished from sight.

For Cromie back in Helsingfors there were three British merchant ships still in the harbour, ships that had been trapped in the Baltic by the outbreak of war in 1914 and since then had been working for the Russians. Nevertheless they were British and neither they nor their cargoes could be allowed to fall into German hands.

With his usual perseverance and unbounded energy he sought out the many committees who now governed every aspect of life and obtained the necessary papers to take over the ships and take them to sea. Then with a scratch crew of Russian ex-officers whom he had recruited he boarded the first ship, the *Obsidian*. The story of this tragi-farce is best told in Cromie's own words.

Now began the trouble with our three transports, all partly loaded with Russian cargo, which I had asked them to remove four weeks earlier. Liquidation, evacuation, Transport Committees, Sailors' Committees and God knows what, all had to be argued with. The Germans circulated a pamphlet threatening punishment for sabotage and rewards for those who handed their ships over in good condition, with the result that I could only get five army officers from the Officers' Employment Bureau to act as crew. I eventually received papers, and then the crews cut up rough; after squaring them I found armed men waiting for me onboard the *Obsidian*, who informed me that I was not to take the ship to sea. However, I walked on board, hauled down the Russian flag, and hoisted a Union Jack pocket handkerchief I had for the occasion, and then pointed out that as we were under the British flag in a neutral port I could not permit armed foreigners on board, and if they wished to guard the ship they must do so from the jetty. This little comedy put us all in a good temper, especially as I had papers and they had none. In the meantime I sent back the tug for half a dozen terrorists to enforce the Commissar's orders, which made the guards think furiously. The cargo was clothing and torpedoes, and they objected to sinking the clothes, so I offered each a pair of trousers and bought them off successfully.

It was a slow job getting through the ice, and I am blowed if another tug did not overtake us before passing Grochara: at first things looked ugly and they wished to board. However, I pointed out that we were an English ship in neutral waters and that any firing or boarding by force of arms was an act of piracy since they were not in Russia, and that I would kill the first armed man that set foot on board, backing my words with an absurd twenty-two pistol. I produced my papers and asked for theirs, so I told them that I did not believe they were anything but pirates. They threatened to tow me back to port, but I said that I would sink the ship in the channel and so shut in the remaining ships. Eventually it looked so like a fight as my fellows were anxious about their trousers; this I could not afford as there were two more ships to sink, and so I compromised by promising to remain where I was for one and a half hours whilst they brought necessary papers to cancel mine, but if they came back with a large force I would blow up the ship where she lay. I was in plain clothes, but took the precaution to put on my cross, which still has great power, otherwise I should have been arrested or shot.

The *Obsidian* was systematically looted before Cromie finally got her, and the other two ships, out of harbour and sunk. The *Emilie* was scuttled in the open sea on the 9th, the *Obsidian* and *Cicero* following her to the bottom the next day, being set on fire and left with their sea-cocks open. Torpedo war heads had been placed on board the ships before the submariners had left, but in the meantime the detonators, batteries and electric firing circuits had all been stolen.

On 11 April, with the sound of the German guns clearly audible, Cromie left for Petrograd by the last train, exhausted by four days of hard labour trying to be stoker, engineer, skipper and deck hand on three cumbersome and unfamiliar ships. He had hoped to block the harbour as well but the Russians whom he had organised to do this ran from the town before Cromie, and on his own it was a task beyond even his ingenuity. Significantly, though Cromie had been working, as always, against the Germans and with the connivance, though little help, of the Reds it was his Finnish White (anti-Red) friends who gave him the warning to get out of town while he could.

Prior to the destruction of the submarines and the departure of all the British from Helsingfors the Finnish business community had offered Cromie the equivalent of £50,000 if he would arrange for the British to prevent Russian sailors from the Fleet landing whilst the Finns dealt with the Reds ashore. Later he received another offer of five million pounds from the Whites to let them have the submarines complete. Both ideas were fantastic but were indicative of the peculiar nature of the times where all standards had been upset by the Revolution and where intrigue and double dealing had become the norm.

Indeed, these circumstances were to set the pattern for the remainder of his time in Russia.

Cromie saw it as his primary duty to prevent the Germans from profiting in any way from the Russian collapse. To do this he was prepared to go to any lengths and there can be little doubt that he became involved in a great deal of under-cover work. His letters back to Commodore Hall and Admiral Phillimore, less frequent than before, record only some of his activities: the evacuation of some 6,000,000 poods (a pood was about 36 British pounds) of metal from under the noses of the Germans on one occasion, 300,000 poods of copper on another, 18,000,000 roubles worth of copper on a third, and so on. Other deals are merely referred to by a reference to his official telegrams back to London. He admitted to having so many irons in the fire that it was difficult to write his official reports!

He was involved in spreading anti-German propaganda amongst the sailors in Kronstadt, many of them from Estonia and Latvia which were occupied by the Germans under the terms of the Treaty of Brest-Litovsk. There was support for the White Russians against the Reds to be organised, though this may have given him some misgivings. He had no greater respect for many of the Whites whose way of life had been so largely reponsible for the events of 1917 and the downfall of the Tsar than he had for the Reds whose excesses had brought the Russian Army and Navy to a state he regarded with contempt. Yet as summer progressed it became more and more the policy of the Allied governments to support the White Russian armies who were prepared not only to fight the Reds but also to resist the German occupation of such areas as the Ukraine and the Crimea. Such resistance would prevent the transfer of large numbers of German troops to reinforce the Western Front.

In all this he had the support of Commander Le Page, a large self-possessed man with a typical naval beard who had spent many years in Russia, having been a liaison officer with the Black Sea Fleet in the early days of the war, and was now attached to the embassy in Petrograd. Another person involved was Bruce Lockhart, the British Consul-General in Moscow, who had managed to get an entrée to, if not the actual friendship of, both Trotsky and Lenin. In May Cromie was twice in Moscow, anxious about the Black Sea Fleet which was in imminent danger of capture by the Germans as they advanced along the coast towards the Crimea. Together, Lockhart and Cromie went to see Trotsky who was full of suspicions as to the motives of the Allies but not unfriendly in his attitude to the two men and reassured them about the Fleet.

It was a strange existence. With the signing of peace terms the Germans were allowed once again to send a mission to Petrograd, and could be seen in uniform openly on the streets and in government buildings working in every way against the Allies. Their flag once again flew over the embassy building in St Isaac Square. They too must have been aware of at least some of Cromie's many activities. Yet until the Allied intervention actually began on 4 August the Bolsheviks remained anxious not to antagonise their former allies, and this coupled with the respect that he had built up with the Centrobalt and the deeds of the British submarines in support of Russia may have given him some immunity.

Once the die of intervention was cast the position of the Allied missions in Russia became untenable. The time had come for the staff at Petrograd to go, something which took time to arrange. The Consulate in Moscow was raided the following day and with the exception of Bruce Lockhart, who was left at large for the time being, the staff were thrown into prison. In Petrograd both Cromie and Le Page led a hand-to-mouth existence, shifting from place to place for fear of arrest. Cromie's flat was broken into and searched, while Cromie himself left over the rooftops before he was discovered. Yet despite this Cromie put off his departure, possibly because the Bolshevik authorities were playing their usual game of taking a long time to process the papers of all the Allied diplomats who wished to leave, while no doubt Cromie himself felt there was still work to be done.

Alas, he delayed too long and events outside his control

dictated the next moves. On 30 August a young Russian officer, a member of a right-wing Social Revolutionary group, murdered Uritsky, the head of the Cheka (Bolshevik secret police — a forerunner of the KGB) in Petrograd. The following evening a young Jewish girl, Dora Caplan, another member of the same right-wing group, fired two shots point blank at Lenin as he was leaving a meeting. That he was not killed outright must be counted as a miracle for one bullet penetrated the lung above the heart whilst the second entered the neck close by the main artery. The immediate sequel was a series of ruthless and bloody reprisals as across the country thousands of non-supporters of the regime were rounded up and shot. With Lenin at death's door and unable to give the cool-headed clear leadership so necessary in a crisis it is not surprising that the events which followed got out of hand and indeed may never have really been intended by the Bolsheviks. Nor is it possible to say to what extent German agents in Petrograd were able to step in and make use of the situation to the discomfort of their enemies.

Among the many legends that have grown out of this affair is the one that Cromie was shot down on the steps of the embassy while defending it either against the mob or from a raid by the Cheka. Like so many legends this one has elements of the truth but glamourises a tragic end unnecessarily. In Petrograd at that time was a young army nurse, married to a Russian doctor, but of an Anglo-Russian family. At the outbreak of war the brothers had joined the British Army while the sisters had become nurses in Russia. One brother had been attached, as an army officer, to the Royal Naval Armoured Car Squadron which had fought in the Caucasus and Galicia for the Russians, and was at that time temporarily attached to the embassy staff. She has left a detailed account of that sad day.*

After a game of bridge at a friend's house the night before Commander Le Page and another officer failed to return to the embassy — a mere five minutes' walk away. The presumption was that they had either been arrested or fallen foul of bandits,

One Woman's Story by Mary Britneiva.

robbed, killed and their bodies thrown into the Neva. The Cheka could hardly be expected to help, the police were almost non-existent, so another officer went to the Bolshevik Party Headquarters to ask for news from a commissar who owed him a favour. From the Russian's behaviour it was obvious that something odd was happening, though there was no news of the whereabouts of the missing two.

At 4.0 p.m. on the 31st Cromie was with a number of other people in the embassy when he was called to collect a letter from the Chancery, a side room across the landing at the top of the first flight of the grand staircase where in happier times the Ambassador might have stood to meet his guests. While Cromie was away the others were all held at gunpoint by some men who had burst into the embassy, members of the Cheka possibly, German agents perhaps, or both, but no one will ever know for sure. When Cromie left the Chancery to return he was unable to see the drama that was unfolding, while at the same time another intruder was coming up the staircase. The two men met at the top of the stairs and almost bumped into one another. Apparently they each recognised the other for suddenly Cromie thrust the other aside and started running down the stairs two at a time. Remaining at the top the Russian drew his pistol and deliberately fired at the fleeing Captain. Several bullets crashed into the great glass doors and smashed them. As Cromie reached the bottom he pitched forward, staggered and fell mortally wounded.

One of the officers' wives was the first to reach him and he died in her arms. She was roughly pushed on one side and remembers vividly staring up into the unshaven face with close-set eyes of the killer. Why Cromie suddenly ran as if he had recognised his potential murderer will never be known, nor indeed whether his death was actually intended when the embassy raid was ordered.

The remainder of the male members of the embassy staff were marched off to join all the other British and French citizens in the Peter and Paul Fortress, where they were to be held in the most primitive and squalid conditions for the next 3 weeks. As they left the embassy they had to pass the body of Cromie by then dragged into a corner and stripped of his cherished St George's Cross.

The rest of this bizarre tragedy belongs to Mr Oudendijk, the Minister to Russia for neutral Holland. A man small in stature but with the heart of a lion and the advantage of being able to speak Russian, it was up to him to represent the interests of the British and French nationals. The Bolsheviks proposed that Cromie should be buried at night, a proposal that Oudendijk indignantly rejected pointing out that in civilised countries only criminals were buried in such a manner, and insisted on a proper funeral. Eventually this was allowed but only after every difficulty had been put in his way and he himself had been made to suffer many petty humiliations hardly in keeping with his status as a diplomat. It was Oudendijk that arranged for a coffin, found a Union flag to drape over it, looked after the wreaths and even arranged for a minister to conduct the service. One curious incident highlights the strange reverence in which this remarkable man was held in revolutionary Russia. As the cortège filed along the banks of the Neva it passed a group of dirty, ill-kept Russian destroyers moored in mid-stream, their guns ready to put down any attempt at counter-revolution. Yet despite this, and all the hatred that the Revolution had bred against officers, the Russian sailors stood silently at the salute as Cromie's body was taken to its last resting place in the Smolensky cemetery.

So this great patriot, brilliant naval officer and submariner and most lovable man died. Winston Churchill, by then Minister for War, wrote that he was a very gifted man, of exceptionally high professional attainments whom he had known personally before 1914. Benson, who had known him so well while serving in the *E19*, was on patrol in the Channel Approaches in one of the new 'L' class submarines and remembers reading a signal with the news of Cromie's death with incredulity and great sorrow. Yet elsewhere in Britain this tragic event caused hardly a ripple. That this should have been so among the general public, engrossed with the horrendous and bloody battles of the Western Front, is perhaps not surprising. But among his colleagues in the Royal Navy, and among submariners in particular, his memory is less well served and his name rarely included with the other heroes of two world wars.

His King did not forget him. Uniquely he was posthumously made a Companion of the Order of the Bath, in recognition of his distinguished service to the Allied cause in Russia, and of the devotion to duty which he displayed in remaining at his post as British Naval Attaché in Russia when the British Embassy was withdrawn. This devotion to duty cost him his life. His widow received the insignia, together with the DSO he had won for the sinking of the German cruiser *Undine* in 1915, at an investiture at Buckingham Palace.

XIV

~~~~~~

'Intervention'

1918, the eleventh hour of the eleventh day of the eleventh month: a time eargely awaited by men of the Royal Navy throughout the world; a time which millions of men on the Western Front, and the other battlefronts of the world, had hardly dared hope that they would live to see; a time which signalled a mass outburst of celebration throughout the countries of the Western Allies. It marked the end of the Great War. But did it? At sea the British submarines on patrol in the North Sea were ordered to remain in their billets, though they were not to take any offensive action unless attacked, and were to be particularly alert for German U-boats which had either not heard of the Armistice or else chose to ignore it. In north Russia and the Caucasus British and Allied troops confronted the Bolshevik Red Army. In the Baltic the British submarines were no more, but the Royal Navy was soon to be back and operations were to continue for many months, involve many ships of the Fleet, including more submarines, and were to result in yet more casualties.

The history of intervention in Russia against the Bolsheviks in the immediate aftermath of the war is a complex story and largely outside the scope of this book. It involved the forces of Britain, France, Italy, the United States, Japan and India. The Czechs, trying to return to their new homeland, were involved. There were several armies of White Russians, seemingly acting with one aim, but with little co-ordination and considerable rivalry. To complicate matters there were over a million German and Austrian ex-POWs in Russia still waiting for transport home after the peace of Brest-Litovsk in March 1918.

Military intervention had begun in north Russia in 1918 when British troops had been landed, ostensibly to prevent thousands of tons of ammunition and stores falling into the hands of either the Germans or the Bolsheviks, and also to oppose a German advance northwards through Finland to Murmansk. It was followed in the Far East where British troops and sailors found themselves with Japanese and Americans advancing westward along the railway from Vladivostok to link up with the Czech Legion. British and Indian troops were in the Caucasus while sailors manned a flotilla of assorted craft on the Caspian Sea. In the Crimea, following the collapse of Turkey at the end of the war, British and French forces provided a backing for the fluctuating fortunes of the White Russian armies, before a final evacuation took place amid the most harrowing scenes as thousands of Russians tried to leave their homeland before the Bolsheviks took over.

In the Baltic, where the Royal Navy played such a prominent part in the immediate postwar years, operations could not begin until after the final defeat of Germany. Yet even here the story is involved and could in itself fill a book, and so details of events must be limited to an outline only to show how they affected the submariners, both British and Russian.

In February 1918, following the breakdown of their armistice talks with Russia, the Germans had completed their occupation of Estonia and Latvia. With the signing of the other armistice in November the situation changed again. Article 12 of that Convention laid down that the Germans were to withdraw from the territory which was formerly part of the Russian Empire in 1914 as soon as the Allies should consider the moment propitious, having regard to the internal conditions of the territories. The added proviso highlighted the dilemma facing the victorious Allies with regard to the German forces in that area. During a Cabinet meeting on 10 November, the night before the Armistice was to come into effect, Winston Churchill stated the possible future need for keeping the German Army as a means of maintaining order and combating the spread of Bolshevism. Applied to Article 12 this simply meant that the German Army should, for the immediate future, hold its positions to prevent a Bolshevik seizure of the three Baltic States, which had appealed to the Allies to guarantee their independence. The Cabinet also hoped, perhaps naively, that not only would the German troops be willing to do this but also that their commanders would co-operate with the Allies.

On 13 November at a conference in the Foreign Office it was decided that the Baltic States should receive supplies of military material when they had governments ready to receive and make use of such aid. A week later an Estonian delegation reached London to plead for immediate aid to protect their country. It was doubtful if the Estonians alone could counter any Red advance and the German troops in the country were in disarray and in some instances in a state of mutiny. The Estonians were told that no troops would be sent but that the War Cabinet had agreed to a show of force by the Royal Navy to deter the Reds and that a supply of arms would also be sent.

Within the Navy there were some misgivings about the plan, showing the purely practical difficulties of carrying out a political decision. With the coming of winter it was pointed out that the port of Revel — proposed as the destination and base of the force — would soon be iced in again. No account had been taken of the possible reaction of the Red Fleet only a short distance away at Kronstadt, for at least on paper it was a significant force despite its ineffective role against the Germans. The Baltic was strewn with mines, the position of many of the minefields being only inaccurately charted. Finally, it was pointed out that this proposal took no account of the effect on the crews of the ships who were expecting some leave with their families after four long years of war, and in the case of the wartime-only ratings, their early de-mobilisation.

Despite these doubts the go-ahead was given and on the 24th of the month — less than two weeks after the Armistice — Rear-Admiral Edwyn Alexander-Sinclair, flying his flag in HMS *Cardiff*,* sailed from the Forth for the Baltic with the 6th Light Cruiser Squadron and the 13th Destroyer Flotilla. The force was to be joined by the seven minesweepers of the 3rd Minesweeping Flotilla and the Admiral was told that a squadron of battleships would be sent to Copenhagen and that he could call on them if required. Also sailing to the Baltic were the minelayers *Princess Margaret* and *Angola*, loaded with rifles and ammunition for the Estonians.

Although British troops were involved elsewhere in Russia, Admiral Alexander-Sinclair's instructions were to support British interests but not to get involved in the land fighting; he was to land the arms and supplies carried in the two mine-layers and then to let the Estonians be responsible for their own defence; he could carry out reconnaissance off the coast but he was not to land any sailors. In the conditions prevailing at the time it was a directive that was bound to lead to doubt, and to need the greatest tact and initiative to implement. One important factor in its favour was that the Admiralty added that the Admiral might consider any Bolshevik naval forces operating off the coast of the Baltic States to be doing so with hostile intent and should be treated accordingly. It was for this reason that the battleships were to wait at Copenhagen.

En route to Copenhagen the collier that was to support the minesweepers ran aground. No replacement was immediately available and it was decided that in view of the urgency of the situation the force should proceed without the sweepers, relying for their safety on accurate navigation along the routes between the supposed minefields. In these circumstances, that the force reached Revel with the loss of only the cruiser *Cassandra* and with only a few casualties, damage to the cruiser *Calypso* on a wreck off Libau and two destroyers damaged in collision, must be regarded as fortunate.

---

*Only a few days earlier the *Cardiff* had led the German High Seas Fleet to its anchorage in the Firth of Forth when it arrived to surrender.

By the time the British arrived off Revel the advancing Red armies were less than 50 miles away, with the dispirited Germans falling back in disarray and the Estonians little more than a guerrilla force. There was only one hope of holding up the Russian advance whilst the Estonians organised themselves to make use of the supply of arms and ammunition landed from the two minelayers — action by the Royal Navy. Alexander-Sinclair considered this to be in support of British interests as laid down in his orders and took the *Cardiff* and *Caradoc* with five destroyers up the coast and bombarded the Russian rear for several hours, bringing their advance to a halt. This was only the beginning of the support that Alexander-Sinclair, and later Admiral Cowan, gave to the Estonians and which in due course played such a large part in enabling them to clear their country of Bolshevik forces and, more important, achieve their independence.

Yet at this time the Russians remained in ignorance of the true strength of the British force, believing it to be led by two modern battlecruisers with six pre-Dreadnought battleships plus cruisers and destroyers. The submarines *Tur*, *Tigr* and *Pantera* ventured out from Kronstadt at various times between the end of November and Christmas to look at the British and try and assess their strength, but their reports did nothing to dispel this inaccuracy. Bad weather and unreliable equipment were blamed for the lack of success. Three destroyers supported by the cruiser *Oleg* also searched to an area just east of Revel but failed to make contact, and they too took back no useful intelligence.

In Latvia the situation was even less stable: the new government was able to keep only a tenuous hold on Riga; the Germans were both unwilling and unable to comply with the Armistice terms, while there was increasing Bolshevik activity throughout the country. In Lithuania, the third of the Baltic States to try to attain its independence, the Germans remained dominant for much of 1919 thwarting local ambitions, while the newly independent Poles also threatened the aspiring state with conflicting territorial claims. But it was Estonia and the Gulf of Finland that was to absorb most of the British efforts in the Baltic during the time to the end of 1919.

At the change of the year Alexander-Sinclair was able to take his hard-worked ships back home, passing another squadron at Copenhagen, led by the fearless Rear-Admiral Sir Walter Cowan, which was to continue the difficult Baltic task. Winter ice meant that there was little that they could do off the Estonian coast and as the Bolshevik fleet was itself iced in at Kronstadt Cowan was able to concentrate his initial efforts to try and sort out the situation in Latvia.

With the break-up of the ice Cowan took most of his ships back to the Gulf of Finland using Revel as a main base and later establishing a new forward base at Bjorko Sound, a roadstead on the southern coast of Finland to the east of the capital and only 40 miles from Kronstadt. There units of the newly-formed Royal Air Force hacked out an airstrip for their aircraft while other planes operated from the converted cruiser HMS *Vindictive*.* HMS *Erebus*, a monitor with two powerful 15in guns and some fast coastal motor boats also joined Cowan's force during the year, the *Erebus* having previously been employed on the northern front around Archangel. In May Cowan's growing fleet was reinforced by HMS *Lucia* with six submarines of the 7th Flotilla.†

The task of the submarines, as signalled by the Admiralty to Cowan, was to act as a menace to the Bolshevik fleet, to operate against any Bolshevik ships attempting to bombard the Estonian coast and to be available to protect Cowan's base at Revel from assault from the sea. In fact should the numerically superior Russian Fleet have put to sea in force the submarines would have been the main line of defence for Cowan's light cruisers and destroyers. Within 24 hours of their arrival in Revel Cowan had ordered the first two to sea to patrol a line between Seskar Island and Kaporia Bay on the Estonian coast

---

*A new ship and not to be confused with the older cruiser used for the assault on the mole at Zeebrugge in April 1918 and later expended as a blockship at Ostend.

†Initially the *L12*, *L16*, *L55*, *E27* and *E40*, followed by the *L11*.

just westward of the Russian minefields protecting Kronstadt, and only some 40 miles from the base itself.

Commanding the submarine flotilla in the *Lucia* was Captain Martin Nasmith, VC — last met with in this story as the Commanding Officer of the *E11* which was unsuccessful in entering the Baltic in 1914 having left England in company with Laurence and Horton. Two other Commanding Officers in this flotilla must have had thoughts of those hectic early days in 1914 as they passed on the surface quietly through The Sound off Copenhagen: Lieutenant Ronald Blacklock, DSC, now in command of the *L12* and earlier the First Lieutenant of Laurence's *E1*, while Lieutenant Charles Chapman, DSC, who had been Horton's First Lieutenant in the *E9*, now commanded the *L55*.

Patrols in the waters of the Gulf of Finland were a very different matter to what most of these submarine crews had become used to during the previous years in the open North Sea and Heligoland Bight. Over half a century later the First Lieutenant of the *E27* recalled his time on patrol there remarking on the small almost landlocked areas they were given and how even, on their first patrol, they had bathed in the fairly fresh, calm and clear water and found it rather enjoyable. Because of the small patrol areas the two boats on operations were stationed one in an advanced position, the other in back-up some miles to the west. The smell of the pinewoods surrounding the patrol areas was very strong and pleasant, and in the still air those on the bridge could hear the noises of dogs barking ashore and occasional bursts of gunfire. The Commanding Officers were warned not to approach too close to the entrance to the Kronstadt Channel as there were lots of Russian mines in the area and their position was in doubt; not a very comforting thought. Most of the patrol time was spent on the surface, something that made them feel very exposed and obvious to the enemy. Fortunately they were able to use the small island of Seskar which was some miles to the west of the entrance of the Channel as a backdrop giving them some natural camouflage. From there they could see clearly any movement of the Bolshevik ships coming down the Channel, and on a clear day the top of lighthouse on Kronstadt itself was plainly visible.

The *L16* (Lieutenant-Commander Alfred Hine, DSO, Royal Navy) was the first of the submarines to make contact with the Bolsheviks, when on 29 May he sighted the destroyer *Azard* escorting six minesweepers and with the distant support of the battleship *Petropavlovsk*. An attack on the *Azard* was not successful, but the meeting was the first of a number of moves which were to take place over the next few days as Cowan reacted to the possible threat to the Estonian army's flank resting on Kaporia Bay. The following day the *L16* was again in action, as was the *E27* (Lieutenant Alec Carrie, Royal Navy) and the destroyer *Walker*. Both the submarines missed with torpedo attacks on the *Azard*, the tracks being sighted as the Russian ship frantically evaded the all-too-close torpedoes, while the only other noteworthy event was the surprisingly accurate and sustained fire of the *Petropavlovsk*. Combined with another attack by the *E27* on 3 June, when both torpedoes exploded short of their target on hitting the bottom, it was not an auspicious opening of the campaign for the submariners. Worse was to follow.

On the 4th there was a brief ineffective engagement between destroyers of both sides, with the *Petropavlovsk* once again appearing in support from inside the minefields. Soon after the destroyers ceased fire Chapman in the *L55* attempted a torpedo attack. To what must have been his utter consternation it went disastrously wrong. The submarine broke surface on firing, not only revealing her own presence to what should have been an unsuspecting target, but enabling the target to comb the torpedo tracks and escape. The tables were turned and the *L55* herself presented a tempting target at which the Russian gunners were remarkably quick to open fire. Before Chapman could get the submarine submerged again she was hit by a shell which holed the pressure hull. The submarine sank with the loss of all her crew. Although Blacklock in the nearby *L12* reported that evening that nothing had been heard or seen of the *L55* since the incident it was several days before either Nasmith or Cowan finally gave up hope that

229

the submarine would somehow turn up safe and sound. Even then it was assumed for many years that she had strayed into a minefield.*

The main events of the next few months concerned the activities of the coastal motor boats, the first two of which arrived at Bjorko in early June. Originally their task was to act on behalf of the Intelligence Service as a means of ferrying agents and their news out of Russia across the Gulf as other methods had proved too costly. Nevertheless on the 18th Lieutenant Agar in one of these frail craft torpedoed and sank the cruiser *Oleg*, a feat for which he was quickly awarded the Victoria Cross. This was followed in August when eight CMBs raided Kronstadt itself. At the cost of three of the boats which were lost and six officers and nine ratings killed the Bolshevik fleet was dealt a serious blow. The *Petropavlovsk* was struck by two torpedoes and was to be out of action for a long time, while another battleship, the *Andrei Pervozanni*, was also put out of action following a hit by another torpedo. A third victim was the old *Pamiat Azova*, for so long the home of the British submariners during their time in the Baltic during the war, and now sunk by British torpedoes. Two more Victoria Crosses were awarded, along with other decorations, for gallantry during this attack.

Little remains to be told of naval operations in 1919 which continued until the winter brought the familiar inactivity. On the Russian side the *Pantera* fired three torpedoes at the *E40*, all of which passed within a few yards of the submarine. At the end of August the same submarine sank the destroyer *Vittoria* off Seskar Island; an action which remains until today as the largest warship to be sunk by a Soviet submarine. Meanwhile the destroyers *Valorous* and *Vancouver* had attacked and damaged the *Vepr*. A contemporary Soviet account records the action.

*The *L55* was salvaged by the Soviet Navy in 1928 and after an overhaul and repairs was commissioned into their fleet under her old name. In an unexpected gesture the bodies of the crew were returned to England for burial in the naval cemetery in Gosport. The submarine herself survived the 1941–45 war and was not scrapped until 1960.

. . . the explosion of one depth charge put out the submarine's lights and caused so much other damage that the boat was unable to maintain depth. But, having succeeded in escaping the attack, the crew set about repairing the damage, and set course for Kronstadt which was reached two hours later, although water was beginning to enter the forward hatch and flood the batteries.

In September Nasmith took the *Lucia* and her submarines home, though not before they had landed their 12 pounder guns which were fitted to the 'E' class boats and handed them over to the Estonians. Arriving in Revel at this time was another old Baltic hand, for commanding the 3rd Submarine Flotilla was Commander Max Horton in HMS *Maidstone*, together with the small 'H' class boats of the flotilla. They were to continue with the monotonous patrols until the ice prevented further operations and ensured that the Bolsheviks' ships were unable to leave Kronstadt. They sailed for home on 2 January 1920, bringing to an end the saga of the British submarine operations in the Baltic, a saga which had started many months before in October 1914 when Laurence and then Horton had forced their way through the German patrols into this inland sea.

Although the Baltic again saw British ships in 1920, and until they were finally withdrawn in 1921, the undeclared war was virtually ended when even before the ice melted in 1920 the ships were told not to take further offensive action against the Bolshevik forces. The Baltic States achieved their independence, albeit only until 1941, thanks in no small part to the actions of the Royal Navy. This was a period of naval operations that again demonstrated the value of sea power. It was a period which set against the standards of the 1980s one may doubt the political motives behind the actions which were authorised. But for all that it was a period for which the British sailor has no reason to feel ashamed, for it was a period which the Estonians, at least, were always thankful for the role played by the Navy in helping them to achieve their independence and freedom from Russian domination. It may be summed up in the words of the message of thanks sent to Admiral Cowan by the Estonians as he left the Baltic for home

. . . [the] fleet has never failed to render valuable aid at the most critical junctions, and the Estonian Government which has recently entered into office after being elected by the Constituent Assembly, wishes to convey to you the expressions of its deepest gratitude in the name of the entire Estonian nation, for the inestimable help rendered by you and your men. They will never forget the bravery and gallantry shown by the British blue-jacket, who has always gone into action with the greatest dash whenever the occasion offered, and has not hesitated to risk his life on behalf of our country. You may rest assured that he will always be a welcome guest in our ports.

Epilogue

At last the guns were silent and the fighting men could return to their homes. What had been achieved? It is all too fashionable, particularly among those who have never had to face the realities of battle, to decry the deeds of the men who fought for their country and to try and draw up a balance sheet of war; to count only the millions of dead and wounded and to ask 'Was it worth it?' War is not like that. It produces untold suffering and casualties among all men and women. It produces heroes and cowards, but mainly it produces men who try to do their duty. Only the politicians can try and assess the results. Even then the view of a Russian whose country had been led to bloody revolution could be different from that of a Serb where it had all started so long ago in July 1914; the view of a Belgian or a Frenchman whose country had been fought over and partly occupied might differ from that of an Englishman whose country had escaped many of the rigours of war but whose young men had fought and died in their millions on land and sea. For the rest of us we can only look at our behaviour and our honour.

So with this campaign in the Baltic by a handful of British submariners we can take comfort that the Admiralty did makee an attempt to help our ally in the most practical way possible, albeit badly planned and supported, and with lack of consultation. Most of all we can be proud of the men themselves who despite all the difficulties maintained the highest traditions of the Royal Navy. At their head for most of the time was Francis Cromie, whose loyalty and sense of duty are unquestioned, while he added those qualities of tact and patience which made him respected by both British and Russians, Red and White alike.

Bibliography

A. Agar: *Baltic Episode*, Hodder and Stoughton, 1963.

G. Bennett: *Cowan's War*, Collins, 1964.

J. Bradley: *Allied Intervention in Russia 1917–1920*, Weidenfeld and Nicolson, 1968.

M. Britneiva: *One Woman's Story*, Arthur Baker, 1934.

W. S. Chalmers: *Max Horton and the Western Approaches*, Hodder and Stoughton, 1954.

W. S. Churchill: *The World Crisis – The Aftermath*, Thornton Butterworth, 1929.

Corbett and Newbolt: *Official History of the War, Naval Operations Volumes I to V*, Longmans 1923.

M. Gilbert: *Winston S. Churchill (Volume III 1914–16)*, Heinemann, 1971; *(Volume IV 1916–22)*, Heinemann, 1975.

H. Graf: *The Russian Navy in War and Revolution*, Oldenbourg (Munich), 1923.

E. Gray: *A Damned Un-English Weapon*, Seeley Service, 1971.

R. Gregor: *The Russian Fleet 1914–17* Ian Allan, 1972.

R. Jackson: *At War with the Bolsheviks*, Tom Stacey, 1972.

B. M. Kassel (Lt.-Cdr. USN): *Russia's Submarine Development (1850–1918)*, Journal of American Society of Naval Engineers Inc, Vol. 63, No. 4, November 1951.

Sir Roger Keyes: *Naval Memoirs of Admiral of the Fleet Sir Roger Keyes, Volume I*, Thornton Butterworth, 1934; *The Keyes Papers*, Naval Records Society, 1972.

'Klaxon': *The Story of Our Submarines*, William Blackwood, 1919.

R. H. Bruce Lockhart: *Memoirs of a British Agent*, Putnam, 1932.

D. MacIntyre: *A Forgotten Campaign*, Journal of the RUSI, 1961.

Arthur J. Marder: *From Dreadnought to Scapa Flow, Volume II*, Oxford University Press, 1965.

Evan Mawdsley: *The Russian Revolution and The Baltic Fleet*, Macmillan, 1978.

Donald W. Mitchell: *A History of Russian and Soviet Sea Power*, André Deutsch, 1974.

F. F. Raskolnikov: *Kronstadt and Petrograd in 1917*, New Park Publications, 1982 (originally published in Russia, 1925).

S. Roskill: *Naval Policy Between the Wars Volume I*, Collins, 1968.

Sir Llewellyn Woodward: *Great Britain and the War 1914–18*, Methuen, 1967.

Also:

Translation of Vice Admiral Schmidt's Despatch: The Conquest of the Baltic Islands, from the original text printed by the German Admiral Staff, Berlin, 1917.

Translation of *Der Krieg in der Ostsee*, Volumes I & II, compiled by Commander R. Firle and published in Berlin.

Unpublished Works and Papers:
Naval Staff Monographs:
  The Baltic 1914
  Home Waters Volumes 1 to 9
The letters of Commander F. N. A. Cromie RN.
Russian Scrap Book 1915–19, by Vice Admiral L. H. Ashmore, CB, DSO.

Index

237

Index

Index

Index

Index

Index

Index